ARABIAN NIGHTS
AND DAZE

Memoirs and Occasional Papers
Association for Diplomatic Studies and Training

In 2003, the Association for Diplomatic Studies and Training (ADST) created the Memoirs and Occasional Papers Series to preserve firsthand accounts and other informed observations on foreign affairs for scholars, journalists, and the general public. Sponsoring publication of the series is one of numerous ways in which ADST, a nonprofit organization founded in 1986, seeks to promote understanding of American diplomacy and those who conduct it. Together with the Foreign Affairs Oral History program and ADST's support for the training of foreign affairs personnel at the State Department's Foreign Service Institute, these efforts constitute the Association's fundamental purposes.

J. Chapman Chester, *FROM FOGGY BOTTOM TO CAPITOL HILL*
Exploits of a G.I., Diplomat, and Congressional Aide

John Gunther Dean, *DANGER ZONES*
A Diplomat's Fight for America's Interests

Robert E. Gribbin, *IN THE AFTERMATH OF GENOCIDE*
The U.S. Role in Rwanda

Allen C. Hansen, *NINE LIVES*
A Foreign Service Odyssey

James R. Huntley, *AN ARCHITECT OF DEMOCRACY*
Building a Mosaic of Peace

Joanne Grady Huskey, *UNOFFICIAL DIPLOMAT*

John G. Kormann, *ECHOES OF A DISTANT CLARION*
Recollections of a Diplomat and Soldier

Armin Meyer, *QUIET DIPLOMACY*
From Cairo to Tokyo in the Twilight of Imperialism

William Morgan and Charles Stuart Kennedy, eds.,
AMERICAN DIPLOMATS
The Foreign Service at Work

James M. Potts, *FRENCH COVERT ACTION IN THE*
AMERICAN REVOLUTION

Howard L. Steele, *BUSHELS AND BALES*
A Food Soldier in the Cold War

Daniel Whitman, *A HAITI CHRONICLE*
The Undoing of a Latent Democracy

ARABIAN NIGHTS AND DAZE

Living in Yemen with the Foreign Service

Susan Clough Wyatt

Association for Diplomatic Studies and Training
Memoirs and Occasional Papers Series

NEW ACADEMIA PUBLISHING   SCARITH

Washington, DC

New Academia Publishing/SCARITH Books, 2010

Printed in the United States of America

Library of Congress Control Number: 2010931476
ISBN 978-0-9828061-2-8 paperback (alk. paper)

SCARITH   An imprint of New Academia Publishing
           P.O. Box 27420, Washington, DC 20038-7420

NEW ACADEMIA PUBLISHING   www.newacademia.com
                           info@newacademia.com

Cover photos by Peggy Crawford:
Front cover: Bayt al-Hilali, Sanaa. The lighted third floor is the author's former residence.
Back cover:
Top: Sanaa Stained Glass
Middle left: Awwam Temple, Marib
Middle right: Terracing with Qat and Coffee
Bottom left: Janbiyya Seller Chewing Qat
Bottom right: Dawn at Mahwit

What Others Have Said

(*From the book's foreword*): "In this highly readable book Susan Wyatt vividly retells with good humor her experiences as a diplomat's wife in one of the Foreign Service's most difficult environments, which she describes without either downplaying or exaggeration. Once she has drawn the reader in with personal anecdotes, told with a sharp eye for local customs, she segues into sound overall observations on Yemeni culture, politics, economics, archeology and architecture."
   —RICHARD W. MURPHY, Career Ambassador and former Assistant Secretary of State

"*Arabian Nights and Daze* describes the everyday—and not so everyday—work rebuilding the US Mission in Yemen in 1970. You find just how critically important spouses are to the success of the mission. Everything distinctly Yemeni is there: qat, malaria, and kidnappings, along with the country's extraordinary hospitality and terraced green mountains. Wyatt presents in a postscript an unusually balanced and thoughtful analysis of Yemen's trials today. Conflict, sectarianism, tribes, regionalism, and, above all, poverty are discussed. The answers to these problems, she suggests, are not quick-fix war and bombings but rather nuanced and patient economic development. A must read for anyone interested in the nuts and bolts of American diplomacy at the height of the Cold War, the book also seeks an explanation of why Yemen's challenges today make the country ripe for terrorist activity."
   —JON MANDAVILLE, Professor of Middle East Studies, Portland State University, Portland, Oregon

"Susan Wyatt's book gives terrific insight into the daily challenges of Foreign Service life in remote and less developed countries in the 1960s and 1970s. What a contrast with today's ease of communication no matter where in the world! I really enjoyed sharing Susan's enthusiasm for this assignment, which occurred several years after my husband and I served there. I was also impressed by her and David's ingenuity at creating recreational and social opportunities to build community, by their respect for the Yemeni people, and by their sense of adventure in that exotic land. This is the best of the Foreign Service, the way it should be."

— MARCIA CURRAN, retired Foreign Service Inspector and former Director, State Department Family Liaison Office

"Here we have a rich and loving portrait of Yemen the way it used to be, before international events and headlines ruined the reputation of this charmingly eccentric country and made it a place to be feared. Susan Wyatt was so deeply moved by her experience of that feudal fortress on the Arabian Sea she continued to dream of it decades later. Reading her remarkable memoir made me dream of Yemen again as well."

— ANGELA DICKEY, U.S. Foreign Service officer and former political officer, U.S. Embassy, Sanaa, 1997–1999.

"Susan Wyatt has given us a fascinating glimpse of a breathtakingly exotic country from a now bygone era. She has also described the kind of life in our Foreign Service I also experienced during three tours in Yemen and remember with nostalgia, a life far different from the glamorous one that most Americans think their diplomats lead."

— DAVID G. NEWTON, U. S. Ambassador to Yemen, 1994–1997

To
Mildred and Forrest Clough, who
taught me there is a world
outside of Texas

and to
David McClintock, who
took me to Yemen

Up into the cherry tree,
Who should climb but little me?
I held the trunk with both my hands
And looked abroad on foreign lands.

Robert Louis Stevenson,
"Foreign Lands," *A Child's Garden of Verses*

CONTENTS

Map of Middle East	xii
Map of Yemen	xiii
Foreword	xv
Preface	xvii
Acknowledgements	xxiii
Abbreviations	xxv
PART ONE — A MEMOIR OF YEMEN IN THE 1970s	1
1 Arabia Beckons	3
A Secret Assignment	3
Cover Orders for Dhahran	7
2 Our New Home	17
A Place to Live	17
The Challenge of Necessities	29
Sanaa, Our New City	39
3 Daily Life at Post	51
Life around the Compound	51
Middle East Security	59
The Justice System	69
Billy Quedens and the Issue of Loyalty	77
4 Family Life	83
Medical Woes	83
Christmas Eve 1970	89

Starting a Family   94
Nurturing Our Mental Health   105
5 Diplomacy at Work   117
A Parade of History and Culture   117
Cold War Politics and U.S. Yemeni Relations   127
Ah, the Diplomatic Life . . .   137
The International Community and Mixed Marriages   147
Famine Relief   159
6 Social Life with Yemenis   171
Yemeni Hospitality   171
Mrs. Al-Aini's Women's Group   180
Chewing Qat and Celebrating Births   184
7 Climbing Nabi Shu'ayb   195

Epilogue   203

PART TWO — YEMEN TODAY   205
8 Friends Compare Yemen Then and Now   207
9 Yemen's Challenges Today   215
Economic Challenges   216
Demographic Factors   220
Domestic Security and Related Issues   222
Solutions to Yemen's Problems   232

Chronology of Yemen's History   239
Glossary of Arabic Terms, People, and Places   249
Bibliography   263
Selected References for "Yemen's Challenges Today"   267
Index   271

MAPS

THE MIDDLE EAST c. 1970

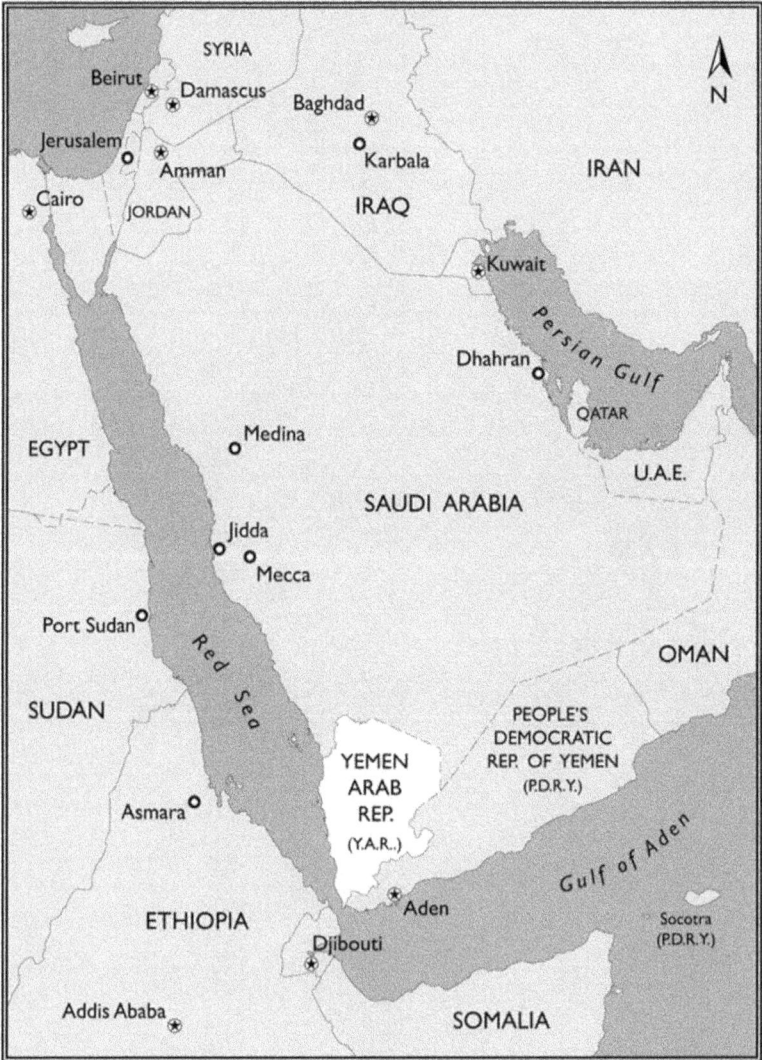

SYRIA

Beirut
Damascus
Baghdad
Jerusalem
Karbala
IRAN
Amman
Cairo
JORDAN
IRAQ

Kuwait

Dhahran
Persian Gulf
QATAR

Medina
U.A.E.

EGYPT

SAUDI ARABIA

Jidda
Mecca

Port Sudan
OMAN

Red Sea

SUDAN
PEOPLE'S
DEMOCRATIC
REP. OF YEMEN
(P.D.R.Y.)

YEMEN
ARAB
REP.
(Y.A.R..)

Asmara
Gulf of Aden

Aden
Socotra
(P.D.R.Y.)

ETHIOPIA
Djibouti

Addis Ababa
SOMALIA

N

YEMEN ARAB REPUBLIC c. 1970

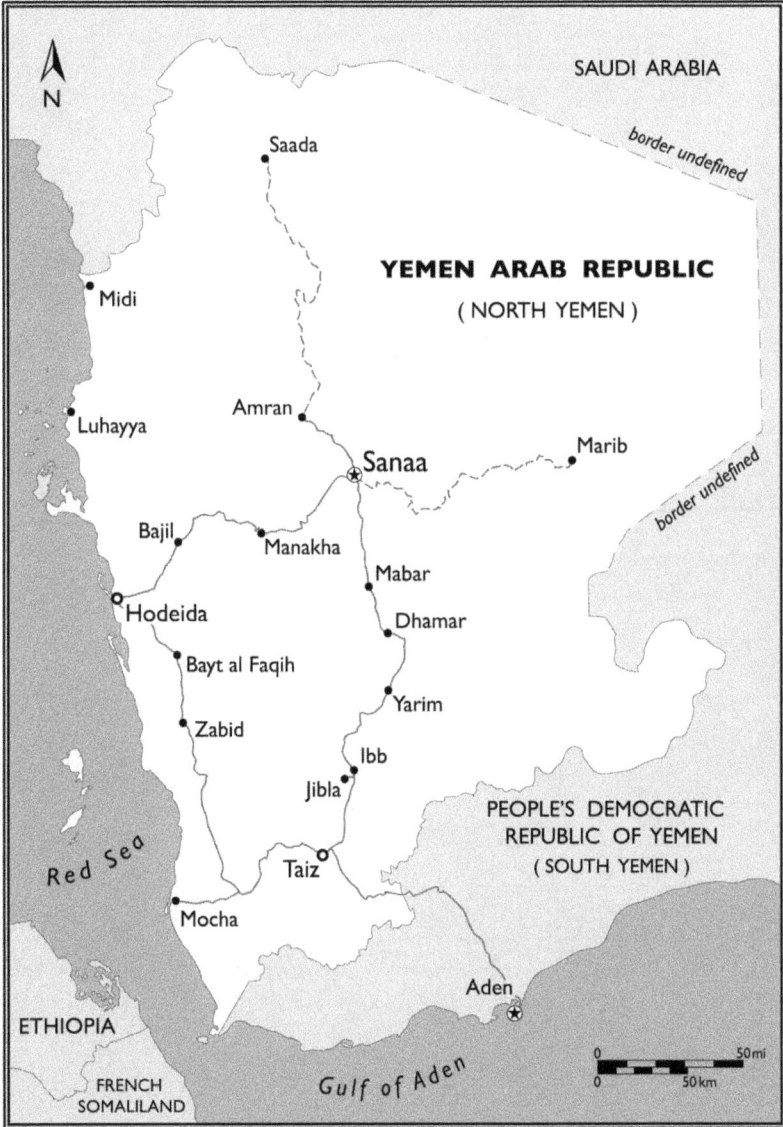

N

Saada

SAUDI ARABIA

border undefined

YEMEN ARAB REPUBLIC
(NORTH YEMEN)

Midi

Luhayya

Amran

Marib

Sanaa

border undefined

Bajil

Manakha

Mabar

Hodeida

Dhamar

Bayt al Faqih

Yarim

Zabid

Ibb

Jibla

PEOPLE'S DEMOCRATIC
REPUBLIC OF YEMEN
(SOUTH YEMEN)

Taiz

Mocha

Red Sea

Aden

ETHIOPIA

0   50 mi
0   50 km

FRENCH
SOMALILAND

Gulf of Aden

© Nathan McClintock

FOREWORD

In this highly readable book, Susan Wyatt presents the relatively little-known history and present-day circumstances of Yemen. She begins with a vivid retelling of her personal experience as the wife of diplomat David McClintock. They arrived at that isolated outpost of U.S. diplomacy in 1970 to restart official relations, which had been severed three years earlier when Yemen joined in the Arab World protest about alleged U.S. policy in the June 1967 Six-Day War. They proceeded to serve with distinction and good humor in one of the Foreign Service's most difficult environments, which she describes without either downplaying or exaggeration.

Yemeni-American relations have undergone major stresses in the past half-century. The Yemeni Revolution in the early sixties pitted two American friends, Egypt and Saudi Arabia, against one another, complicating Washington's relations with both. In 1990 Yemen earned American wrath when, as a member of the Security Council, it abstained from voting on a resolution condemning the Iraqi invasion of Kuwait. A decade later came the attack on the U.S. naval ship USS *Cole* in the Yemeni port of Aden, which led to the arrest of the ringleaders and their subsequent escape from a Yemeni prison. Since then the increased activity of al-Qaeda supporters in Yemen has complicated Yemeni-Saudi relations and raised sharp concern in Washington about the direct threat these Yemeni-based extremists pose to American citizens.

I first met the McClintocks in 1971 on a visit from Washington, where I was serving as country director for the Arabian Peninsula. That visit taught me that the sometimes difficult conditions my family and I had experienced a decade earlier at the U.S. Embassy in

Jeddah, Saudi Arabia, had in no way equaled what the McClintocks found awaiting them in Yemen.

Wyatt and her husband spent two years in Yemen during the early 1970s. In this account she brings a welcome depth of understanding to Yemeni society of that period and then updates her account through exploration of the limited published literature and interviews with colleagues who both preceded and followed them in Sanaa. She lived through the earlier Cold War competition and the country's first steps toward building a republic after its centuries-long heritage of harsh autocratic rule.

Clearly a hardy survivor, Wyatt covers the problems of helping set up an official office virtually from scratch, foraging among long-discarded pieces of furniture, while caring for her own family. But once she has drawn the reader in with personal anecdotes, told with a sharp eye for local customs, she segues into sound overall observations on Yemeni culture, politics, economics, archeology, and architecture.

Her book concludes with an excellent chronology of Yemeni history from antiquity to today, along with an extensive bibliography and welcome explanations of Arabic terms used in her text.

RICHARD W. MURPHY, Career Ambassador and
Assistant Secretary of State for Near Eastern and South Asian Affairs 1983–89.

PREFACE

I am in Washington waiting for my assignment to Yemen. Because of my four years in the Family Liaison Office, I have been drafted out of retirement and back into the Foreign Service along with David. He appears healthy again, although he seems to have been called directly from his sick bed. He is being assigned as ambassador, a reward for his previous time there as chargé d'affaires. We are no longer married, and I am going out to post as a single person.

At the State Department ceremony some women present me with a crystal ice bucket and other gifts, which make me realize they are sending me out with more visibility than I first thought. I soon learn they want to give me credentials, too. I will be like a co-ambassador or backup in case something happens to David. At the swearing-in ceremony, I meet other women being assigned to Yemen. I ask how we will fare in Yemen today as women, and who will carry back the American flag to be hung up at the Embassy.

So went the dream I had in July 1998. It was one of many about Yemen I have had over the years since accompanying my late husband, David McClintock, to that country on his U.S. Foreign Service tour from 1970 to 1972. In the 1980s and 1990s, after we had divorced, I began recording my dreams. These nightly visitors often featured scary, fiery, warlike situations in Yemen or other parts of the Middle East. In more recent years, what few Yemen dreams I have remembered have focused on the people, the marketplace, the colors and costumes, the striking scenery of mountains and desert—the more memorable and pleasant aspects of my time in this remote corner of Arabia.

For years I felt I needed to refresh my memory in order to tell David's and my story about our "never in a lifetime" experience opening and running the U.S. interests section within the Italian Embassy. On several occasions over the last twenty years I contemplated visiting friends assigned there with the State Department or traveling there with friends doing research, but I aborted those efforts for various reasons. Deep down, I guess I was just scared. At a gut level, I feared going back as a woman traveling alone and speaking no Arabic. Although I felt my friends would be welcoming, I would need to impose on them to help me find services and resources (including a translator), and I hesitated to do that.

In October 2000 I realized my feeble efforts to return were over for the foreseeable future. The USS *Cole* disaster occurred in unified Yemen's Aden harbor and launched this little-known country bordering the Red Sea and Indian Ocean into world consciousness. Osama bin Laden's family hails from Yemen. A few of the September 11, 2001, hijackers who crashed planes into the World Trade Center were Yemenis and the operations center for the attack was allegedly located in Yemen. Yemenis have been tried for terrorist attacks or conspiracy around the globe. As of February 2010 approximately 100 Yemenis were still being held at Guantánamo.

Terrorist attacks have increased in Yemen in the past two years, and al-Qaeda in the Arabian Peninsula (AQAP) announced in early 2009 that it had combined forces with similar jihadist organizations and made its new headquarters in Yemen. The aborted December 2009 attempt to bring down a Northwest airliner over U.S. soil by a Nigerian who had reportedly trained with AQAP in Yemen added a more ominous dimension to the world's view of this previously little-known country. For good or ill, the world and now, especially, Americans know about Yemen. It will not retreat into obscurity any time soon.

These sensational news events do not reflect the Yemen I knew. I believe they paint an unjustified, negative picture of a people with a proud and remarkable history. Even if I did not return to see the changes for myself, I felt that writing this memoir was important — perhaps urgent — in order to tell a story of Yemen and its people that contrasts starkly with the *Cole* attack of 2000 and subsequent terrorist activities launched by al-Qaeda operatives both inside and outside that country.

Yemen presented David and me with issues and difficulties different from Foreign Service life in other, more progressive Middle Eastern posts. The notion that "we had a great time in spite of ..." is part of the reason I developed such affection for the Yemeni people in their struggles to become an equal, respected player in the Middle East. In part, this memoir is about my experiences with a people who are proud, loyal, unpretentious, friendly, and hospitable. When I was there, I found that some were naïve and unsophisticated in Western ways. However, none were known to be terrorists.

Arabian Nights and Daze documents a twenty-one-month effort to rebuild the American presence in Yemen following the break in diplomatic relations that began during the 1967 six-day Arab-Israeli war. Although it covers Yemen's history, politics, and foreign policy in several chapters, the memoir is mainly about the complex challenges of our daily lives in Yemen, considered in the 1970s to be the highest level of hardship post by State Department standards. The story also offers a glimpse of my life as a Western woman living in Yemen, a working spouse who also has both family and diplomatic responsibilities that take me into the international and Yemeni communities.

I rely on my memories and impressions as well as those of others who ventured to Yemen during the 1950s, 1960s, and 1970s. I am at last "okay" with the fact that I have not returned to Yemen for a personal update. Seeing the changes imposed by modernization would likely tarnish my memories of a country that almost forty years ago made me feel I had stepped several centuries back in time.

Instead, I have written two postscript chapters, both in Part Two, that compare Yemen in the 1970s with contemporary life and describe challenges facing Yemen today in 2010. The first postscript, "Friends Compare Yemen Then and Now," includes the views of three American friends about changes they observed through 2004, based on their return to Yemen several times after I left. The second postscript, "Yemen's Challenges Today," offers a discussion of major interrelated problems the country must handle successfully to survive and draws on numerous secondary sources as well as on the informed views of several people who know Yemen well.

The chapters are topical and partly chronological. Many acronyms, mostly referring to governments, agencies, organizations, and titles, appear throughout. In the text, I initially give the full name of each entity, followed by the acronym in parenthesis, and then generally use the acronym in subsequent references. A listing of abbreviations and acronyms appears at the front of the book.

Since we called many things by their Arabic rather than their English names, I have used italics for each Arabic or foreign word that does not appear in Webster's Collegiate dictionary. Dr. Dan Varisco of Hofstra University kindly provided me with the accepted Yemeni Arabic transliteration for each word used. I have taken the liberty of Anglicizing with an "s" or an "i" Arabic words used in the plural form. A glossary of those terms and phrases appears at the end of the book.

A chronology of history dating back to ancient times supports and expands the historical narrative found in chapter 14. References for that chapter, the chronology, and parts of chapter 15 on U.S.-Yemeni relations are drawn from the following sources:

—David McClintock's two textbook chapters, personal notes, and letters;
—Interviews with current and retired Foreign Service officers;
—Oral histories of Foreign Service officers on file with the Association for Diplomatic Studies and Training (ADST), especially those of Hermann Eilts, William Stoltzfus, William Crawford, William Wolle, Marshall Wiley, Michael Sterner, Jim Cortada, and Ted Curran; and
—Books by Khadija al-Salami; Marta Paluch; Caroline Singer (ed.); Fritz Peipenberg; Tim Mackintosh-Smith; Mary Quin; and Victoria Clark.

A comprehensive bibliography of these and other references used appears at the end of the book.

The many black-and-white photographs sprinkled throughout

the text were either taken by David, me, or a friend or given to David as enlarged professional photographs during his first tour in Yemen (1962–64). Sadly, I have no information that would allow me to give credit for those photographs. Alain Bertaud, who lived in Yemen at the same time we did, was the source of a few of the photographs. Manfred Steffan donated the photo of Bill Stoltzfus and a camel caravan on the Sumarra Pass in 1961, and Marco Livadiotti supplied the 1977 photo of his father Mario. Professional photographer Peggy Crawford provided four of the photos in the text and all of the color photographs on the book cover, all made during her nine trips to Yemen between 1985 and 2004.

Yemen was the first of two overseas tours I had with the Foreign Service, and I loved my time in this fascinating corner of the world. I also very much enjoyed my two years in Amman, Jordan, our second post, and the later years in Washington, D.C., where I worked in the State Department's Family Liaison Office. But, it is Yemen I have dreamed about over the past forty years. Before I began writing, it was as if something about that time in my life were unfinished. Reviewing my journals, letters, and tapes sent from Yemen, reconnecting with old friends, and writing about our tour there have all been satisfying. It now feels as if I have achieved closure, although I would be eager to visit again should the opportunity present itself.

Because Yemen was so different from other more modern Arab countries I visited over three decades ago, I look back on the experience as if in a daze. My memories of this foreign land are surreal, dreamlike, almost as if they had not really happened. That is why I want to share them before they are lost. I now realize my role as David's embassy backup in the dream described earlier is that of storyteller.

Susan Clough Wyatt

Albuquerque, New Mexico, and Eugene, Oregon
July 2010

ACKNOWLEDGEMENTS

Special thanks to:

Dr. Lealan Swanson for editing and critiquing a final draft of the manuscript, and most important, for her invaluable support and numerous resources (knowledge of Yemeni foods, social customs, and traditional Yemeni costumes); **Peggy Crawford** for her wise counsel, for editing a draft of the manuscript, and for the use of her fine photographs of Yemen; **Dr. Daniel Varisco** for translation of Yemeni Arabic terms into English; **Ambassador David Newton** for reviewing the final manuscript and providing many factual details and helpful comments from his three tours in Yemen; **Nathan McClintock**, my son, for his editing of an early draft and for his fine maps in this volume, made with the assistance of Jenny Cooper and Darin Jensen of the U.C. Berkeley Cartography Lab; **Judith Sawyer** for her editing of a draft manuscript and for making the index of names that appear in the book; **Margery Thompson**, ADST Publishing Director, for editing the final manuscript and, along with **Anna Lawton**, New Academia Publishing, for their patience and persistence in guiding this project to completion; **Dr. Richard Williams,** my husband, for his support, encouragement, and technical expertise; and my children **Lesley, Nathan**, and **Anna McClintock**, who gave me the reason to write this part of our family history and without whose encouragement this manuscript would never have been completed.

Sincere appreciation goes to the following individuals and organizations:

For editing, reviewing, or critiquing a draft of the manuscript: Judy Fitzpatrick; Kathleen Anderson; Betsy Messeca; Stephanie Kinney; Ella Joan Fenoglio and Sonya Ewan (members of my Southwest writers [SWW] critique group); Helga Wood; Ambassador Richard Murphy; Angela Dickey; Marcia Curran; Dr. Jon Mandaville.

For comments or critiques regarding individual chapters, research tidbits, verification of facts, technical support, and help in locating contacts and information: my SWW critique group (Gail Rubin, Kay Lamb, Kathleen Hessler, Nancy Costea, Ann Euston, Sherri Burr); Gloria Zamora; Alain Bertaud; Lew Reade; Marjorie Ransom; Ted Curran; Ambassador David Newsom; Dr. Raufah Hassan Al-Sharki; Muhammad Abdul Ghani Nagi; Abdul Kadir Farhan; Eddie Bos; H.E. Ali Hamid, Arab League Ambassador to London; Selwa al-Radi; Ambassador William Eagleton; John Shipman of the British-Yemeni Study Association; Khadija al-Salami; Merilyn Phillips Hodgson; Dr. Maria deJ. Ellis of the American Institute for Yemeni Studies (AIYS); Mathias Oppersdorff; Michael Sheehan; Marco and Mario Livadiotti; Marilyn Sobke; Betty Case; Dr. Brink Messick; Rob Syslo; JoBeth Wolf; Jan Hartsough; Dwight McAnally; Ambassador Joyce Leader; Bill Heenan; Dr. Emile Nakhleh; Dr. Robert D. Burrowes; June Young; Debbie Carrick; Lucy Dorr; and, from the Association for Diplomatic Studies and Training (ADST), Ambassador Kenneth Brown, President, Margery Thompson, Marilyn Bentley, and interns Rebecca Davidson and Rita Hawkins.

ABBREVIATIONS

Admin – administrative
ADST – Association for Diplomatic Studies and Training
AIYS – American Institute for Yemeni Studies
ALF – Arab Liberation Front
APO – Army & Air Force Post Office
AQAP – Al-Qaeda in the Arabian Peninsula
BOQ – bachelor officer's quarters
BRAT – banana, rice, applesauce, toast
BSO – Black September Organization
Chicom – Chinese Communist
CPI – Corruption Perception Index
CRS – Catholic Relief Services
CTU – Counterterrorism Unit
DCM – deputy chief of mission, second to the ambassador
DDR – Deutsche Demokratische Republik (East Germany)
EPLF – Eritrean People's Liberation Front, or ELF for short
FLOSY – Front for the Liberation of Occupied South Yemen
FRG – Federal Republic of Germany (West Germany)
FS – Foreign Service
FSN – Foreign Service national
FSO – Foreign Service officer
GCC – Gulf Cooperation Council
GDP – gross domestic product
GEC – General Electric Company
GOY – Government of Yemen (referring to unified Yemen in recent
    years)
GPC – General People's Congress (the party of President al-Saleh)
GSO – general services officer

HP – horsepower

INR/RNA – Intelligence & Research, Near East–North Africa in USDS

JMP – Joint Meeting Parties (the coalition alliance of opposition parties)

KGB – Russian acronym for the Soviet intelligence organization (intelligence counterpart of the U.S. Central Intelligence Agency)

LOU – limited official use

MEA – Middle East Airlines

Medevac – medical evacuation, usually by air ambulance

NGO – nongovernmental organization

NLF – National Liberation Front

OER – Officer Evaluation Report in USDS

PADCO – Planning and Development Collaborative International

PDRY – People's Democratic Republic of Yemen (Southern Yemen)

PLO – Palestine Liberation Organization

PM – prime minister

PX – post exchange, a discount store on a military base; also BX, or base exchange

ROY – Republic of Yemen, new name of the united YAR and PDRY since 1990

R&R – rest and relaxation (or recreation)

TDY – temporary duty

UAR – United Arab Republic (union of Egypt and Syria 1958–61); also Egypt

UAS – United Arab States (confederation of Egypt, Syria, and North Yemen 1958–61)

UK – United Kingdom

UN – United Nations

UNCAC – United Nations Convention Against Corruption

UNDP – United Nations Development Program

UNESCO – United Nations Educational, Scientific, and Cultural Organization

UNFAO – United Nations Food and Agriculture Organization

US – United States

USAID – United States Agency for International Development

USDS – U.S. Department of State, also referred to as State or the department

USG – U.S. government

USINT – United States interests section (in a foreign government's embassy)

USIS – United States Information Service

USSR – Union of Soviet Socialist Republics

WASP – white Anglo-Saxon Protestant

WFP – World Food Program

YAL – Yemen Airlines (today called Yemenia)

YAR – Yemen Arab Republic (Northern Yemen)

YARG – Government of the Yemen Arab Republic (prior to unification with the PDRY in 1990)

YSP – Yemen Socialist Party

PART ONE

A Memoir of Yemen in the 1970s

Arabia Beckons

A Secret Assignment

The telephone rang in Ann Arbor one afternoon in early December 1969 while David, my husband, was studying for his statistics final. Bob Paganelli in Near East personnel at the U.S. Department of State in Washington, D.C., had a new assignment for us. Original plans had us destined for the Indian Ocean seaport of Aden, capital city of the People's Democratic Republic of Yemen (PDRY), in the southwestern corner of Arabia. (Located directly south of the Yemen Arab Republic [YAR], the PDRY would not unify with its neighbor to become the combined Republic of Yemen [ROY] until 1990). Our Aden assignment had fallen through in October 1969 when the Communist-run PDRY suddenly broke diplomatic relations with the United States. We had been anxiously waiting to hear what would happen next.

David listened to Bob's carefully couched words emphasizing the secrecy of his phone call. "How would you like to return to the place where you previously served and open up a U.S. interests section under the protection of the Italian embassy?"

What a question! Knowing that Bob meant Yemen (YAR), David hung onto every word. He could hardly wait to tell me when I got home from work. Forget the statistics exam.

Bob continued, "Since discussions are still going on with the country in question concerning resumption of relations, we'll have to give you 'cover orders' for Dhahran so you can proceed with shipping your household effects."

At last, some news. We started telling everyone we would be going to the Persian Gulf and a climate similar to what Aden's would have been. Family and friends were almost as anxious to learn about our assignment as we were.

David's Yemen stories would at last become a reality for me. His abilities as a storyteller and apparent wisdom in dealing with adversity had been major attractions for me, an awestruck summer intern who had met David, an experienced U.S. Foreign Service officer (FSO), three years earlier. The opportunity to go to Yemen, the ancient home of the legendary Queen of Sheba, had arrived sooner than we dreamed — at the end of our first year of married life. This would be our chance to live some of those adventures together and make new discoveries of our own. I could not wait to explore the Middle East, especially Yemen, with David as my tour guide.

Spending Christmas with my family in Texas (and reassuring them that we would be "safe" in Yemen), getting David through his doctoral prelims in early January, and packing up our apartment consumed every moment of the next few weeks. Should the Yemen assignment in Sanaa (with its high altitude and cool dry climate similar to New Mexico's) fall through, we had to be prepared with appropriate clothing and provisions for the hot, steamy Saudi port of Dhahran. We sorted items to meet all climate contingencies: for storage, for sea shipment, and for airfreight.

At the end of January 1970, in a state of near exhaustion, we drove to Washington with two huge airfreight trunks weighting down our car. We needed medical exams, and David had two weeks of consultations with various State Department offices. We also socialized with some of his FSO colleagues who were back in Washington from the Middle East. Feeling insecure in my new role, I hoped I passed scrutiny as David's new wife among his oh-so-worldly friends. I had traveled abroad, but never in the privileged circles of these Foreign Service (FS) officers and their wives. I had a lot to learn.

We headed for Beirut on Friday, February 13 (not so auspicious, if one is superstitious), stopping first to visit friends in Copenhagen and Berlin. We then spent four cold and rainy but fascinating days in Istanbul, a perfect psychological introduction to the Byzantine drama that lay ahead.

Istanbul's Galata Tower

Only after we were packed and on our way did I have time to reflect on the chain of events that propelled me to the Middle East. My parents had instilled in me an early curiosity about a world different from my middle class WASP beginnings in Texas, and I vowed to see as much of it as possible.

By the time I graduated from Whittier College in California, I had traveled from coast to coast, to Canada and Mexico, spent a semester in Denmark, a summer at a youth work camp in Pakistan, and visited several countries in Europe. Receiving a fellowship at the University of Michigan to complete my master's degree in international relations, I made my first trip to Washington, D.C., in September 1965 to attend the American Political Science Association's convention and do a little advance job hunting.

In Washington I had a fortuitous meeting in the West Wing of the White House with my father's friend, Horace Busby, who was Lyndon Johnson's cabinet secretary. Busby orchestrated a spontaneous encounter with the president, which led to my getting an internship on the Japan desk at the State Department the following summer. Before beginning the internship, I funded my third trip to Europe for six weeks with money I had saved from the fellowship. By the age of twenty-three, I was hooked on traveling to foreign lands.

Spending the summer of 1966 in Washington was exciting after the drudgery of my master's work in graduate school. When the internship ended, I walked the halls of the State Department, knocking on doors, and found a research analyst position in the Near East section of the Intelligence and Research division (INR/RNA). I served as the Iraqi analyst and shared an office with the Arabian Peninsula analyst, David McClintock, who had recently returned from his posting in Sanaa, capital of the YAR. At that time, the Department referred to the YAR as North Yemen to distinguish it from the Communist-led PDRY, or South Yemen.

David, eleven years older than I, was married and had a young daughter when I met him. As a supportive office colleague, he listened patiently and gave advice like a big brother when I told him stories about the singles scene in D.C. A year later he was going through a divorce, and his life was in upheaval. It was my turn to listen. We eventually began dating, fell in love, and married in December 1968.

Growing up in Los Angeles, David seemed to have been born with the same wanderlust as I. An international relations major at UCLA, he managed to take a trip to Europe in the summer of 1952. After marrying a Greek exchange student at the university, he served two years in the U.S. Army before beginning the arduous task of written and oral tests for entrance into the Foreign Service.

Finally his ticket to freedom and adventure arrived when he was invited to join the December 1959 class of new Foreign Service officers. He spent his first tour in Manila as a consular officer, opting for two years of Arabic language training in Beirut after that. He and his wife adopted their baby daughter Anna in Greece before being assigned to the YAR in 1964. They returned to the States in 1966 so that David could begin his tour in INR/RNA.

Three years later found us married and living in Ann Arbor, Michigan, where David was on a sixteen-month paid educational sabbatical from the Foreign Service. He chose the University of Michigan as the place to complete his master's degree as well as the coursework for his PhD in international relations, a program

I had abandoned four years earlier in favor of the lure of Washington. Knowing the professors there, I was convinced it would be possible for David to accomplish his goals in so short a period of time. He was already thinking about becoming a college professor when he retired from the Foreign Service. I had not yet developed any long-range career goals and at the time was just happy being David's wife and looking forward to some exotic adventures with my never-dull husband.

Bob Paganelli's phone call to Ann Arbor at the end of David's sabbatical launched us into the Middle East on our first international wanderings together. Istanbul was the gateway, and Beirut our initial destination.

Cover Orders for Dhahran

Arriving in Beirut on February 22, 1970, we ostensibly devoted our next two months to Arabic language refresher work for David. The sojourn also represented something of a holding operation while officials in Washington reached a final policy decision about re-opening the post in Yemen. That decision would be based, in part, upon David's findings following a reconnaissance trip he was to make to Yemen in March.

Having told so many people we were headed to Saudi Arabia, it was easy to continue the charade among the friendly but curious Lebanese (as well as most of the American community) whom we met. The Hotel Charles on Rue Rustom Pasha in Ain Mresse, a section of Beirut near the Corniche and hotel district and an easy walk to the embassy's Foreign Service language institute, served as our headquarters.

The hotel owner, a Lebanese man named Khalil (for Charlie, as we called him) had long catered to Americans assigned to Beirut on temporary duty (TDY). David had stayed there several times before and considered Charlie a friend, though figured he might be reporting the comings and goings of his American clientele to his Lebanese security connections. Every time David had anything sensitive to convey to me, we made sure we flushed the toilet or turned the radio on loudly to interfere with any bug that might have been planted in our hotel room. Middle Eastern intrigue had begun.

Along the Corniche in Beirut

When David was not studying, we made new acquaintances (official U.S. personnel as well as expatriate Americans, Lebanese, and other nationalities) and explored Beirut together. David had several contacts he renewed from his earlier time as an Arabic student at the language institute. We took *services* (taxis), buses, or rode with friends into the Lebanese countryside and went on a one-day shopping spree to Damascus, Syria. David also traveled alone for several days to Rome, Cairo, Asmara (Ethiopia), and Yemen to make preparations for our new assignment. We ended our time in Beirut with an exciting official four-day trip to attend a conference in Tehran, Iran.

These two months of adventure and discovery served for me as a relaxed, storybook introduction to the charms of the Middle East. While David studied Arabic by day, I luxuriated in our one-bedroom apartment, staring with my historically land-locked eyes at the magnificent blue-green Mediterranean. It was my first time ever without work or study obligations. I read books, especially mesmerized by the exotic, romantic stories of four nineteenth century adventurous women in Lesley Blanche's *The Wilder Shores of Love*. Although I attempted to study Arabic on audiotapes David brought home, I was much more interested in exploring Beirut.

I bought fresh-squeezed orange juice and ripe, local vegetables and fruits from the street vendors in front of the hotel. I window-shopped on busy Hamra Street and bought a Lebanese cookbook at Khayyat's. I wandered through the campus of the American University of Beirut and found some colorful Hebron glass items at a little shop tucked into a side street near the ocean. It was easy to understand how the bustling, balmy, affluent seaport had earned Beirut the label "Paris of the Middle East" in the days prior to Lebanon's devastating and lengthy civil war (1975-1990). Acclimating myself in patient stages, I found, in retrospect, that Beirut facilitated my transition to the much less developed environment of Yemen.

Because the new U.S. interests section (USINT) in Yemen was to operate under the auspices of the Italian embassy in Sanaa, David made a two-day visit to Rome on March 23. Viewing the trip primarily as a matter of protocol, he received assurances of maximum support and cooperation from the Italians. Working with officials at the Italian foreign ministry, he drafted a *note verbale* that he and the Italian ambassador in Yemen would present to the Yemen government (YARG) officially announcing the opening of the interests section.

Those two days of separation were easy for me compared to the two weeks that lay ahead when David headed to Yemen. Hurrying back to Beirut from Rome, David repacked his bags to begin the more rigorous fact-finding trip to Yemen on March 27.

How I wished I could have gone with him. This would be the first lengthy separation since our marriage. I was somewhat nervous about it and also concerned about his safety. In those days communication occurred only through letters via the unclassified diplomatic pouch and usually required a week or more to reach someone. However, before he returned, I received from the Asmara consulate two of his letters, which allayed my anxiety about him and our new post.

Cairo was David's first stop. There he consulted with Minister Donald Bergus and other U.S. interests section (USINT Cairo) officials about the mechanics of operating a mission under the protective arm of a foreign embassy. From Cairo he proceeded to Asmara, Ethiopia. (Asmara was part of Ethiopia in 1970, but today is the capital of Eritrea, which gained its independence from Ethiopia in

1991 after a thirty-year civil war.) The consulate general there, as well as the U.S. Army's Kagnew Station military base, planned to serve as USINT Sanaa's main logistical support for everything from weekly mail pouches to case-lot commissary and liquor shipments. Yemen Airlines (what we called YAL, or Yemenia, as it is known today) would bring our supplies directly to Sanaa.

A telecommunications specialist from our embassy in Athens (I'll call him Tom since his name escapes my memory) was dispatched to Asmara to join David for the secret fact-finding trip into Yemen. They flew Ethiopian Airlines to Taiz, YAR, on March 31 and were met by Italian Ambassador Romualdo Massa-Bernucci and his assistant, Counselor Fausto Pennacchio. David and Tom traveled by Land Rover north to Sanaa over the gravel road built by the U.S. Agency for International Development (USAID). The approximately 150-mile trip, which took a minimum of five hours, involved a memorable climb through three spectacular mountain passes between Taiz and Sanaa.

At one point they stopped and got out of their vehicle to look over the steep drop-offs at the beautiful terracing. A truckload of turbaned Yemenis passed them and David could hear one of them yelling, "It's the American!" So much for hush-hush reconnaissance trips. By April 7, French and English language newspapers had published the news that David was back in Sanaa to work in the American interests section of the Italian embassy.

David and Tom checked out the former American Embassy compound in Sanaa, taking inventory of what had been destroyed or damaged in the hasty retreat of 1967. They were the first official Americans to return to the country following the closure of the embassy three years earlier.

In Sanaa, they met up with a Foreign Service National (FSN) named Muhammad Abdul Ghani Nagi, who had worked for the U.S. government (USG) since 1962. He was then employed by the Italians to watch the American compound. David and Tom needed Muhammad's help to locate a sledgehammer and break into the steel communications vault in the chancery building, since keys to the room were non-existent. The three took turns wielding the hammer against the thick, adobe roof until they broke open a hole big enough to drop Muhammad down by rope into the pitch-black, windowless vault. Using a flashlight, he made his way across the room and unlocked the deadbolt on the door from the inside and let David and Tom in. All the equipment that that been destroyed with sledgehammers three years earlier was still there to be removed, which they proceeded to do, shipping it out in large diplomatic pouch bags during their twelve-day stay.

The Italians were supposed to have guarded the compound to prevent pilfering, but it was clear that furniture was missing, both in the chancery building and in the five apartments where American families had lived. However, David found stored in the apartment building a large quantity of older surplus furniture, some of which had been brought to Sanaa when the embassy had relocated there from Taiz in 1966.

Back in Beirut, I was well cared for by embassy friends. The Friday after David left, a number of explosions occurred at the Bank of America and several people were killed near Place Martyr in downtown Beirut. Reportedly, the Phalangists and a Muslim group, two of the several groups fighting for power in Beirut at that time, caused the fracas. They reached an accord that evening, so I felt secure enough to resume my busy social schedule, going out with friends nearly every night. I actually felt safer at night in most parts of Beirut than I had in Washington, D.C. in the late 1960s.

After his return from Yemen, David and I made last-minute preparations for our move to Sanaa before embarking on a delightful four days in Tehran for the chiefs of mission conference. Surprised that he had been included in this ambassador-level group, David bought me a plane ticket to accompany him, because other wives would be there.

We hastily threw together a wardrobe for the occasion. I had nothing suitable because I had not expected to need formal clothing in Yemen. A Lebanese dressmaker whipped up a long white crepe, sleeveless dress with a black cummerbund. It would match my black leather pumps, since I knew I would never find any formal dress heels in Beirut to fit my long quad-A feet. Fortunately, David had thrown his tux into our luggage at the last minute. All he had to do for the occasion was to borrow a shirt, tie, cufflinks, and cummerbund from another FSO posted in Beirut, who was about his size.

David at Golestan Palace in Tehran

Arriving in Tehran, we joined all the American ambassadors stationed in the Middle East. Undersecretary of State Elliot Richardson and his team of U.S. officials from Washington were welcomed by Shah Reza Pahlavi and held a two-day meeting April 20–21. We may have been low on the totem pole, but I got a taste of life at the higher levels of diplomacy.

Our first night in Tehran, Ambassador Douglas MacArthur (nephew of the famous general) and his wife hosted a formal dinner party for our group at their palatial residence. I wore my new gown and tried to act as if I were comfortable and belonged in such rarified company. I had heard tales from other FS wives who had served under Mrs. MacArthur. They had nicknamed her "Dragon Lady," but I found her pleasant, and we had a most enjoyable evening.

Another night we went out to an elegant local restaurant where I ate a fresh salad with Black Sea sturgeon and caviar. Although I had been warned not to eat raw veggies unless I knew they had been specially cleaned, I did so anyway, naively believing that such an upscale restaurant would have Western hygienic standards. "Tehran tummy" hit the next day, and I paid the price for my indulgence, missing my once-in-a-lifetime opportunity to visit

Isfahan. The shah was providing special aircraft for a red carpet tour of this Persian jewel for Mrs. Richardson and the other wives. I felt miserable and did not want to delay the group in any way with my ailments. I was also leery of flying on a chartered aircraft, even if it was to be provided by the shah.

Since appearances were very important in this high-level circle, David did not want to do anything that would embarrass or blackball us. So, at five o'clock in the morning, the appointed time for the entourage's departure for Isfahan, David rose, dressed in a business suit and tie, and went downstairs to the Hotel Semiramis lobby to tell Mrs. Richardson personally that I was too ill to accompany her group. As a reminder of my missed opportunity, I still have the note she sent me later wishing us well in Yemen. I hear that currently Isfahan is under siege by developers who want to modernize this historic wonder and have already torn down many old buildings.

Two days after our return from Tehran, we boarded a Middle East Airlines (MEA) flight for Cairo. MEA, feeling generous upon seeing our diplomatic passports, I suppose, put us in first class where we were served a gourmet meal—the perfect way to begin our first diplomatic assignment together.

We stayed in a hotel room at the Cairo airport until our five a.m. Ethiopian Airlines flight for Asmara. I watched out the window in awe as we climbed through the early morning fog over the Nile, the plane following the river toward our destination. The fertile green river valley slithered like a snake between vast sand dunes and grayish-brown hills that became more rugged as we crossed over Sudan en route to Ethiopia.

Asmara, then the second largest city in Ethiopia next to Addis Ababa, offered us several days of warm tropical sunshine. From our Nyala Hotel balcony and on walks around town we saw reddish-purple bougainvillea and lilac-colored jacaranda, many-hued wild parakeets, and palm and eucalyptus trees. Asmara's 7,000-ft.-plus altitude, dry climate, and clay-like hilly terrain with cedar and fir trees reminded me of northern New Mexico. The fifteen-degree latitude created a tropical atmosphere I had not experienced before.

David tried to prepare me for what lay ahead. "This climate is much like Sanaa will be, but don't expect as much color as you see here. Everything will seem much more primitive, too."

Asmara skyline

People of Asmara

The fine-featured, olive-skinned Eritreans with their white robes and dresses, and the horse-drawn taxis as well as numerous bicycles all added to the charm of this former Italian colony in East Africa. (Italy conquered Eritrea in 1895 and Ethiopia in 1935.) The consulate stabled twelve horses owned by several employees for recreational use and most of the staff rode or played tennis. Once I recovered from the lethargy created by the high altitude, I figured I could easily fit right in to this little paradise the Americans were enjoying.

In Asmara we ordered commissary provisions for later shipment to Yemen. We met with consulate and military officials at Kagnew Station about logistical support we would need in Yemen, indulged in our last shopping at the PX (post exchange), and enjoyed hamburgers and milkshakes at the officers club. Asmara would be a nice place for rest and relaxation (R&R), and I looked forward to those courier runs with the diplomatic pouch we would take every few months.

The big day finally arrived in late April. We hopped into an Ethiopian Airlines DC-3, a reliable old propeller airplane, to fly into Taiz, the second largest and more commercial city in Yemen. David looked very dignified in his navy poplin business suit, blue oxford cloth button-down shirt, and tie. I had trimmed his hair before we left Asmara and he had slicked down the few wisps that still adorned the top of his head. Slim but muscular, at 5'11" David was three inches taller than I. Dressed in a tailored, avocado-colored cotton suit with A-line skirt, hose and pumps, I tied up my shoulder-length brown hair into a ponytail. We were to be greeted by Counselor Pennacchio when we arrived in Taiz and wanted to at least look the part of a chief of mission and his wife, even if we were a bit unsure of ourselves.

After flying over the Danakil Depression, the plane set down on a dirt landing strip to pick up mail at Assab, near the Red Sea coast of Ethiopia. I noticed only a tin shed and no other structures. Oh, my gosh, I thought. Although I had visited large cities in the developing world, it finally hit me that we were going to someplace really remote.

The Taiz airport was little more impressive than the one at Assab, something I was forced to acknowledge as we swooped down over a mountain onto a crooked, dirt landing field. Automatically tensing for impact, I felt the pilot slam on his brakes so we would not sail off the cliff at the end of the runway. David had warned me about this tricky landing field.

"Whew, we are safely down," I exclaimed, swallowing hard and relaxing back into my seat. Not wanting to display my nervousness any further, even to David, I made small talk as I gazed out the window while the DC-3 taxied to a stop, "Oh, look, that must be Mr. Pennacchio over by that mud-colored building."

Although it was almost May and there was some greenery around the airport, I could not help but notice the huge amount of sand and dry vegetation everywhere. Nor were there any lights at the airport for nighttime flights should we need to get out in a hurry. Hmm, no pavement and no lights—at the airport of the second largest city in Yemen. I was beginning to see the picture David had been trying to paint.

2

Our New Home

A Place to Live

Our Italian host, the man I had spotted from the plane window, greeted us warmly. He located assistance for our bags and had his driver take us to our overnight quarters in the old USAID compound. Left over from the road project, the compound was now under YARG control. However, the Yemen government had returned keys to David so he could use one of the still-furnished cement-block, ranch-style houses as a guest facility. David and Tom had stayed there in March and cleaned out several years of accumulated dust and debris. Wanting to help me land gently, my considerate husband had made the place presentable for our first night in the country. After a quick shower and a little rest, we joined Mr. and Mrs. Pennacchio in their nearby compound home for a quiet dinner.

As one of its major contributions to the development of Yemen's infrastructure, USAID built the well-cambered gravel road from Taiz to Sanaa during the early 1960s. Traversing narrow passes, the new road finally made it possible to get to Sanaa overland through the high mountains without risking one's life. We headed to the capital city over that very road the next morning, driven by Abdul Kadir Farhan, who had been hired by the Italians to work with us.

My first ride through those striking, green-terraced mountains to Sanaa in the Italian embassy's Land Rover offered the magnificent views I had long heard about. We climbed slowly over the

Cultivated fields on the Yarim plain

al-Sayyani pass before reaching the fertile, green basin of Ibb, which experiences the most rainfall in Yemen. Between Ibb and Sanaa we crossed two more mountain passes, first the Sumarra, at 8,775 feet the highest point on the road between Taiz and Sanaa. I was awestruck with the breath-stopping beauty each time we paused for a look down the steep ravines and terraces. Although sometimes covered with coffee bushes, the terraces more often sported qat plants, a more lucrative cash crop than coffee. Chewing the mildly stimulant qat leaves is a national pastime for most of the Yemeni population.

Next we passed through the towns of Yarim, Dhamar, and Mabar, all situated on cultivated agricultural plains, before climbing the Yislah pass and descending to the Sanaa plateau for the final thirty miles. Eventually, we neared Sanaa and spied the two *jebels* or mountains (Nuqum, the highest, and Barish) that sheltered the capital city on its east side.

At last, we arrived at the Bab al-Yemen, the southern gate to the city of Sanaa. I marveled at finally seeing in person this famous structure. Sure enough, there was the Pepsi sign David had

Bab al-Yemen with Pepsi sign

mentioned, plastered on one of the massive pillars that supported the tall gates. The gate, which was part of the thick, mud and brick wall that had surrounded the old city for centuries, had been locked at 8 p.m. each night during the time of the imam (the Shiite religious leader and ruler of Yemen prior to 1962). By 1970 a few parts of the wall and some of the other gates had fallen into disrepair or been intentionally destroyed by the new Republican government.

A camel or two lumbered by, turbaned men pushed carts, and black-draped women carried huge bundles on their heads as they scurried about their daily tasks, paying no attention to us. Without entering the old city, we negotiated around donkey carts and bustling activity to head west on dust-filled Zubairi Street. Spotting a mix of multistoried houses, a couple of minarets, and modern cement-block buildings, we soon turned right onto Abdul Mugni Street. In this newer part of the city, the main streets had been paved by USAID self-help projects in 1966–67, so David was pleasantly surprised to see the changes. We finally arrived at the United Nations guesthouse, which became our headquarters during the initial days we were making the American compound livable.

Our residence was located in the old Turkish garden quarter of Sanaa, the Bir al-Azab, not far from the big square and *hammam* (public bath) at Maydan al-Tahrir. Many trees, including palm and eucalyptus, and large prickly pear plants forested themselves in grassy or garden spaces among the houses and narrow unpaved alleyways. Like other large homes in the Turkish garden quarter, ours was part of a four-acre compound surrounded by a high mud brick wall.

Looking from the outside at our American compound one could see three buildings above the wall. The tallest was a traditional five-story chiseled stone apartment building, solidly built, where we lived with three other American families. The office building, or Chancery, was a more modern two-story stone building. Each building was decorated with stained glass windows. A smaller stone building next to the Chancery served as the consular office. At least two adobe-mud brick buildings (each one story with one or two rooms) also dotted the grounds. One served as a house for the guards on duty and the other a home for Muhammad Abdul Ghani, our stalwart FSN employee who had climbed down into the vault for David and Tom, and his wife, Rashida. Within the high compound walls, plenty of private open space with trees and oleander bushes around the buildings allowed us to enjoy the outdoors away from the eyes of curious spectators.

We slept at the UN guesthouse our first night in Sanaa and ate meals there for five days afterward. Over long dinners on those early nights in our new city we enjoyed meeting Tony Hagen, the Swiss director of the United Nations Development Program (UNDP), and some of his colleagues. They had led fascinating lives in the developing world, and their stories left me, an inexperienced twenty-seven-year-old, wide-eyed and open-mouthed. I felt as if I had dropped in on a different planet. We understood Tony Hagen's view that other Westerners would think us rather eccentric for being someplace with so few amenities and so different from the familiar. At times, as our tour unfolded, I wondered that myself!

Because Americans had not lived in the embassy compound for three years before we arrived, there was a mess to clean up. Numerous broken windows in the buildings had let in enough sand and dirt to fill a truck. The chancery building looked the way it

Bayt al-Hilali

probably had on the day of evacuation. Dead birds and rats, which had partially eaten the carpets, were scattered over the floors. Old, dried coffee sat in the bottoms of mugs as if waiting for the water to be poured. Photos of former Secretary of State Dean Rusk and President Lyndon Johnson graced several rooms. Calendars on the walls read June 1967 and left us with an eerie feeling of time standing still, as if we were in a ghost town.

The second night in Sanaa we slept on the top floor of our apartment building. Called Bayt al-Hilali, it was named for the family who had built the buildings and from whom the Americans had long rented the compound. The top apartment had some twin beds and was the cleanest of the residences. With a little dusting, we could create a place to sleep, using sheets borrowed from the Italians since our airfreight had not yet arrived.

Bayt al-Hilali had not fared as well as the chancery, however, and looked like a warehouse, with pieces of furniture piled to the ceiling in some rooms. The Italian caretaker, D'Amico, had replaced or simply mingled much of the good furniture left in people's homes at the time of evacuation with older, unmatched pieces of furniture brought up from the American compound in

Taiz. Reportedly, D'Amico, whom we labeled "a scoundrel and a thief," had sold much of the good furniture on the open market or distributed it to his friends, leaving us with the mishmash dregs. Since we were initially to be only six U.S. employees, two single men and two married couples, we located just enough furniture among the rubble to set up four apartments. We converted the bottom, windowless floor into a warehouse for the remaining odd pieces.

Luckily, we found six straight-back dining chairs in the warehouse and made it a priority to have replacements as well as other furniture shipped from the regional General Services Office (GSO) warehouse in Beirut. Muhammad Abdul Ghani had tried to guard U.S. property in our absence, but because he received his pay from the Italians, he basically had to do things their way, keeping his lips sealed about D'Amico's unorthodox "caretaking" efforts. "There is American furniture all over town," Muhammad commented, something we verified when visiting foreigners around Sanaa.

David discovered what should have been his leather office sofa in the Italian ambassador's office upon his first visit to Mr. Massa-Bernucci. Diplomatic decorum prevented him from saying anything, for the Italians were our "protecting power" and we were grateful to them. But David secretly delighted in ushering Ambassador Massa-Bernucci on a reciprocal visit to a straight-backed chair in his office, saying, "I'm terribly sorry not to be able to offer you the chargé's comfortable leather sofa. It was missing when we arrived." ("Chargé" is a French term for "envoy." The chargé d'affaires is the diplomat in charge of a mission in the absence of an ambassador or minister.)

Most of the appliances had also been pilfered, but we did find three partially working stoves, a few freezers, one washing machine, and three refrigerators. We bought one Egyptian-made fridge on the local market and waited for new appliances to arrive from the Beirut GSO warehouse. One hard-to-find man, trained in France, put new Freon in the fridges. Miraculously, the freezers were in operating condition.

After three long weeks we managed to make all the apartments clean enough for habitation, though we had been eating and sleeping in one of them for over two weeks. An efficient contracting crew from Taiz conducted the major clean-up operation and made the apartments sparkle with white *guss* (gypsum paint), which they slathered on the dingy walls. I found a sewing machine in the warehouse and made white curtains of sheer organza that I bought in the suq (market).

In June, seven weeks after arriving, we received word that four new electric stoves, two Land Rovers, and some rugs shipped from Beirut had been delivered to the docks in Hodeida. On the Red Sea coast, Hodeida was about four hours from Sanaa. Picking up the shipment with David would be an opportunity to visit the Tihama, a part of Yemen I had not seen.

We drove down in our only vehicle, the VW van, which the Italians purchased for us, having sold *all* the American vehicles left in the compound in 1967. Abdul Nu'man, one of our drivers, and Terry, a TDY communications expert who had come from our embassy in Athens to help us get the mission operational, accompanied us. David and Terry would each drive one of the new Land Rovers back to Sanaa. We planned to make an overnight of it and stay in Hodeida at the Red Sea Hotel recommended by our UN friends. This was a good deal at only $2.50 a night per person.

As we drove to Hodeida and descended to sea level, we scanned the mountain peaks on both sides of the Chinese-built paved road, noticing several villages perched like lookout posts. Reachable only by foot, their strategic locations had historically been a strong deterrent to invaders.

Closer to our target the terrain flattened out and we began to see villages with round grass huts and high-peaked thatched roofs, some at least thirty feel tall. Thorny hedges, looking like tidy fencerows, surrounded groups of houses. Men along the road wore cone-shaped, fine-woven straw hats with flat tops that looked like upended wastebaskets. Women exposed their hair and faces and were dressed more colorfully than in Sanaa. Black robes for women or jackets for men were not needed in this hot, humid climate. Their African features and skin coloring made me think I was in Tanzania or Uganda, not Arabia

Sanaa's high altitude gave us dry but bearable heat June through August. In our excitement about the journey to the roughly

Tihama beehive house

thirty-mile-wide Tihama coastal desert, we had not considered that we would be descending dramatically through the rugged terrain to a tropical climate, where temperatures regularly exceeded 100 degrees in the summer. Approaching the coast, we began to feel a wall of heat rising up the valley from the sea. We figured this would be no problem, since the hotel where we planned to stay had air conditioners (window units, but A/C nonetheless).

We headed straight to the seaport area. It was bustling with wiry, thinly clad laborers, who earned only seventy-five cents a day for guiding donkey carts overloaded with goods through the dusty streets. Our shipment had come overland from Beirut to Aqaba (Jordan), and then by sea to Hodeida. We found the dock and our stoves with the help of an agent we had hired. Still in their cardboard containers banded with steel, the stoves sat in boxes marked with "Up" arrows, which were all pointed downward!

It took four hours in that day's extremely sticky 110-degree-plus temperature for the agent to clear the Land Rovers and stoves through customs. Leaving the docks with our cargo and dripping with sweat, we cooled off by driving our new vehicles, windows open and warm air fanning us, up the coast to Jiinana. There we saw mango groves, date palms, and fishermen in loincloths holding a small stingray they had caught.

After a while, we returned to Hodeida and headed to the main part of town to find our hotel. "Oh, yes, sir, we have two air conditioned rooms for you. I will send someone to turn on the window units right now," declared the hotel clerk in his best English. The nondescript cement-block hotel exceeded our expectations. It was new enough not to show the telltale signs of bubbling, flaky paint that often appears in humid, seaside communities.

David and I eagerly settled into our room and turned on the ceiling fans to augment the A/C. Two single cot-like beds, each with a thin mattress over metal springs, and an old wooden dresser decorated the Spartan but clean room. White *guss* covered the walls, and the woodwork was an apple green. There was a bathroom and shower. The floor was linoleum, easy to sweep and mop in a town that had little paving and regular sandstorms. We closed the scraggly thin curtains and stripped to our underwear, stretching out on the cots to wait for the cooling that was due to arrive any moment.

After thirty minutes or so, we heard a knock on the door and quickly pulled our clothes back on. Terry, still in his jeans and a tee shirt, announced that his A/C was not working. The fan just stirred up hot air. He had been downstairs to find the manager, who told him, "I am sorry. There are no more air-conditioners in this hotel, but we will send someone up to fix it."

The hotel mechanic, who turned out to be the same fellow who had showed us to our room, was unable to get Terry's unit working. So, Terry decided to see how we were faring. Our A/C unit was not functioning at peak capacity, but it was still something to be grateful for. Since it was too late to go back to Sanaa that evening, we suggested to Terry that we all just camp out in our room for the night.

David went out to a couple of appointments that afternoon and returned to the hotel after each with his only shirt dripping wet. He hung it over a chair to dry before his next foray into the outdoor oven.

To cool off, we walked down to the beach that evening, stopping at a small open-air restaurant with a few tables to get something to eat. Several oil slicks caught our eye as we tromped along the beach, as well as some cement-block beach homes built by the many Russians living in Hodeida. We saw fishermen, some scantily clad but wearing big brimmed straw hats, hauling in their daily catch.

Back at the hotel, we found a third cot had been moved into our room. Sprawling onto the cots, we soon realized our air conditioner was no match for the body heat of three people. Throwing modesty aside, the three of us stripped down to our underwear to endure the night. We were thankful we had no flies and that only eight hours stood between us and the relative cool of the mountains en route to Sanaa. The hum of the languid A/C unit drowned out the noises of the street.

When our new furniture arrived in September, it was Spanish style, the latest craze, and dark, carved wood heavier than the older Danish modern–style Kroehler. At last we had eight chairs and four table leaves so we could seat twelve. A monstrous breakfront/buffet arrived with broken glass we had to replace. The flowery sofas and chairs were not to our taste, but they were comfortable, and we decided to relinquish the old, tailored, cream cotton faille upholstered furniture in the living room.

In the large reception room we installed an imposing plywood bar found in the warehouse and covered it with an attractive orange, red, and yellow-striped cloth we had bought in Beirut. The bar stored all our glasses and liquor and was perfect for parties. It must have been a USAID fixture in a club or group facility, perhaps in Taiz, in the early 1960s when the post was much larger.

We also received a new refrigerator, freezer, gas range, washer, and dryer, all the comforts of home. We prayed the fluctuating electricity would not damage them. As much as we appreciated the State Department's support, we both wondered why we really needed all this elaborate furniture in a remote hardship post. The basic necessities would have been more than acceptable. All we had really needed were a few more dining chairs and appliances that worked.

Finally in October, six months after arriving, our 900 pounds of airfreight appeared. It sat in Taiz almost three weeks, so near yet so far away. After much cajoling and pleading from us, Yemen Airlines (YAL) sent a special plane to bring it to Sanaa. The State Department deemed airfreight to be faster than sea freight and authorized it for shorter eighteen-month tours, such as ours. This did not work for us because a moving company in Asmara had repacked it, creating further delays and hazards. My powdered Tide soap had been punctured and decorated our clothing. Someone filched the cranberry sauce for Thanksgiving, but the pumpkin pie mix arrived safely.

Once we unpacked the freight, we put up a few familiar pictures and trinkets to create a cozy home. We basked in the novelty of twelve-foot-high ceilings, two-foot thick walls, crooked wooden roof beams, tile floors, beautifully hand-carved front doors with gray metal door knockers, and eight-inch long heavy metal keys for opening them.

The magnificent stained-glass windows with greens, yellows, blues, and reds shaped into graceful semicircular, fan-shaped

Our living room before new furniture arrived

designs and held in place by a carefully carved network of plaster and white *guss* were the most stunning feature in each apartment. A separate fan-shaped window superimposed from outside onto the inside window had a different design outlined in *guss* and was inset with white glass in lieu of colored. Some of these windows on the outside of our apartment boasted Star of David designs that cast lovely shadows through the pinwheel and floral designs of the inside colored windows.

Wooden-framed, clear glass windows that opened like shutters were situated below the fan-shaped windows. Sometimes it took two or three pieces of the clear glass carefully fitted together to create one window, which left minute air gaps between the individual panes and defeated the insulation effect of the double fanlight windows at the top. However, intricately carved wooden shutters that opened to the outside could be closed over the clear windows below the fan-shaped ones to halt blowing sand and occasional rain.

Whereas the carved-wood shutters were generally made by artisans in South Asia and shipped to Yemen through the Indian

Sanaa skyline from our rooftop

Ocean, local Jewish artisans years ago had designed and made most of the fan-shaped windows in these old buildings. Fortunately, before about 45,000 Jews were airlifted to Israel beginning in 1948 on the Operation Magic Carpet flights, they taught their skills to the local craftsmen, who continued the art in post-1950 buildings. There are now only a few hundred Jews left in Sanaa and the northern part of Yemen.

We had chosen the west-facing third floor apartment (the one whose windows are highlighted on the front cover) rather than the top two-level apartments primarily because we (and our guests) would have fewer steps to climb. Our apartment still had plenty of entertaining space and was higher than most other buildings in the neighborhood. We loved to gaze through the panorama of eleven-plus windows in the dining and living rooms, for they gave us a sweeping 270-degree view of the city below and mountains in the distance.

Dust suspended in the air cast a magical aura over the rooftops, creating an "other-world" picture and wonderful feelings I can still evoke today. We were living in a home that was by far the most exotic we ever had, before or after.

The Challenge of Necessities

At first, water was our major problem. Laborers pulling donkey carts delivered it to the compound in the weeks before we could hire a man to come and clean out the well. The cleaning allowed good water to flow for a week until the old Czech pump broke. When that happened we called in the one man who supposedly could fix it. By reputation, we knew he was a qat chewer who only worked from eight until noon each day.

Webster's defines qat as the leaves of *Catha edulis*, a southwest Asian and African shrub, which is a member of the staff-tree family. It is chewed as a stimulant or made into a tea. However, many Yemenis do become "addicted" to the ritual of the daily qat chew and spend numerous hours chewing, to the detriment of their productivity.

The pump repairman always appeared "stoned" and was referred to by Westerners and our FSNs as a qat addict. Although we had hoped his shop would reopen in the late afternoon following the qat chewing, he said he could not come for five days to fix the pump. We borrowed water from the Italians, resorted once again to buying tanks of water hauled in on donkey carts, and scrounged enough for the bare necessities.

Finally, we grew tired of waiting for the qat addict to finish the job he started, so we bought a new East German pump. After a week without baths, we had water again. The addict wanted his parts back from the old Czech pump. We relinquished them, but refused to release the whole pump for fear he would repair and resell it to some unsuspecting customer.

Whether our water came from the well or off a donkey cart, we had to make it potable through a complicated process. The well water was pumped to holding tanks on the roof, where it stayed until the kitchen tap was turned on. We collected a gallon or so of water, adding a few drops of Purex to kill germs. We poured that water into the top half of a filter so that it could seep through two ceramic "candles" into the bottom half. Detailed instructions that we gave the servants continued: "After water goes through filter number 1, fill the large teakettle from the bottom of filter number 1. Boil that water on top of stove (with fire on highest flame) to a rolling boil for 30 minutes. When boiled water has cooled, pour that water into filter number 2. Fill water bottles, ice trays, teapot for coffee water, etc., from filter number 2." Boiling the water also helped distill the alkali out of it. It was at least a one-hour process to get a glass of water into our hands, but it was our best hope for staying well.

Butagas was another problem. Gas cost $2.50 a bottle and lasted three weeks on average. The gas fueled our kitchen stove and the old British hot water flash heaters. Finding valves for the bottles and flash heaters, as well as parts for various appliances and machines, often required a trip to Taiz or Hodeida.

Invariably we would run out of butagas at nine p.m.—just at my bath time—forcing the pilot lights on the flash heaters to go out. I would have to dress and go find Muhammad Abdul Ghani to bring in and hook up a new bottle and then relight the pilot. Even when the butagas bottle was full, the pilot lights on the flash heaters frequently went out, often leaving David all lathered up to shave just as the hot water disappeared. He finally gave up trying to shave and grew a beard, which he kept for the next seventeen years.

Having electricity was not guaranteed either, since the whole apartment building needed new wiring. Hundred-watt light bulbs would frequently dim to fifty watts. The fluctuating 220-volt AC current placed a terrible strain on the appliances. The voltage was often too low to trip the refrigerator's relay and keep the fridge running, resulting in lots of groaning and clicking on and off. Our freezer and toaster operated only on 110 volts and we had to use a small step-down transformer to run them.

When a major power failure occurred we never went for more than a day or two without electricity, but we had enough electrical appliances, including fridges with frozen food in them, to put us in a dither when an outage occurred. We did purchase an old Fairbanks-Morse backup generator that would power our communications gear through lengthy emergencies, and eventually we used that to power our homes in the evenings as well. When parts for that backup generator broke and we had to send someone to Taiz to replace a simple $10 item, we really got nervous.

Communication with the outside world was another challenging priority. It was several weeks before we got the chancery phones hooked up to the Yemen phone system. We had a four-digit phone number (7290, later changed for some reason to 2790) to make local phone calls, but that proved unreliable. Phone service cut off frequently, just like the electricity.

We could not call outside of town or place international calls during our time there. Only after Cable and Wireless, a British company, set up a satellite between White Plains, New York, and Sanaa, which relayed through Bahrain, were we able to receive international calls. Jack O'Donnell got the first such call—loud and clear— regarding a visa case, but even this new capability did not improve our ability to send messages home.

Our own expert from Washington, John Cole, and his wife Diane did not arrive until the end of June to set up the mission's telecommunications gear. So, initially, we had to rely on the Italian embassy in Taiz to get out our official cable traffic. Only in an emergency could we send personal messages through official channels.

Since phone calls were impossible and commercial cables expensive, letters and tapes became our best means of communication. When feasible, we asked visitors headed to Europe or the States to carry our letters. We also instituted a weekly unclassified pouch for personal mail to the United States sent out on Yemen Airlines (YAL) to the consulate in Asmara for routing through the State Department in Washington or the military's APO system. Later, when Saudi Airlines inaugurated regular air service into Sanaa, we shipped out unaccompanied mail pouches through Jidda.

For mail that was classified, in ascending order of secrecy, from administratively controlled Limited Official Use (LOU) to Confidential, Secret, or Top Secret, we set up a twice-weekly pouch run. Handled by a U.S. government (USG) courier, official classified correspondence as well as personal letters and tapes, could be sent and received more frequently.

We took every opportunity we could to send reassuring letters or tapes to our parents, but these often took ten days or more to reach them via the pouch. Only now that I have my own children who travel to remote parts of the world can I look back and imagine how worried my parents must have been about me living, practically incommunicado, halfway around the world. And they did not have the instantaneous phone communication, much less email we have today, to assuage their fears.

Even the airlines had problems that caused us to experience courier and pouch delays. In three consecutive weeks Saudi Airlines had to cancel flights into Hodeida or Sanaa due to mechanical problems such as loss of hydraulic fluid, a blown tire, navigational equipment failure, or lack of lights for a delayed, after-dark landing.

Sometimes it was not the airline's fault. Once, when Saudi Airlines got within the twenty-five-mile navigational range of Sanaa airport, the pilot called the tower for directions. A voice came over the radio: "Sorry, the air traffic controller is away in Jidda on a scholarship." That pilot had to come in on a wing and a prayer.

Yemen Airlines flew Russian planes the USG regarded as unsafe at the time and discouraged us from using these aircrafts. During the late 1960s and early 1970s, YAL had two plane crashes within six years, which reinforced the State Department's concern. Fortunately, these were only cargo flights, so fewer lives were lost. Still, we relied heavily on YAL's cargo flights and occasionally a courier had to use YAL when a Saudi Airlines flight was cancelled.

Ambassador David Newton told me an "airline story" that occurred in 1972 after we left Yemen. A Saudi Airlines (Saudia) Convair was unable to find Sanaa airport and landed on the Sanaa-Taiz road near Mabar, taxiing off the road, with no one hurt. Saudia personnel stripped the plane of avionics, seats, and other items and painted over the name. When Newton traveled on the road periodically, he watched the plane slowly disappear as Yemenis disassembled it.

One of the first things we did after getting our place cleaned was locate servants. Having someone to do the shopping, mopping, laundry, and cooking was essential because of the entertaining we were expected to do and my working fulltime as USINT's secretary. We had a servant allowance that covered only one employee, so we wanted to find someone willing and able to handle both cooking and housework. I had never worked with hired help before and figured our small two-bedroom apartment could not handle two employees even if we had wanted to spend our own money for the additional person. We knew we could hire extra help for parties.

Abdullah Muhammad Saad, our first dual-duty servant, had worked for the previous two chargés, primarily as a house servant who assisted the cook as needed. Hoping he had learned something about cooking during his previous employ, we had new khaki uniforms made for him for everyday use and white ones for entertaining. To finish off his uniform, he wore a beanie or skullcap, as they did in Jibla, where he came from.

His assistance was an absolute necessity for our many spur-of-the-moment guests. A real jewel, he was a quiet, shy, small man, age about forty. He was the father of four girls (five others had died, illustrative of Yemen's child mortality rate of 50 percent in 1970). I do not know where he lived, but, like most working-class Yemenis, he had no refrigerator and probably little furniture. He welcomed the gift of a baby bed we found in the storeroom.

Abdullah did not speak much English. When I could not make myself understood, I grabbed David or one of our FSN employees to translate. He could not read English recipes either. For anything new and special, I took time off from the office to supervise his work and often ended up cooking it myself. But he was helpful in many other aspects of housekeeping that made up for his limitations as a cook.

Initially, we did not find it difficult to locate qualified or at least "trainable" help. Retraining servants who had worked for the British and tended to boil everything was always a challenge. We taught them how to spice up food for the American palate and how to serve correctly. (Once, Abdullah set the platter of food down on a chair rather than the table or buffet.)

Teaching servants to use kitchen equipment was a particular problem since modern gadgets and appliances were practically unknown to them. Abdullah once poured hot grease into my Tupperware plastic container and could not understand why it crumpled. He could never remember to use plastic utensils in Teflon pans, which he scratched down to the aluminum. Then I was more worried about damaging my new pan, whereas today the flaking Teflon on an aluminum pan would be considered a health hazard.

Abdullah also struggled to understand how the stove timer worked. Once he set it to go off twelve hours later than intended. At one a.m., David was awakened by a strange ticking noise in the kitchen. "Is that the butagas bottle about to explode?" my panicked husband asked as he shook me awake. We jumped up and stood outside the kitchen door, which was right next to our bedroom, listening carefully. "That sounds like the stove timer. Abdullah must have set it wrong," I calmly responded. Relieved, we finally decided it was safe enough to enter and turn it off.

One evening during Abdullah's employ, I was excited to have purchased some imported bacon from a friend. It was our first since Asmara. I wrapped the bacon around well-tenderized pieces of local filet and showed Abdullah how to cook them under the broiler. Unfortunately, despite his training, Abdullah's penchant for cooking things to oblivion won out. The saving grace for the meal was a delicious baked potato that accompanied the crispy, charred meat. Imported Danish butter, far superior to the local brand of canned margarine, topped the potatoes. To his credit, though, Abdullah tried hard and often baked David chocolate cakes in an effort to fatten him up.

Another time, when we expected luncheon guests, Abdullah did not show up for work. I quickly arranged for another employee's cook to come and help. Worried about Abdullah, who was always reliable, we sent Muhammad Abdul Ghani to look for him. Muhammad found Abdullah in the Yemeni hospital, recovering from an operation. Earlier that week Abdullah had complained of hemorrhoids to David, so we sent him to Dr. Mario Livadiotti, a respected Italian doctor in Sanaa, for some nonsurgical solution (probably an antihemorrhoid salve like Preparation-H). Abdullah had been too embarrassed to tell us he preferred to have a Yemeni doctor surgically remove the problem rather than follow the Western doctor's prescriptions. He said Dr. Mario's medicine had prevented him from sleeping.

To our surprise, Abdullah was back at work in an amazingly short time. He never mentioned the surgery or asked for a reduction in household duties due to pain. We paid him 250 riyals a month, about $43, a high salary by Yemeni standards for a cook at that time. We were told that senior Yemeni government ministers made only $95 per month.

Muhammad Abdullah Radub from the Hujariyya (south of Taiz) replaced Abdullah, who resigned after four months to join his immigrant brother in the United States. Far superior to Abdullah as a cook, Muhammad did not need much supervision. He could even read my English recipes in the cookbooks. With Muhammad's custard and mince pies, homemade rolls, and imaginative recipes, David soon began regaining the weight he had lost from stress and illness.

On a Monday night in September 1970, we hosted our first big dinner party for about twenty-five people—a successful buffet that came off with no hitches. Although we had managed a large cocktail party while Abdullah was with us, this dinner party was payback for the many social obligations we had incurred. After four months at post, I had at last assembled the ingredients and mustered the confidence to attempt such a feat, thanks to Muhammad's support and expertise.

Muhammad had faithfully worked for us for seven months when, in March 1971, we acquired Fritz, a cute waif of a puppy we found wandering along the road to Hodeida. We took Fritz home

Abdul

Sayf

and kept him in the bathroom until he was housebroken. Muhammad refused to go into the bathroom to clean. Whereas Americans love dogs and treat them like family, Yemenis do not like them, much less tolerate them inside the house. So, we had to let Muhammad go. He quickly found another job where he did not have to clean and could focus on his cooking. When Fritz got bigger and could fend for himself with the other dogs, he began staying outside, but not before we'd lost Muhammad. This particular cultural difference in perspective and priorities, one of many we encountered, turned out to be his gain and our loss.

We had two more house servants during our tour, Abdul and Sayf, whose stories were similar to our first two and to those of most other servants working in Sanaa. Many had worked for foreign embassies in Sanaa or Taiz, for the British in Aden or the Americans at Aramco in Dhahran, and were happy to see Westerners returning to Sanaa and giving them work.

Servants did make life a lot easier for us and also more engaging—their stories added a different perspective on Yemeni life than we were getting from the upper echelons of society. Some of their mistakes or misadventures thirty years ago amused us and were typical of those found in other hardship posts. Today, in our global economy, I suspect that servants in places like Yemen are a lot more

Fritz as a puppy

sophisticated and knowledgeable of Western ways.

At first, before we had trained the servants to function effectively for our purposes, we lived off canned goods from the Arab Unity store. A small grocery store where Westerners shopped, it imported such items as tuna from Japan, Chinese green peas and egg rolls, and Russian green beans. Local flour was often buggy, so we imported both white and whole wheat from Asmara. We could not get pasteurized milk products and reluctantly drank the powdered variety. I remember once trying to make whipped cream for a dessert out of powdered Richning, but it tasted nothing like the real stuff. Canned Velveeta made us long for a trip to Asmara or Jidda, where fresh cheeses were available.

As soon as we were set up in the apartments, we brought in commissary goods from Asmara by airfreight. Vienna sausage, two-ply toilet paper, Cheez-Its, and soda crackers, and items from Asmara Frozen Foods might seem mundane to some, but to us they were pure luxury. Shipped in on YAL at $.17 a pound, these reminders of our Western heritage were well worth the added expense. Since we had to order in case lots (twenty-four boxes of chocolate cake mix, forty-eight cans of pie cherries, twelve boxes of Bisquick), we divided the lots up among the families. What spices and seasonings I could not find locally or in Asmara, I had my mother send me via APO.

We ate local lamb liver and bony, free-range chicken. Once our cook brought a live chicken with its legs tied together into the house. He wrung its neck and hacked off its head right there in the kitchen. Though I refused to watch the deed, I felt confident the meat was fresh.

Because the local chickens were hard to chew, we often resorted to buying frozen imports flown in from Taiz or Aden for $1.75 each. Local beef was also tough. So, we ordered Kenyan beef along with other luxuries, such as lobster tails, ice cream, and Birds Eye frozen orange juice flown up from Aden Cold Storage in the PDRY.

We learned one trick from the cooks for making local meat tender: let it age for several days in the refrigerator while the blood drips out. The local filet of beef tenderloin at eighty-five cents per kilo responded well to this technique, but it was also quite passable if I beat it and added tenderizer when there was no time to let it age. I tried every possible recipe I could think of with tenderloin and we got spoiled eating it several times a week, something we could never afford in the States.

I abhorred the idea of going to the local meat market, which had no inspections and was reportedly unsanitary. Fortunately, our cook spared me the task. Had I ventured there, I would probably have become a vegetarian before it was fashionable.

Occasionally we got a treat when friends brought seafood up to us from Hodeida: shrimp, lobster, roe, and flounder, welcome diversions from red meat and chicken. Since Yemen was a Muslim country, there was no pork to be found locally and we had to import it. Once when Abdullah's brother came from the States to visit, they slaughtered a sheep and brought us a tender leg of lamb as a wonderful treat.

Our cooks made nice green salads that did not make us sick because they cleaned the veggies in potassium permanganate and double-filtered water. We got fresh limes from Taiz in the summer months. Abdullah was resourceful and made homemade mayonnaise with twenty eggs and a whole bottle of olive oil beaten together. When certain items were scarce or nonexistent locally, he also went to his hotel friends and, for a little baksheesh, could get eggs, lettuce, and other items, depending on how much we were willing to pay.

During the first few months in Yemen we spent most of every day just dealing with basic needs like water, electricity, food, and administrative crises. There was little time for photographs, and I discovered very few from those early days of chaos. It was even a challenge to stay healthy, as discussed later. Our household servants and several folks working for USINT Sanaa helped us through those stressful early months. Eventually things improved, and we began to enjoy our new home in this exotic location so far away in both distance and style from life in the United States.

Sanaa, Our New City

Far different from the chic of Beirut, Sanaa would be my new home for almost two years. Fortunately, David had prepared me well and I was not shocked by the stark contrast between the two cities. I looked for and saw the magic in my exotic new home—the otherworldliness of it. I soon discovered for myself, after meeting some of the Yemeni people, what David had raved about ever since he left the post the first time in 1966.

Sanaa, which means "well fortified" in ancient South Arabian, is one of the oldest continually inhabited cities in the world. It served as one of the centers for the prosperous caravan trade route some two thousand years ago. When we arrived in 1970, the city had about 80,000 inhabitants.

Situated on a plain surrounded by mountains, Sanaa is not far from Jebel Nabi Shu'ayb, the highest point in the Arabian Peninsula. Sanaa's 7,500-ft. elevation fifteen degrees above the equator made the climate a pleasant 30°F–85°F year-round. Its overall setting—dry, dusty mountains in one direction, plains with distant mountains in the other—reminded me of New Mexico near Albuquerque. Rains came in the spring and early fall, providing enough moisture for crops and gardens, sprinkling Sanaa with some greenery amidst the dirt and mud-colored buildings.

Many of Sanaa's adobe houses (made of clay, sand, and straw blocks) resembled older homes on Indian reservations in the American Southwest. These one-story buildings were interspersed with minarets atop an estimated 100 mosques and 14,000 multistory, basalt or lava stone and fired brick "tower house" buildings. A few of the tower houses around town were as tall as nine stories, according to Ronald Lewcock (1986), but most were four or five stories. Many had the semicircular fanlike stained glass windows in their higher floors, as did our house, while other older buildings had smaller windows of translucent alabaster.

Guss delineated the various floors and external features of the buildings, making these houses resemble a square, multilayered, milk chocolate wedding cake, with white lace icing separating the tiers and draped in intricate patterns along the sides. They re- minded me of the ginger cookie houses—minus pitched roof—that Americans make at Christmastime.

In the early 1970s, the sanitary conditions in the old part of the city shocked most Westerners. We had to walk carefully through the narrow passageways between houses. The beautiful multilevel, wedding-cake buildings had little stone chutes with openings (like gutter pipes) that stuck out the sides of each floor. Carved out and plastered over, vertical channels ran down the buildings' sides, connecting the chutes and allowing gray water and urine to drain into a septic basin at the houses' street level.

In contrast, an internal pipe carried feces from each floor's bathroom down several stories to a holding area at ground level, where it dried and was shoveled out periodically by men who carried the residue by the donkey load to the public *hammam*. There it was burned to heat water for the baths. Later, the ashes were dumped on gardens as natural fertilizer. In the dry climate of the old city of Sanaa this Yemeni drop-toilet sewage system, still found in 1970 and regulated by the authorities, was remarkably ingenious, and certainly more sustainable than the flush toilet system that apparently has now largely replaced the old method.

The peoples' dress and customs distinguished Yemen from its more modern Arab neighbors. In 1970, walking along the main streets or in the old city of Sanaa, we could usually tell whether the

Tower house in Sanaa

men were highlanders or lowlanders merely by their headdresses. In the Sanaa highlands turbaned men, often with beards or mustaches, wore *zinnas* (ankle-length dresses with long, tight sleeves) or knee-length *futas* (skirts) of solid or striped cotton cinched with a belt of leather or bright cloth that held a large *janbiyya* (curved dagger) or an *asib* (smaller, straight dagger used by nontribesmen).

The *janbiyya* or the *asib* was a sign of manhood, a social marker akin to the Western necktie. It was rarely removed from its scabbard and almost never used as a weapon. A man's status in society was also announced by how the turban was wrapped and knotted.

Turbaned man with *lihfah* and bowl

A cotton jacket or polyester Western-style suit coat covered the long-sleeved dress or shirt stuffed into the skirt. Some men wore a striped cotton cloth or shawl thrown over one shoulder (*lihfah*), which indicated they were sayyids, descendants of the Prophet through his grandson Hussein. The *lihfah* also served the practical use of carrying groceries or qat from the market.

Rather than the turban, men from the lowlands near Taiz often wore a knitted beanie or skullcap (*kufi*) along with the traditional dress. Flip-flops, plastic sandals, or regular men's close-toed shoes, with or without socks, adorned their feet unless they chose to go barefoot. In 1970 in Sanaa, one saw military uniforms and Western clothing sprinkled only lightly amidst the traditional dress.

Lealan Swanson in *sharshaf* and *lithma*

The Sanaani women balanced enormous bundles or buckets on their heads as they traveled on foot throughout the city to the suq or the nearest water well or public fountain. One prominent style of dress seen on the streets was the black two-piece *sharshaf*, circular cape that covered the head, arms, and shoulders across the back. The lower half of the outfit was a long black skirt, tied or pinned at the waist. Some younger women wore the black *abayah*, a tubelike garment one slipped over one's body, covering a street dress and held at the top with one hand.

The other outfit worn on the streets of Sanaa at that time was the *sitara*, an Indian cotton paisley print spread or tablecloth. Featuring blues, reds, blacks, and whites, the cloth covered the body from head to foot. The face was covered by a light silk or cotton square cloth called a *moghmuq*, dyed in red, black, and white circles like bulls' eyes and attached to a *rais*, a heavier hat/cap that held the moghmuq in place.

Underneath the outer garments Sanaani women usually wore the black *lithma*, a long chiffon head scarf that encircled the head and was wrapped in such a way as to completely cover the hair and allow a narrow opening for the eyes. Long-sleeved dresses with pants underneath or, even more daring, fashionable miniskirts among the younger women, accompanied the *lithma* and were exposed to female friends and family when indoors. Passers-by on the street saw only figures covered from head to foot, veiled or partially veiled faces, dark eyes, and perhaps hennaed hands to indicate there was a mysterious human being behind the flowing robes.

Besides walking, the main modes of transport for the average, nonmilitary Sanaanis were old cars, motor scooters, or donkey carts. A few camels with riders and cargo lumbered along the streets as well. Dogs, sometimes packs of them, roamed the streets as scavengers, not pets. Tan, brown, or black, these mongrels were thin and bony. The females had sagging teats. All cowered because of their poor treatment by the Yemenis, who believed dogs were filthy (*wassakh*). Nevertheless, these packs cleaned the garbage, so no one wanted to shoot them. We saw one poor dog eating chicken feathers, as there was no other food for him to forage.

Finely decorated minarets dotted the skyline and offered up their haunting call to prayer. "*Allah-hu akbar! Allah-hu akbar!* (God is great)," wailed the muezzin through a loudspeaker near our house between four and four thirty each morning. The muezzin's call always set off hundreds of street dogs howling and usually woke us up. Other than the dogs yapping at the slightest provocation and the muezzin's calls to prayer, our neighborhood was quiet.

Everything was *bukra*, tomorrow. Big meals were eaten at noon, followed by naps, qat chewing, and back to work for some by late afternoon. We learned that if we desperately needed something, we had to plead that it be done before noon. Otherwise, it would be *bukra* before the workers showed up again. In Sanaa, life was so focused on meeting daily survival needs no one thought much about time. The muezzin's call to prayer five times a day was the only clock people needed. Except for Friday, the Muslim holy day, they paid little attention to what day of the week it was.

Wandering through the suq in the old part of Sanaa took me to a surreal world. At night, I felt as though I were walking through a foglike forest of huts, sheds, and tall buildings. I expected a goblin to jump out at each turn.

One crisp evening during our first October there, we ventured into a smoky maze of buildings in the old suq with our friend David Ransom, who was visiting from the States. A Foreign Service officer who had also had "the Yemen experience," David enjoyed returning to his familiar haunts in Sanaa. Our friend seemed to know every narrow passageway and specialty shop in the suq, and we delighted in learning his secrets.

As we turned one corner after another, kerosene lanterns and alabaster oil lamps, the primary means of lighting in the old city, cast an eerie glow upon the wizened faces of the shopkeepers. The scents of cinnamon bark, ginger, cumin, cardamom, and other spices blended with the smells of oil, incense, and smoke. Normally, the shops were closed in the evenings, but now it was Ramadan. During this holy month, eating, drinking, having sex, and visiting could occur only after sunset, which encouraged shopkeepers to stay open for their friends and the possibility of making a few riyals (at that time, a riyal equaled about U.S. fourteen cents).

Sanaa minaret and woman in *sitara*

Sanaa was a study in contrasts. Where we lived—outside the old city and its exotic suq—there were shops and businesses similar to those in more Westernized Arab countries. The next night we treated David Ransom to dinner at the newly opened European-style Romantic Restaurant in this newer part of the city. After ushering us to a table for four, complete with a white cloth set with forks, napkins, and knives, the waiter brought us menus written in their best English. The menu featured "asprey grass soup and paper stake," which I ordered and which tasted better than it was spelled.

While we were eating, a loud noise drew our attention to the Japanese ambassador accredited to Yemen, who was sitting at a nearby table with his back to the wall. We turned to see him carefully lifting an oil painting off his head and shoulders. The restaurant's collection of artists' works left there on consignment had apparently not been nailed securely to the wall. The ambassador took it in good stride, amidst vigorous apologies from the waiters.

Later that fall, I asked Abdul Nu'man, our driver, to take me to the suq to buy a very special Christmas present for my husband. Having been there on numerous occasions, I was not afraid to meander through the streets in a trench coat and jeans, with a scarf covering my hair. After all, Abdul Nu'man was with me to run interference and translate if needed.

We located the tiny, packed stalls of "antique alley," where David and I had found his 1840 Ottoman rifle with its cushioned shoulder padding and decorative brass on the stock. During our tour we also purchased other rare souvenirs in these narrow alleyways: a brass Torah finial that predated the Jews' departure from Yemen; old metal and wooden locks; silver and gold bracelets containing intricate filigree; amber beads; a gold necklace linked with tiny stars of David and holding a pendant of rough pearls set in a delicate filigree design; an 1878 French-made pistol; carved wooden tobacco boxes with mother-of-pearl, camel bone, or button inlay; alabaster lamps; and a 17-inch woman's belt (too small for any Western woman!) with silver amulets and inlaid red glass, purportedly worn by the first lady in a harem.

That particular day I spied amongst the hoards of trinkets a small silver *janbiyya* with lovely filigree on the case. David had told

Spice seller in suq wearing *kufi*

me the young princes of the royal family had worn these small silver daggers after they reached puberty. It would make a perfect mate to the large one we had already purchased, the kind worn by an adult male of prominence or royalty.

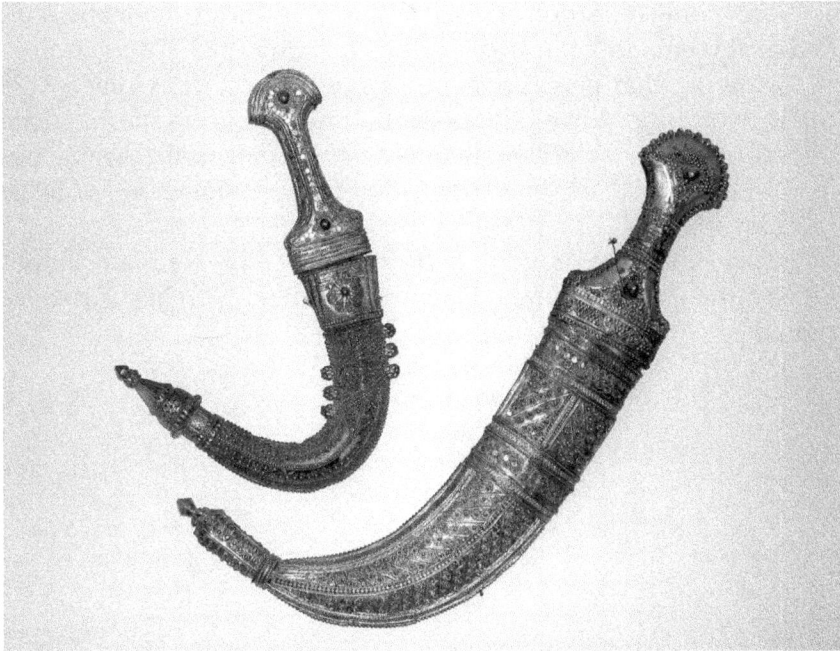

Our silver *janbiyyas*

But, how could I get it for a good price? I had had several lessons in bargaining, beginning with a thirty-minute tea-drinking chat we had in Istanbul when we purchased our award-winning Russian samovar, which we named Anatoli. Now was my chance to see if those lessons worked in Sanaa.

I quickly turned my focus to a larger silver *janbiyya*, also heaped up among the antiques on the floor. "*Adaysh?*" I asked, pointing to the large dagger.

He answered in Arabic, "300 riyals," and raised three fingers in the air.

Shaking my head, I pursed my lips and frowned, indicating it was too much. He shrugged his shoulders and gestured with his hands that he was not bargaining. I turned my back to walk away and "suddenly" spied a much smaller silver *janbiyya*.

Pointing to the object of my desire, I asked "*Adaysh?*" I quickly added, "It contains *swiyah* silver compared to the larger *janbiyya* over there."

After some reflection and scratching of his head, he finally nodded in agreement that it was smaller and suggested 200 riyals.

Knowing that he expected a counter offer, I threw back "175 riyals," (or twenty-five dollars at the time), holding the requisite fingers in the air, which came faster than speaking the Arabic numerals. He smiled and handed me the *janbiyya* while I pulled riyals from my wallet.

I was extremely proud of myself. Even Abdul Nu'man complimented me on my feat. And David was thrilled with his Christmas present.

3

Daily Life at Post

Life around the Compound

Daily life at USINT Sanaa brought its own surprises. Equipment breakdowns, administrative crises with the Yemen government, expected and unexpected visitors, or some personnel problem with our faithful local employees determined each day's priorities. These uncertainties kept us on our toes, creating more challenges and excitement than we ever bargained for.

Many of the crises affected our personal as well as official living regimen. It seemed we were always trying to climb from the bottom rung of Maslow's hierarchy of physical and security issues to the next rung of social well-being. We would make it for a while until the next problem. Then we would slip back down a rung.

David believed the jinn had cast a spell on us, making life much more difficult than it should be. He concluded we were not being sufficiently respectful to these spirits, since we were constantly having mechanical breakdowns. One day he put cookies out under an obviously magical tree with five trunks that our guard Salah said was where the jinn lived. That whole day went so smoothly we decided it would be to our advantage to feed the jinn regularly with some sweet delicacy. We continued to do so, but appeasing the supernatural proved only partially successful.

Although every day was different, the unexpected was the norm. Some of our most memorable times around the compound were those days on which the diplomatic pouch was due to go out.

The twice-weekly classified pouch was hand-carried to Jidda or Asmara by an American official, one of us, or a courier who'd flown in.

One typical pouch day, completely unannounced, a fellow from Catholic Relief Services (CRS) walked into my second-floor secretarial office, adjacent to David's. "I'm here from New York and need to find out about the wheat I'm to help distribute for the U.S. government in the famine areas," he advised as I jumped up to alert David in the adjacent office.

Quickly shedding his surprise, David greeted him as if we had known he was coming. David also wanted to cover up what was often some mix-up in communication between Washington and Rome or Sanaa. Since there were no phones, I ran over to our apartment. "Abdullah," I ordered, "put on an extra plate for lunch and whip up some of your vanilla custard for dessert."

After a politely brief lunch, David excused himself from the table, leaving me to complete the pleasantries. He ran out the door to clean the *shadrawan* (Persian fountain) for the children's weekly swimming party. Since David's jerry-rigged filter system did not work very well, his personal attention was needed each time we invited friends over.

By four thirty, the New York visitor was on his way. Our swimming guests, the German (FRG) ambassador's wife, Ulrike Vestring, with her three children and a Yemeni general and his children, were sitting around the pool. "I wonder where Abdullah is with our tea and cookies," I said to my guests. "He was supposed to be here at five. He's usually prompt."

I excused myself briefly to look for him, but no Abdullah. He showed up with the tea at five thirty, to my great relief, telling us his wife had given birth to their fifth daughter that afternoon! (In his quiet, self-effacing way, he had gone home after lunch without mentioning what was up. If I had known, I would have told him to take the day off.)

While I was at the pool, David petitioned to get our driver Abdul Nu'man out of jail. When driving the Land Rover through Sanaa, Abdul had been hit by a motorcycle. Although the accident was not his fault, it took some effort to get him released. David's official request to the YAR did the trick. We did not want him to languish in jail overnight, and we desperately needed him to drive us to Taiz on a pouch run the next morning. Otherwise, David, who had been running a temperature of 103 degrees all day, would have had to drive the long trip himself.

But the day was still not over. At six thirty FRG Ambassador Alfred Vestring summoned David to his office for an urgent message, which had to be conveyed to Washington that evening due to the eight-hour time difference. We gobbled down a late dinner of leftovers and rushed back to the office to seal official papers in the pouch and write a carbon-copied letter to our parents. Last-minute crunches made personalized letters rare, but we did not want to worry them by noncommunication. Pouch day always seemed to turn into a photo finish, often close to midnight.

That was pouch day. Once during that first August we had an entire week when almost everything that could went wrong. In

Abdul Nu'man with our daughter Anna

letters home we labeled it "the week that was." We were between administrative officers, which left David responsible for handling all the crises even though he was still weak from what doctors called a blood infection. Our water pump broke while the carriers who delivered water from donkey carts were on strike. In the midst of the water crisis, our consular officer's servant left the faucet open in our apartment building, allowing all the water we had managed to save in the roof storage tank to drain out. Going several days without baths in the heat of summer was the least of our worries, but it was an uncomfortable annoyance.

That same week, two banking officials from the United States arrived unannounced, and we had to entertain and make appointments for them. Our embassy translator disappeared, and we had to get him out of jail for something he did not do. YAL lost two of our mail pouches, which did not turn up for several days. Rick Rauh, our consular officer, had an accident with the Land Rover, leading to one man's death and a run-in with some angry tribesmen. John and Diane Cole had their kitchen demolished by fire when their cook failed to hook up the butagas correctly. We were afraid we were going to have to evacuate the whole apartment building until someone found a fire extinguisher in the storeroom.

In the midst of all that chaos, we did enjoy hosting two small dinner parties and even attended three parties that week. Visiting with friends gave us a chance to relieve the tension and to look back and laugh at our misadventures.

Getting the mission to function smoothly took a while. We had two lines of defense against the problems that arose daily, both involving personnel. The first was our American staff—four men and three women—all working for the mission. The first five months were difficult because these American employees dribbled in slowly through the end of August. Administrative problems were our biggest headache, and it did not help that we lost our first administrative officer, a bachelor who found Yemen too isolated. It took two months to locate and bring on his replacement.

Temporary assignee Rick and his replacement, Jack O'Donnell, had their own problems at the consulate, which was always a busy place. As many as a hundred visa applicants crowded around the entrance daily. Once, they were so eager they knocked over the guard at the door, requiring a trip to the hospital, where the poor fellow was given a bottle of vitamins to help him feel better.

One of the more humorous situations occurred at the hands of the Yemeni consular assistant Rick hired. After wasting hours trying to find some files, Jack discovered the fellow had filed all the visa applications backwards. It made perfect sense to him because Arabic is read from right to left, the opposite of English.

When our replacement administrative officer, Walt O'Grady, and his wife Peg arrived at the end of August, the State Department had by then become convinced the consulate needed some efficient help and hired Peg as a temporary employee during her tour. The job was a benefit to Peg, too, since she was a non-Arabic-speaking housewife with no work to occupy her time in those early days. Long hours of inactivity would probably have tried her sanity. Having lost one American, we did not want others jumping ship. With Peg's help, the consulate managed to process the backlog of visa applications left over from the forced closure of our consulate in Aden in October 1969, when the PDRY broke relations with us. Before then, the Aden consulate had taken over issuing visas to Yemenis after the United States had been forced to evacuate Sanaa in June 1967.

People popped into our offices constantly until we found a Yemeni receptionist to run interference. The many interruptions forced us to do major work at night, making ten- to twelve-hour workdays for both of us in our first months of operation. Theoretically, we worked Saturday through Wednesday, though Thursdays usually found us at the office, too. The mission recognized the Muslim holy day of Friday for its day of rest. We were indirectly compensated for these stressful six-day workweeks because the State Department paid us a differential of a half-day's pay for working on Sundays.

Our second, and often most important, line of defense against daily challenges was the local Yemeni staff, Foreign Service National (FSN) employees of the USG. When anything broke down either in the apartments or at the office, we usually called on two FSNs: Muhammad Abdul Ghani Nagi and Abdul Kadir Farhan, both of whom I've mentioned earlier. Both in their twenties, these young men were our right hands. They knew how to fix things, find obscure items in the local market needed for repairs, and generally how to solve any problem "Yemeni style." Other employees helped out too, but these two reopened the U.S. mission with us and were indispensable.

Muhammad Abdul Ghani, who hailed from Taiz, served as guard, gardener, and janitor, doing repair and maintenance on all of our appliances and machinery. Hired by the USG in 1962, Muhammad continued working for the Italians to oversee our property from 1967 until our return in 1970. Of medium height, thin and wiry, he was very clever mechanically and was designated the chief engineer for watching over the water well repair and helping to build the tennis court. He could do electrical work as well and continually wrestled with the butagas bottles, kerosene stoves, and flash and space heaters in our apartments. Since he was handy and lived close by, we called on him at all hours to fix a heater or find a new butagas tank and repair its valve. And he was fearless. We were always afraid he would hurt himself because he was not as careful as we would have been working with live electrical wires, gas, or kerosene.

Muhammad and his young wife Rashida (probably around age fifteen or sixteen) lived on the compound in a one-story, two-room mud-brick house. When we first met Rashida, she was pregnant. We were told she had a dislocated shoulder (due to a fall) and burn scars on her hands. A year earlier when the shoulder problem had first occurred, the Yemeni cure was to burn her hands—a remedy that merely changed the locus of pain. When she became pregnant, the Russian hospital was unable to x-ray her shoulder to reset it for fear of hurting the baby.

She delivered a stillborn baby, her first, in their little house after two days of labor, with the help first of a midwife and finally a Russian doctor who came to assist. Yemeni women are so tiny and have such narrow pelvic areas that childbirth is often quite difficult for them (see Claudie Fayein, *A French Doctor in the Yemen*). They also observed the superstition of not eating protein during the last two months of pregnancy in order to make the baby smaller, a belief that probably did not help either mother or baby.

Abdul Kadir, also from Taiz, was shorter and slightly stockier

Muhammad Abdul
Ghani Nagi

Abdul Kadir Farhan

than Muhammad. He was our jack-of-all-trades. While Muhammad took care of breakdowns and malfunctions within the compound, Abdul Kadir served as the mission's administrative/general services assistant, handling problems with merchants and the authorities in town. Hired by the Italian embassy in 1969 to work with American interests, he drove us from Taiz to Sanaa when we first arrived and continued to function as a driver, messenger, translator—anything we needed.

From day one his goal was to get to America. He knew that if he worked fifteen years for the Americans he could immigrate to the States. Eager to learn how to type, he could not find a typing school in Sanaa. My mother shipped over an instructional typing manual so he could study on his own. Because of this strong desire to emigrate, he worked tirelessly, was scrupulously honest, and always eager to be of assistance at any time, day or night.

Abdul Kadir also spent a brief time in jail. In July of our first year, an employee of the Ministry of Foreign Affairs ran a motorcycle into Abdul Kadir, who was driving one of our vehicles. The motorcyclist demanded 3,000 riyals ($500–$600) in damages, thinking he could shake down the wealthy Americans for something Abdul

Kadir did not do. He kept pressing his claim, even though Abdul Kadir had caused no harm and had lots of witnesses to prove it. However, the police picked up Abdul Kadir and put him in jail in late October, forcing David to drop everything and deliver a huge verbal protest to the chief of protocol. This got Abdul Kadir released but not until after he had spent the weekend in jail.

Thirty years later I was able to track down Abdul Kadir and Muhammad Abdul Ghani, who both had large families and were living in the States, awaiting their turns to become U.S. citizens. I was thrilled to speak with each of them by phone and exchanged several emails with Abdul Kadir. Muhammad and Rashida had two children with them, and two others were married and living in Sanaa. They were living on his $1,200 per month USG pension while he did maintenance work for an auto parts company in Detroit. One of his daughters was in college studying accounting. Abdul Kadir was spending half his time in the States and half in Yemen. He was trying to get visas for his new, younger wife and family. He wanted to bring them to the United States to join him and the two older children of his first wife, who had died.

Muhammad Qassim was another FSN who had worked for the Americans before the 1967 evacuation and also served a few months in jail because of his association with us. He was our administrative (admin) officer's chief assistant. Once he got into a brouhaha with the other local employees. They accused him of showing favoritism to Zaydis as vendors for things the mission needed to purchase. (Zaydis, of Shi'a lineage, were the ruling Muslim sect of Yemen for hundreds of years and lived in the northern mountainous part of the country. Shafi'is, of Sunni lineage, were the business class who lived in the southern part of Yemen.) Eventually, because of the accusations, Qassim was arrested and thrown into jail. I still have his handwritten notes sent from prison pleading for assistance to get him released. What actually happened and how long he stayed there I cannot remember, but I'm quite sure David and our admin officer won his release with official protests to the YARG.

To handle his reporting efficiently, David needed someone to act as his political consultant, doing background research on key people and current issues. Ali Hamshari, a somewhat aloof Yemeni from Aden, came well recommended. Always immaculately attired

USINT staff

in suit and tie, Hamshari had been educated in the British system in Aden. He and his family had left that country for northern Yemen when FLOSY (Front for the Liberation of Occupied South Yemen) and the NLF (National Liberation Front) forced the British out in 1967. His wife and daughters appeared freer, at least in dress, than the average north Yemeni family. His girls loved to dance to Western rock music, something I never saw among the other Yemenis in Sanaa.

I always got along well with our local staff, finding all of them personally helpful—with one exception. I had sewed lightweight white polyester-and-cotton curtains for several of the offices where our locals worked on the first floor of the chancery. I ironed them carefully and draped them over a table in one of the offices to await David's or Muhammad Abdul Ghani's assistance in hanging them. I returned later to find them wadded up and thrown on the floor because someone needed the table. That was probably the angriest I ever got at our hard-working FSNs, because ironing was not one of my favorite activities! What was a thing of beauty to me that I had made to enhance their offices was not something at least one particular staff member, whom I never identified, understood or appreciated.

During the year that followed those stressful first five months, the unexpected continued to keep us alert. Looking back now, I see we were happy, perhaps closer to equilibrium than we felt day to day at the time. Somehow finding clever ways to deal with the obstacles we faced gave us great satisfaction as well as many amusing stories to share with friends and family. In fact, the unpredictable daily adventures endeared Yemen and the Yemenis to us in ways a "normal," more Western, post would not have. And, dealing successfully with our challenges was a necessary part of the groundwork we laid to facilitate the arrival in 1972 of a much larger U.S. embassy staff, six months after our departure.

Middle East Security

Everyone living in the Middle East in the early seventies was supersensitive about security. The airlines were concerned about hijackings. Western governments were fearful about kidnappings of their diplomats. Several governments in the region, such as Jordan, Egypt, Lebanon, and Ethiopia, were trying to keep the lid on Palestinian and other dissident groups threatening their internal stability. U.S. Secretary of State Henry Kissinger was engaged in "shuttle diplomacy," trying to broker some kind of Arab-Israeli agreement. Those of us living in the eye of this storm felt varying degrees of trepidation and took what precautions we could.

Ethiopian Airlines had stringent rules, even for diplomats, and rightly so. They had guards on every flight and checked all baggage. About the time of our R&R trip to Kenya, the DC-3 we often took to Asmara was hijacked between Bahardar and Gondar in Ethiopia. It was flown to Khartoum, Cairo, and Benghazi before authorities could negotiate with the hijacker. While we as diplomats complained about Ethiopian Airlines' suspicion of us (for example, when we suddenly changed our return reservations from Kenya) and were occasionally offended by an inconvenient handbag check, today we would think nothing of it.

Living in such an unpredictable environment, we routinely looked over our shoulders and checked out mysterious people, activities, packages, or objects. We felt relatively safe in the Yemen Arab Republic in 1970 because of the government's strong desire to improve relations with the United States and the West. If there was unrest, the YARG was quick to establish curfews, and did so several times. As diplomats, we were told we were free to ignore the curfews around town. We took precautions and did not travel to rural areas the YARG did not consider secure or pacified. Yemen's eye-for-an-eye system of justice generally kept robberies, murders, and local crime rates down. However, we knew that, as official Americans, we could be the target of a bomb or a kidnapping, because Palestinian terrorists were active throughout the Middle East.

Given David's high profile as an American diplomat, I held only a remote fear that he would be taken hostage or kidnapped in Yemen. Perhaps, because we were far from center stage of all the unrest, I did not take things as seriously as I should have. That changed dramatically when we arrived at our next post in Amman, Jordan, in 1972, and the regionwide terrorist threat against official Americans became a tangible reality.

In Sudan, FSO George C. (Curt) Moore had opened up USINT Khartoum in 1969 under the auspices of the Netherlands embassy. He and David had been in touch over operational matters about running their respective interests sections while we were in Yemen. In 1973 Curt was in the process of turning the post over to his replacement, the newly arrived U.S. ambassador, Cleo Noel, when the two of them along with the Belgian chargé d'affaires were taken hostage during an official reception in their honor at the Saudi embassy in Khartoum.

I will never forget the moment early one morning, after David had left for work at the Embassy in Amman, when the BBC broadcast that negotiations with the eight Palestinian terrorists of the Black September Organization (BSO) had broken down, and all three diplomats had been executed. The BSO operated under the umbrella of al-Fatah, the secular political party that took control of the Palestine Liberation Organization (PLO) in 1969. According to subsequent reports, PLO and al-Fatah chairman Yassir Arafat ordered the executions of the diplomats. (For a full account, see David Korn's *Assassination in Khartoum* [Indiana University Press, 1993].)

Beginning in September 1970, less than a year before we arrived there, Jordan engaged in its own lengthy confrontation with Black September. King Hussein's army finally defeated the militants in

July 1971 and expelled the entire PLO, only to have them set up new headquarters in Lebanon. Despite the defeat, tensions remained high throughout the Hashemite Kingdom during our tour. The Khartoum assassinations, as well as a thwarted plot during our tour by Abu Daoud and his BSO terrorist friends to launch a rocket attack against the U.S. Embassy in Amman, increased my anxiety and vigilance.

Each morning at our home near Fourth Circle, I checked our car for bombs—under the hood and in the tailpipe—because it was not sheltered in a locked garage. One time I ignored someone I had noticed watching me from his car at Third Circle in Amman. Soon after, I spied him following me on a lonely road leading out of town. Quickly crossing a median, I raced back to town, but not before memorizing backwards the Arabic numerals on his license plate as I looked through my rearview mirror. After returning to the Embassy and reporting the license number to the police, I actually had to identify the man in a lineup. Apparently, he told the police he had heard there was a blonde Western woman driving a black car who was an "easy pick-up."

We befriended a Palestinian, whom I will call Rashid. Although he had a good position in the Jordanian government, he turned out to be a double or perhaps triple agent. We found Rashid interesting and were entertained by him many times, including at a huge *mansif* (feast) near the Dead Sea. However, we became leery of some of his friends, who kept popping in "to meet us" at various venues he had arranged. We wondered if we were being set up for some nefarious deed. I last saw him when he visited us on Christmas day in 1973, telling us he was headed the next day to Cairo, where he vanished. Although we heard he had been killed, he reappeared several years later and told David over lunch in Washington that he had been kidnapped in Cairo and spent five years in a Libyan jail. I was quite ready to return to Washington after the Jordan tour because there I knew we would only be random targets and could choose our friends more carefully.

We experienced a few incidents in Yemen worth noting. The State Department had warned us about mail bombs. One afternoon, David brought home a mysterious package addressed to him that had been sent through the APO military mails. We did not recognize the return address. We had no Marine guards such as larger embassies had whom we could ask to investigate and open the package. So we took matters into our own hands.

David and I turned our dining table on its side and both crouched down behind it. Protecting his face, David gingerly reached his arms around the table's end and carefully opened the scotch-taped wrapping. So far, so good. The paper came off easily and did not require scissors. No explosion.

In the box David found a camera and a note: "Please give this to our son Jerry Erbach. We could think of no other way to get the camera safely to him." Jerry was a young American who worked with PADCO, an international development consulting firm that had a contract with the UNDP. Whew!

Although greatly relieved, we would have been spared a lot of sweat and anxiety if Jerry had only told us to expect a package! When he had arrived months earlier, he had asked to use our APO address for the one-time shipping of an emergency medical prescription to have on hand should it be needed. The prescription never arrived, and we forgot about his request.

When our new consular officer, Graham Fuller, and his wife and two daughters arrived in Sanaa, they decided that living in one of the small compound apartments would not serve them well. They received permission from the State Department to rent a house outside the compound. One evening the entire Fuller family was sitting around their living room when suddenly the house shook with an explosion. Someone had thrown a bomb through one of the girls' bedroom windows. Fortune was smiling on them that day, as no one was hurt. I do not know if they ever caught the perpetrator, but my guess is that it might have been someone dissatisfied with a visa application decision.

Adding to our underlying wariness while living in Sanaa was the fact that Yemenis always carried guns—big guns—and fired them into the air as a part of celebrations. They did not use guns to kill. Like the *janbiyya*, the weapons were part of their persona and a sign of their manhood.

One story my friend Lealan Swanson tells is about a boy who wanted a motorcycle when he finished school. His parents thought it

Graham Fuller (L) and Jerry Erbach

safer, because of the large numbers of motorcycle and car accidents in Yemen, to give him a Russian Kalashnikov assault rifle—but they refused to give him any ammunition.

In another incident, the local movie theater in Sanaa was showing *Bonnie and Clyde* one night when the power went out. Perhaps the movie's violent content spurred an outburst, as the spectators became agitated and fired off a few shots inside the theater before the movie resumed. No one was killed, and, fortunately, we were not there.

With the huge numbers of guns and their uncontrolled use, accidents were frequent. One day we visited the beautiful medieval town of Jibla north of Taiz, arriving in our Land Rover. Seeing women washing clothes in a stream and no motor vehicles, we felt as though we had jumped backwards in a

Tribesman with Kalashnikov and *janbiyya*

time machine. Not only was Queen Arwa, venerated by Muslims as far away as India, reputedly buried in the local twelfth century mosque, but Jibla was also the site of a holy mountain where a Christian Nestorian archbishop was buried. The Nestorians (called by Yemenis *Nasranis*, for Christians or foreigners) came from the Najran oasis in southern Saudi Arabia around the year 500 CE.

After we finished our sightseeing, we wandered over to the Baptist hospital to call on the doctors and staff, arriving just as they

Arwa mosque and town of Jibla

were conducting emergency surgery on a little boy. The governor of Jibla was on hand to tell us what had happened. The boy had been waiting in the hospital lobby with his family. A soldier nearby was cleaning his rifle and accidentally discharged a bullet, which went through a refrigerator, through the boy's stomach, and lodged into a man's leg. Emergency surgery saved the boy's life—and the man's leg.

The Yemenis' guns may have looked fierce, but they offered us only a limited feeling of security. It really depended on who was wielding them whether or not we felt safe. We initially relied as guards on four local *qabili*, or tribesmen, complete with armed rifles. We inherited them from the Italians, who had hired them to "protect" the compound. Three disheveled old men who lived in a small adobe house near the gate were charged with guarding everything inside the compound. They wore turbans, long skirts (*futas*), and old U.S. Army khaki shirts left by our military attaché during the 1967 evacuation. We had ripped off the insignia and offered the shirts to the guards to help them look more official.

The fourth guard, Salah, in his mid-thirties, lived in a space about four-and-a-half feet high under the Consulate. Claiming to be a sayyid, Salah had an eleven-year-old bride named Samura, who was his third wife. As she was prepubescent, she cooked for him but did not provide other wifely duties. Salah received those from his older wives, or so we understood from Muhammad Abdul Ghani. A goat and a sheep lived in the stooped quarters with them and dined on our recently planted, colorful gladiolas. One day we also noticed four guinea pigs outside their front door. The next day they were gone—eaten. Muhammad told us they are quite tasty.

Besides guarding, Salah did odd jobs around the compound to help Muhammad Abdul Ghani. But Salah was calamity-prone. While pruning branches from a tree, he cut a 220-volt electric wire. Amazingly, he was not hurt, but David had to console him and send him off for a nap. Another time, a scorpion stung him, and someone had to minister to his wound. He also tried to carry some enormous baggage and nearly ruptured his abdomen. Finally, he chased a boy who was throwing stones and got into an altercation with the boy's father, who seized his *janbiyya* and carved up Salah's hand, which required stitches at the local Yemeni hospital.

Two old guards with Salah (white tee shirt and *janbiyya*), four children,
and Muhammad Abdul Ghani (on right)

Never trained by anyone in the fine art of maintaining security, these guards were not much good for protection. Others similar in experience had been on duty in 1965, during David's first posting to Yemen, when a mob climbed over the wall at the U.S. compound in Sanaa. While our guards could not keep mobs at bay, they did know how to open and close gates, which made it convenient for us and for our visitors as we came and went in our vehicles.

The three old *qabili* were always complaining, asking for more money, new clothing, or time off, and tried our patience on many occasions. We gave them a raise when we first arrived, then we gave them an intercom. The first thing they used it for was to ask for another raise! The fellows slept right through a robbery at the Chancery that first June. The night I went out at two thirty in the morning to find Dr. Mario for David, I caught all of them sound asleep.

Eventually, we learned the YAR government was willing to provide us with some government-trained *askaris* (security guards) to protect the compound. These guards worked six-hour shifts and carried machine guns, and the army provided them food three times a day. All we had to do was give them a mattress to sleep on. It was the perfect excuse for David to fire all of the *qabili* except Salah, who performed other necessary chores for us.

The old guards were indignant, using reasoning that seemed illogical to our Western minds: "If we refuse to accept the final two weeks' pay in riyals that the boss offers us, then surely we cannot be fired." They claimed they had given loyal service for five years and demanded certain benefits. David could not convince them that he had worked at the U.S. mission five years earlier and not one of them was there. Muhammad told us that the Italians had hired these *qabili* only six months prior to our arrival. Unable to persuade them, David made arrangements to have their severance pay held for them at the labor and welfare society. We knew the cash money would not last long there and urged them to claim it immediately.

The Justice System

Yemen's system of justice was based on *Sharia* law developed from teachings in the Qur'an (Koran) and from common practice in the more traditional Middle East, especially the Arabian Peninsula. The harsh system ensured that the local populace toed the line rather carefully. We saw people walking about town dragging chains, sometimes with lead balls, attached to their ankles. Occasionally their feet were chained together, allowing them only short steps. The punishment depended on the crime. Criminals who owed blood money (*diya*) were allowed out of confinement to beg for money to buy their release but had to return to jail at night.

Others less fortunate were missing hands, a typical punishment for robbery. During our tour I heard that hands were hung over the old city's entrance gate. Lealan Swanson saw the rotting hands of thieves nailed to the old Taiz city wall as late as 1974. Fortunately, I was spared the ghastly sight of severed heads hanging from the Bab al-Yemen, although David said that was still occurring during his first tour.

Man reading Qur'an in old city of Sanaa

There was also the sad tale of several Russian women, married to Yemenis, who wore miniskirts to the only cinema in town. Young Yemeni men, angry at the affront to their culture, threw acid on these women, seriously injuring some of them. The Yemen government did not side with the young men. In true eye-for-an-eye fashion, they dressed the men in black women's cloaks and put them in the middle of a public square to be mocked and have acid thrown on them.

Our gardener was arrested in town while carrying a green garden umbrella David had given him. The police maintained that no Yemeni owns a garden umbrella so he must have stolen it. David had to drop everything and write a formal letter to the criminal section of the local police station to get the poor fellow out of jail. Even a minor transaction required a letter with an official seal. Initially, David had to send a letter in the form of a diplomatic *note verbale* to request the official stationery upon which to make these routine requests. Had David not intervened, the poor gardener might have lost a hand.

After a thief broke into the chancery at night while the guards slept, we found footprints outside the window where our first administrative officer, Dick Maresca, worked. He was known as the "money man" and someone on the inside may have tipped off the thief about where his office was located. We turned the problem over to the authorities, calling the chief of protocol and demanding police protection. We got bars for the windows of the chancery after that and used the incident as another excuse for firing the three old *qabili*. When the police broke up a local robbery ring some months later, they displayed ten hands over the door of a mosque, cut a leg or an arm off the ringleader, and summarily executed the three military officers involved.

U.S. Chancery

Yemenis were not the only ones to wrangle with the local officials. One of our American staff members had a run-in with the Yemeni justice system. After Rick Rauh had an accident with his Land Rover, he calmly relayed what had happened to him:

> While I was driving down the highway between Hodeida and Mocha, I hit a local tribesman who had run out in front of my Land Rover without warning. The impact was so hard it mutilated the sturdy Rover fender as well as the poor man who jumped in front of it. Before the man's companions would let me drive him to the hospital to get medical assistance, they insisted I return to their village to speak with the Sheikh. As I approached the village, I got really nervous watching all those long-skirted fellows with their rifles and clinched fists waving at me.

Rick, a good Arabist with lengthy experience in the Middle East, had to do some fast talking, as angry mobs descended upon the car. Finally, with the Sheikh's approval and Rick's promise to pay $600 in *diya*, Rick was allowed to drive the injured man to the hospital. Unfortunately, the man died en route, as it had already been forty minutes after the impact before Rick could leave the village to seek help. Although Rick was completely absolved by the Taiz police and by the village's Sheikh, I suspect that someone paid the requested blood money to keep peace with the local population. Rick was thankful he got away with his life.

Sadly, it was easy for powerful men to overextend their authority and punish anyone who crossed them. Even if it was not fair, they usually got away with it. While David was on a trip with Prime Minister Muhsin al-Aini to visit the drought-stricken Tihama, the PM's brother-in-law, the governor of Hodeida, Sheikh Sinan Abu Luhum, rode in the first jeep and led the entourage through many villages. According to David, a Land Rover pulled out from a side street in one town and almost hit Sinan's car. Sinan took matters into his own hands and confiscated the offending vehicle, putting its driver in jail.

An even more bizarre event occurred at the end of our tour that showed yet again how men in positions of power sometimes abuse their authority. In September 1971, the Egyptian Middle East

News Agency (UPI Beirut) reported that the Yemeni premier and commander-in-chief of the armed forces, Lt. Gen. Hassan al-Amri, had resigned. In office for only two weeks, he had killed a local photographer during an argument. The incident began when the telephone lines between Gen. Amri's office and those of the photographer, Ali Jazaery, became crossed and the men traded insults with each other over the phone. Gen. Amri found the photographer's name and summoned him to the ministry of communications, where he killed him.

Paying *diya* between family clans was often the ex-officio method under customary law (*'urf*) for solving such problems. Considering his position and influence, I suspect al-Amri remained in exile for a while and paid some blood money to the victim's family, but otherwise received no penalty for the murder. Given the cultural differences between Yemen and the United States over the handling of a life-and-death matter, we could see the impact of this custom on future efforts to modernize Yemen and its legal system.

But for the hardcore terrorism manifest in Yemen in recent years, this harsh system of justice has been counterbalanced generally by the notion of Arab chivalry toward strangers and women. We encountered this code of conduct on more than one occasion, most memorably three months after we arrived in Jordan in 1972. David and I had been traveling by *service* (pronounced serveese) taxi from Beirut to Amman via Damascus. When we reached the Jordanian border, two plainclothes Syrian intelligence agents got into our car, saying we had been in a traffic accident back in Damascus and that we must return to the Syrian capital 100 kilometers away to appear before the magistrate at one p.m.

Our mouths suddenly turned dry, and we were petrified by the arrest. Squeezed closely together in the backseat with one of the agents, David and I, with daughter Lesley on my lap, quietly plotted what we should do to get us out of the mess. "Get to the Belgian Embassy [our protecting power in the absence of diplomatic relations with Syria at that time] any way you can," he urged, knowing it was he they were most interested in.

Upon arrival at the Syrian intelligence headquarters in Damascus, the agents took David into a room where an official was sitting at his desk slapping a heavy-headed blackjack across his hand.

Roman ruins on Straight Street in Damascus, site of
Apostle Paul's conversion

Fifteen-month-old Lesley and I were led into the adjacent room, where I took a seat next to the door, letting her crawl out into the hallway so I could keep my eye on David's room. I got knots in my stomach when I saw an ashen-faced David being escorted out of his room and back down the stairs. A few minutes later, I was immensely relieved to see him return to the same room, carrying our bags from the trunk of the taxi, presumably to be searched.

In my room, I pleaded with several of the guards to allow me to call the Belgian embassy in Damascus. Lesley was running a mild fever from her measles shot the week before. I claimed she needed to see a doctor, but to no avail.

After a while the two agents said they were taking Lesley and me to their car. I insisted on carrying along Lesley's diaper bag containing Evian water and powdered milk so she would not starve. I feared the worst and mentally tried to memorize the turns the car took as the men drove it across town to a group of vacant cement-block, high-rise apartment buildings. A woman and some children, who lived in one of the ground-floor concierge apartments, greeted us. She was the wife of one of the agents. I relaxed a tiny bit. She took Lesley and me into a back bedroom where she had me undress so she could search me for Israeli spy papers. Finding none, she reported this to her husband, who then drove us back to headquarters.

There we saw David drinking tea with his captors, a telltale sign in the Middle East that tensions had eased. Apparently there was no woman on staff at headquarters who could search me, and Arab chivalry would not allow the men to touch me.

The Syrian intelligence agents released us, and our taxi driver took us to the Belgian Embassy, where David sent an urgent cable to alert the U.S. Embassy in Amman about the incident. The Belgians then drove us in their car with diplomatic plates to the Syrian-Jordanian border, where we got back into our taxi driver's vehicle for the rest of the trip to Amman. The agents had even quizzed the taxi driver about our conversation prior to arrest, and he had responded, "Do you want a baloney or tuna fish sandwich?"

We discovered in Amman that the Syrians had picked up the U.S. military attaché traveling from our Embassy in Amman to Beirut that same day. Although he possessed a diplomatic passport, for some reason he chose to travel through Syria using only an official passport that did not convey diplomatic immunity. Thus, the Syrians must have believed that keeping him was not a violation of the Vienna Convention, as it would have been had they detained us. Traveling alone, he was also accused by the Syrians of stopping his vehicle to photograph military installations along the way—a real no-no.

Because there had been an Israeli air raid over Homs, Syria, the day before, the Syrians chose this as their way to retaliate. They kept our military attaché for seven weeks; the U.S. government prohibited Americans from traveling to Syria for a year; and our incident with Syrian intelligence made the front page of the *New York Times*. I guess this will go down in Andy Warhol's terms as my fifteen minutes of fame.

Despite our scary experience with the Syrian government's intelligence apparatus operating near the heart of the Arab-Israeli conflict, kidnappings in remote Yemen were not a problem in the 1970s. However, many years later kidnapping foreigners became a way for tribesmen in remote areas to put pressure on the central government to pay up on their promises, such as a needed village school. From 1996 through 2001, 157 foreigners were kidnapped in 47 incidents.

In keeping with their code of chivalry, the tribesmen generally treated their kidnap victims as honored guests and released them within a matter of days. Peggy Crawford, my photographer friend who lived in Paris for many years and has made nine trips to Yemen, told me that *Le Monde* once featured a cartoon about a French couple kidnapped in Yemen. The wife, who is being carried in a sedan chair by her hosts, calls back to her husband riding a camel, asking: "How do you say 'I love you' in Arabic?"

In 1999, tribesmen near Marib kidnapped an elderly couple and their daughter, Marta Colburn, a British woman who had lived in Yemen off and on since 1984 and who was director of the American Institute for Yemeni Studies at the time. According to her published statement, the incident was resolved peacefully with no payment of ransom.

Prior to 2007 only two kidnappings that I am aware of did not end well: in December 1998 four foreign tourists were killed near Aden when Yemeni soldiers attempted to rescue them from the Islamic Army. A militant group loosely networked with other Middle Eastern terrorist groups, the Islamic Army was trying to win the release of some of their comrades. In June 2000, a Norwegian diplomat was killed at a roadblock after he and his nine-year-old son were kidnapped.

We could probably date the arrival of international terrorism to Yemen's shores with that December 1998 incident. Mary Quin, who wrote *Kidnapped in Yemen,* and her fifteen tourist friends all believed—based on stories they had heard—that they would simply be held overnight and their release negotiated quickly. However, the kidnapping turned deadly as Yemeni soldiers approached. The terrorists showed their true colors and turned against them, killing four tourists outright, according to Mary. She had to run for her life, grabbing her captor's rifle as he lay wounded from the gunshots of the Yemeni soldiers. The kidnappers were apparently receiving instructions from the same Muslim imam in London who was the spiritual mentor of Richard Reed, the shoe bomber.

Billy Quedens and the Issue of Loyalty

Our receptionist at USINT Sanaa that first summer was Ahmad Ali Hizam, better known to us as Billy Quedens. Billy had lived and worked with the Americans in Taiz prior to the 1967 evacuation. When we met him in 1970, he had quite a story to tell, one that underscores Yemeni loyalty and resilience. We were so taken by Billy and his desire to improve his situation that David and I, along with other Americans living in Yemen that summer, worked hard to help him.

Billy told us he was born on or about September 14, 1952, in the Hujariyya village of Demnah in the southern part of the YAR. He lived with his family of many brothers and sisters until the age of nine, when he ran away from home by hitchhiking about twenty miles to the commercial city of Taiz. His mother had died and he was unable to get along with his father's two new wives.

Wandering alone in Taiz, trying to locate his older sister's family, he came upon some American children. Their father was with the American legation in Taiz and invited Ahmad into their yard for some food and to play. After three days with this family, another American took him in. He had no bed for Ahmad but was able to feed him and let him sleep in the cab of his truck. Finally, Ahmad was "adopted" by the Quedens family and assumed the name Billy.

The Quedenses kept Billy in their home for about a year until their tour of duty with the Yemeni/USAID road project was finished, probably in mid-1962. They had wanted to adopt Billy and take him to the States. They petitioned Yemen's ruler, the elderly Imam Ahmad, who denied their petition because Billy was Muslim and might be corrupted by Christian influences.

At the end of their tour, the Quedenses left Taiz after enrolling Billy in the American school and finding him a room in a boarding house. Billy spent the next five years attending school and supporting himself by part-time jobs (messenger, switchboard operator, typist, movie projectionist, and bartender) with the USAID mission in Taiz.

In late 1966, when anti-Western tensions were mounting throughout the Middle East, Billy was put in jail temporarily because of his American ties. In February 1967, fourteen-year-old Billy, by then in the eighth grade, was confined to jail a second time. Sympathetic Americans provided his only source of food in the overcrowded Sanaa jail cell. Amazingly, following the full-scale American evacuation in June 1967, Billy survived conditions of near-starvation and unsanitary cramped quarters in eight different jails. When asked, he said, "I was forced to sleep sitting upright for lack of space." During that time he experienced complete intellectual isolation from the Western ideas he had come to know and appreciate.

Released from jail in March 1968, he returned to the small room he had called home before his internment and discovered he had been stripped of his possessions. All of the clothing provided to him as gifts from the Americans was missing, as well as the $900 he had carefully saved for his long-dreamed-of trip to the States to attend school. For five months he subsisted on the $85 USG severance paycheck that had been held for him at the Italian Embassy.

Eventually Billy found a job as a clerk in the accounting section of the department of public works in Taiz. A year later he was transferred to the chemical lab of the Kennedy water project. When we

Taiz mosque

arrived in May 1970, Billy tracked down David and me in Taiz and traveled to Sanaa with us to open the interests section.

When we first met him it appeared that Billy had a benefactor in the States, an elderly woman from Massachusetts who had visited Yemen and met Billy. Her address scribbled on a piece of scratch paper was all that he found in his ransacked room. Two years earlier he had written to this address describing his plight and received a favorable reply regarding some financial assistance once he got to the States. However, subsequent efforts to locate a home for him in the States had produced no results by the time we met him. Billy came to Sanaa with us hoping we could help him. He wanted to work for the mission again until he was able to get to the States.

I wrote to friends back home and spoke with everyone we knew locally trying to find support for him. By midsummer, through the Baptist missionaries in Jibla, we had located someone to sponsor him and a school for him to attend in North Carolina. As of August 29, his plane ticket was the one remaining obstacle. Catholic Relief Services (CRS), in the person of Monsignor Harnett of their Rome office, came through at the last minute so Billy could enroll in September. We took great delight in knowing we had the Baptists and the Catholics helping a Muslim boy go to school in the States.

Billy Quedens and Rick Rauh
on picnic in Hadda

Billy attended school in North Carolina that fall and remained there during our entire Yemen tour. We received a letter from a Mrs. Ruby Doar, the mother of a surgeon serving as a missionary at the Jibla Baptist Hospital. She reported that he was doing well and making a B average. Someday I hope to learn what happened to Billy and where he is now. Abdul Kadir heard a rumor recently in Yemen that Billy stayed in the States for thirty years but may be back in Yemen now.

Billy had demonstrated that once you became their friend, Yemenis were fiercely loyal, sometimes to their own detriment. Others like Billy who had been affiliated with the Americans before the embassy was evacuated in 1967 had also suffered. I do not know how they demonstrated their loyalty, whether they spoke out on our behalf or simply did not deny their association with Americans.

Muhammad Hassan, an FSN who had worked at the embassy in Taiz and Sanaa, was jailed for a few months after the U.S. departure in 1967 because of his friendship with the Americans. By 1970, he had become a commission agent with lucrative self-employment. We once visited him, his unveiled wife, and their two children in their modest home. Like many Yemeni residences, their bedroom and *mafraj* (living room, often the top floor in a Yemeni tower house) were the same room.

Muhammad told us, "You know, we named our son Mark after David Newton's son." David Newton was the FSO friend who followed my husband David to Sanaa in the mid-1960s, was posted to Jidda during our tour, and served as ambassador to Yemen in 1994–1997. Despite Muhammad's punishment at the hands of the YARG, he remained a friend of the United States.

FSN Muhammad Abdul Ghani had barely escaped being jailed for his affiliation with the United States. As an employee of the USG since 1962, he transferred to Sanaa when the embassy relocated from Taiz in 1966. He told us how he stayed up all night to guard the suitcases of the American personnel when they were given 24-hour-notice to evacuate the country in June 1967. He declared when we first arrived at post, as if to prove his loyalty to me, "After the Americans left, I continued to live in the compound to guard U.S. property and almost got thrown into jail a few times. Once, I had to climb out a rear window and hide in the toolshed to avoid being arrested with some of the guards."

Leaving loyal FSN staff to guard U.S. property when we have been forced to depart suddenly is a common practice often fraught with difficulties for those employees. For example, following the U.S. departure in 1989, Afghani FSN staff risked their lives to protect embassy property from harm by the Taliban. The FSNs lived in a bomb shelter (constructed on the compound in Kabul in 1997) until the post's reopening in December 2001.

The need for a living wage sent many Yemeni men abroad to seek their fortune. Their remittances sent back to families in Yemen, from Saudi Arabia and the Gulf States in particular, represented a major part of the country's economy. The imam had begun to allow a small number of Yemenis to study in the Eastern bloc as well as in the West at least a decade or two before the U.S. legation opened in Taiz in the late 1950s. Many leaders of the Republican Revolution had studied abroad and brought their modernist ideas and experiences home with them. These cultural exchanges likely helped plant the seeds of revolution, nurtured and watered by the Egyptians, which sprouted in September 1962.

Those who managed to work and study abroad opened their minds and hearts to the modern world, including the United States. Yemenis in the early 1970s had a strong fascination with America, evident in the large numbers who immigrated to the States and settled in places such as Dearborn, Michigan, Youngstown, Ohio, and Lodi, California. Being good U.S. citizens yet loyal to their roots, they sent money back to their families in Yemen from jobs they held in the auto industry in Michigan, steel mills in Ohio, and agricultural work in California.

One of David's old Yemeni friends, Vic Mawry, lived in the Yemeni community in Dearborn, Michigan, where he worked on coaling boats in the Great Lakes. He visited us in Sanaa on a trip back to see his family. Vic took us out to eat at the Mocha Hotel and, knowing how finicky American stomachs can be, worried the whole time that we would pick up a bug. We were much less concerned, as we had been in the country long enough to know what was safe for us to eat.

I suspect that the Yemenis involved in the USS *Cole* attack, as well as the young men from Buffalo, New York, arrested for having trained in Afghanistan, were not even born when I lived in Yemen. Their parents' generation immigrated to the United States, eager to work hard and improve their lot in life with the same hopes and ambitions as those of immigrants from other countries. For some reason, their parents' loyalty to America did not rub off on their children. A myriad of complexities lured this younger generation of Yemeni youth, some of them U.S. citizens, to the side of al-Qaeda and its terrorist war against the West.

4

Family Life

Medical Woes

Medical care in Yemen was iffy at best. Yet one could stay healthy with personal vigilance, a good immune system, and the ministrations, both curative and preventive, of a few local doctors. For appropriate medical attention for most ailments, we relied on Dr. Mario Livadiotti, an Italian doctor with the YARG's Republican hospital, two Hungarian doctors, or the American doctors in Jibla four hours away. For emergencies, there were the Russian and Yemeni hospitals, but we hoped we would never have to use their services.

A few weeks after our arrival in Sanaa, Dr. Jim Young, a doctor from the Jibla Baptist mission near Taiz, came to visit, bringing medicines to add to the few supplies we had on hand. Jim had been the medical director of that facility for at least six years, as David had known him during his first Yemen tour. The Baptist mission had not closed down during the official U.S. evacuation in 1967, and the staff borrowed our movie projectors while we were gone, returning them in 1970. We also worked with the mission to help our young Yemeni friend, Billy Quedens, obtain schooling in the States. They were always willing to offer sound medical advice, although we had to drive four hours to see them.

Occasionally, the regional medical officer from our embassy in Beirut or the embassy nurse from Jidda came to visit us in Sanaa. More than a year after our arrival, we were fortunate enough to have a new communicator, Larry Koehnen, join our team. His wife, Sue Koehnen, was a nurse who reassured us by giving necessary shots and vaccinations, taking our temperature and making diagnoses, prescribing medication from her in-house kit, and treating minor illnesses. We prayed we would never get anything serious enough to require a medical evacuation (medevac) by plane to Asmara, Beirut, or Germany.

We knew of a respected Chinese woman gynecologist in Sanaa and one fine Yemeni internist, who had been trained in Egypt and worked at one of the hospitals in Sanaa. During our time there, however, Yemenis had access to medical training only in Russia, where scholarships were available. Our FSN political consultant, Ali Hamshari, had a son studying medicine at one of the better universities there. He saw one problem with Russian training versus an education at the American University of Cairo; a student had to learn the difficult Russian language before beginning his medical studies! Additionally, the quality of education varied from one university to another. The whole Russian medical education experience required a minimum of eight years even for a quick learner.

A few days after arriving in Yemen, the dust and increased stress of settling in got the best of me. For three weeks I coughed all night and had to sleep sitting up. In desperation, I finally called on the Hungarian doctors, who had a small clinic in Sanaa, and one stopped by the compound to check on me. In good English, he responded to my exhausted, sleepless situation: "Here are some codeine tablets. These should stop your cough very quickly. They are the perfect medicine for the dry Sanaa cough everyone seems to get here."

Knowing the tablets were something we would never be able to obtain over the counter in the States, I was happy to try the Hungarian remedy. None of my mild Western syrups had worked. The medicine did the trick, and soon I was a new person.

Within a day or two after my miracle cure, David came down with intestinal flu or food poisoning. We were not sure which. He became deathly ill with vomiting and diarrhea, the sickest I had ever seen him. He could barely get out of bed yet somehow managed to perform his official duties. I gave him paregoric for his stomach cramps, but Dr. Mario had to rush over in the afternoon to bring more potent medication. We hoped Dr. Mario's ministrations would enable David to entertain the visitor from telecommunications company Comsat who was in Yemen for a brief visit and whom we had invited for dinner that evening.

David survived the social necessities of the evening but later became quite ill. In the middle of the night, I had to rouse a driver to get Dr. Mario again. David's fever was 103 degrees, and he could not keep down the pills the doctor had given him earlier. I kept cold towels on his head all night. Fortunately, his fever dropped by daylight.

The next day David faithfully returned to Dr. Mario's tried and true treatment for intestinal bugs—bananas, rice, applesauce, and toast (known as the BRAT diet). We could add chicken broth in a day or two after things stabilized internally. Dr. Mario was the first person ever to recommend the BRAT diet to us, a treatment we profusely thanked him for. I used his recipe with my children and later learned it is standard procedure for Peace Corps volunteers the world over. Although a few friends advised us to include carrots and/or carrot juice in that diet as well, over the years I typically stuck to BRAT.

Dr. Mario was always willing to come day or night and offered thoughtful and reasonable medical treatment. However, when we were really sick and needed relief fast, we often called in our Eastern bloc friends, the Hungarians, for a second opinion. Whether it was codeine cough syrup, a tetracycline shot, or a stitch to the head, the Hungarians generally had a quick fix. We did not want to offend Dr. Mario, a respected member of our community, and usually consulted him as well. We felt lucky to have good advice from not one but three doctors in remote Sanaa.

The Hungarian doctors were two young, single fellows whose names I no longer remember. Their motor scooter had a little sidecar so both could ride in it. If only one doctor dropped by for a visit, he occasionally brought along their pet monkey, who loved to ride in the sidecar. Seeing either of the doctors with that monkey was always a delight. They were truly a breath of fresh air and helped ease our health adjustment to Yemen.

Another time that first summer David became very ill with a high fever that scared me. I had summoned the Hungarians but had to wait awhile before they could get to the compound. In the meantime, I called Dr. Mario, who arrived promptly with something

Dr. Mario Livadiotti

to reduce the fever and the pain. As he and I were standing at David's bedside, I heard through the open window the noisy motor scooter of the Hungarian doctors pull up outside.

Since I did not want to embarrass or anger Dr. Mario, I quickly excused myself, raced down the stairs, and pleaded with the Hungarians, "Can you please come back in an hour?" I explained the delicate situation, "Dr. Mario will not understand why you are here too. His pride may be hurt."

They immediately grasped the diplomatic faux pas that might arise should Dr. Mario realize we had called other doctors. I did not want to offend a well-meaning and responsive friend or allow Cold War politics to interfere with our health. The doctors understood, turned off the engine, and quietly rolled the motor scooter out of the compound.

True to their word, they came back within an hour after Mario had left, bringing their "quick fix" magic remedy. Although they believed David had a viral rather than a bacterial blood infection, they gave him over a few days several injections of Terramycin (a tetracycline antibiotic) as a precaution, and David was finally able to get out of bed.

A month later in Asmara, doctors thought David had had viral meningitis. By the end of our first summer, David had suffered a couple bouts of dysentery, the viral blood infection, and food poisoning and had lost over twenty pounds. His weight loss was likely due to the stress and long hours of our first few months at post, but the fevers he kept having remained a mystery.

It was December 1971, just prior to our departure from Yemen, before doctors in Asmara were able to diagnose his periodic fevers, which had been recurring every three or so months for well over a year. At last able to obtain a live blood sample while David was experiencing the undulating fevers, the doctors declared them to be caused by the vivax strain of malaria and administered appropriate treatment. Each time those fevers returned occasionally over the years, they were less debilitating. Eventually the episodes stopped altogether.

Where, we wondered, had he contracted malaria? We spent most of our time at over 7,000 feet in Sanaa, where we did not regularly take the weekly malaria preventive. Only when we traveled to Taiz and Hodeida, both much hotter and lower in altitude, did we do so. However, David had left in such a rush on the hastily organized trip to view the Tihama famine with the prime minister in June 1970 that he forgot to take the chloroquine tablets (one of several types of malaria preventives issued to all Westerners headed to tropical climates). Mosquitoes relished the heat and humidity of the Red Sea coast. Even though David never remembered the bites, he was an ample target over his three days of exposure while traveling in the Tihama.

We had our surefire methods for curing ailments—the BRAT diet, paragoric for stomachaches, enterovioform as a preventive against contamination from eating questionable meat—but one remedy I witnessed left me squeamish. While I was in Jidda and eight months pregnant, I visited a shop in the old suq used mostly by Bedouins. There I watched a bloodletter shave the backs of the heads of several men lined up in a row and put leeches on each to suck blood, using three silver cups sticking out the back of each head. I was glad the Hungarians and Dr. Mario never recommended that remedy for either David or me. However, I have recently read about the modern practice of using leeches and maggots to clean wounds and necrotic flesh. The old ways usually endure for a reason—they often work!

Our medical complaints were manageable without hospital-
ization or medical evacuation, but our friend Alain Bertaud had
more serious problems. He got lead poisoning from some locally
purchased pottery, suffered an infected tailbone, and required an
emergency appendectomy during his tour. While the first ailment
was serious and required detoxification by the Baptist doctors at
Jibla, the infected tailbone was treated by a Russian doctor who
nearly poisoned him. Alain learned later from a Russian working
for the UN International Labor Organization that his Russian doctor was really a KGB intelligence operative and that being a doctor
was his cover!

As for the appendectomy, Alain is lucky he survived. When his
appendix ruptured, there was not enough time for a medevac to
a European hospital. He consulted Dr. Mario, who was a general
practitioner, not a surgeon, and he referred Alain to the Hungarian
surgeon working at the military hospital built by Kuwait. The surgeon first suggested using Novocain as a local anesthetic, but none
was available. Thus, there was no anesthetic for this serious abdom-
inal surgery. Alain learned they amputated legs with only a local
anesthetic, if available, which gave him some comfort in retrospect.

Marie Agnes and Alain with our
daughter Lesley in Virginia, 1977

While Alain was lying on the table in the operating room, he looked over to see an orderly sweeping the floor and dust flying everywhere. As he recently explained to me, "I was told I was the first *Nasrani* (Christian) to be operated on in that hospital, and they wanted to make a good impression!" So much for a sterile environment!

Somehow Alain endured the painful surgery. When it was time to take him to his room, the hospital orderlies could not find a gurney to transport him. So two male Yemeni nurses supported him as he walked from the operating room on one level up to the second level to his room! There was no ramp between the two levels.

Yemeni hospitals did not have facilities to offer food to patients. Families had to bring food and water and alert the staff about anything the patient needed. David and I visited Alain soon after the surgery. Finding our way through the dingy corridors, we entered a dark, windowless room with one small nightstand and a mattress on the floor. Huddled over his bed, Marie Agnes, his wife, was feeding him some soup. Far from the cheerful appearance of some hospital rooms I have seen, this one was truly Spartan.

We visited briefly, then left the two, wondering how we would cope in a similar situation. According to Alain, "Marie Agnes sat with me for as long as we could endure, then she brought me home in her Volkswagen Beetle during the night."

Surely things have improved in Yemeni hospitals since then.

Christmas Eve 1970

It was December 24, our first holiday season in Sanaa. I was three months pregnant and just starting to wear maternity clothes. Donning the fiery-hued, paisley print pants suit a Beirut tailor had made for me, I was pleased with my alterations. To accommodate my enlarging measurements, I had simply moved the buttons over several inches on the double-breasted vest and let out the pants drawstring. I was eager to model my new outfit at our oyster soup supper with John and Diane, who lived in our building. Tom Seibert, a volunteer with CRS, unexpectedly joined us for the dinner. He had tried to leave the country for the holiday, but YAL brought him back to Sanaa because he had not had his cholera shot. Presumably, a neighboring country would not let him transit.

Zabid fortress painted by Hashim Ali

About eight thirty, after dinner and conversation, David and I climbed a short flight of stairs from their apartment to ours to open our presents. We had brought back our own four-foot fake Christmas tree from a recent trip to Asmara. Although it was made of metal and plastic, it was green and reminded us of home. I can still see it standing near the exit door behind the seats in an Ethiopian Airlines' DC-3 as we flew across the Red Sea to Taiz. Snuggling with each other around our beautifully decorated tree, we were determined to make the most of our first Christmas together so far from the United States.

We began opening presents sent from our families in the States, shipped in by APO through Asmara. We took turns admiring each other's gifts, extending the process as long as possible. Ribbons and colorful wrappings festooned the furniture as we tore into one gift after another.

David surprised me with a 14"x16" oil painting of a fortress in Zabid done by Hashim Ali of the Modern Era Studio in Taiz. We had first admired it at Claudie Fayein's national art exhibit at the

Egyptian school following the September 26 independence parade. There we had met the artist, who was half Yemeni, half Indonesian, and had studied art at the University of Java. Later we saw the picture on display and consignment at the Romantic Restaurant. I was thrilled to own the painting we had both admired so much, our first art purchase since marriage. David built a frame for it and it still hangs in my home.

Ripping the paper from his last gift, David realized he needed a pair of scissors to get into a smaller box inside. Like a kid eager to see what the box contained, I jumped up to help, racing through the dining room and into our bathroom to retrieve the scissors. The bathroom door was only about five-and-a-half-feet tall, high enough for the short Yemenis but not for this 5'8" American. David and I both had to duck when we went in—and step up over a five-inch-high wooden threshold. By the time I reached the bathroom door, I was flying.

Wham! I saw stars for the first and only time in my life. Just like in the comic strips when someone gets hit over the head, **#!! *#*! *##*! The next thing I knew I was flat on my back, neck stretched over the threshold and blood dripping from a gash in the top of my head just above my hairline.

Hearing the thud of my body hitting the floor, David came running. "Oh, my gosh, Sweetie, what did you do!" he shouted in horror. Cradling me in his arms while I tried to regain my senses, he pressed a bulky towel against my wound, half-covering my eyes.

Struggling to lift myself up, I tried to see around the towel and assess the seriousness of the situation. I had slammed into the squared-off edge of the top of the doorframe so hard it flipped me backward. Although the crown of my head was bleeding profusely, I did not feel any blood or cut on the back of my neck. I seemed to be able to move my limbs so I had not broken my neck, though it hurt quite a bit.

Then, David's voice penetrated my dazed reverie, "The cut on the top of your head needs a few stitches. Since the Yemenis don't celebrate Christmas, maybe their hospital will be open."

Trying to act confident and mollify his fears, I asked David, "Can you get some ice to put in this towel to stop the bleeding? And see if John can go with us."

"Yes and let's stop by the Hungarian clinic first—maybe they'll be back from any Christmas party they might have gone to. It's nine thirty," David rationalized as he tried to calm his own emotions, "and it'll be ten before we can get there." It never occurred to me that my pregnancy might be at risk because I was focused on the pain in my head and neck. David immediately thought of the baby but did not want to scare me, so he waited until much later to share that concern.

After helping me up off the floor and getting some ice from our kitchen refrigerator, David ran down to get John. Draping a trench coat over my shoulders and each taking an arm, they escorted me down the three flights of stairs in our apartment building, carefully stepping up and over the front-door threshold, which was similar to the one into the bathroom. While I held the towel filled with ice over my wound with one hand and hung onto David's arm with the other, John steadied me on the opposite side as we walked through the dark compound courtyard toward our vehicles.

David carried the keys to the VW van, telling me, "No need to rouse any of the drivers. We've given them the evening off, too." He helped me up into the high shotgun seat, while John climbed into the back seat. David was anxious to get moving and see if the Hungarians were home. Gunning the engine, with gears slamming into place and tires spinning, he charged rapidly toward our front gate, which needed to be opened by the guards posted there.

Compound guardhouse

Startled by the noise and aroused from his slumber, one of the *askaris* came rushing out of the guardhouse with loaded rifle pointed straight at us, yelling things like: "*La!* (no) *Bass!* (stop) *Khalas! Khalas!* (finished, time is up!)" to get our attention.

While turning on the internal car lights so the guard could see who it was, David screamed, "*Iftah al bab! Iftah al bab!* (Open the gate!)" Stunned by the rude awakening and realizing this was his boss yelling at him, the guard lowered his weapon. He quickly opened the compound gates so David could maneuver the van in the dark of night through the narrow dirt alleyways to a lighted street.

Just as we arrived at the Hungarian clinic, the two doctors pulled up in their motor scooter-cum-sidecar, surprised to have a visit from the Americans on Christmas Eve. Feeling rather jolly after an evening of food and drink with their Hungarian colleagues, they invited us in to see how seriously I was bleeding.

"Yes, we should do a few stitches, though the bleeding seems to have stopped. There's a deep cut and it will not close nicely without stitches. We'll need to shave your hair off around the wound," one of them explained as I lay down on his examining table. "Here, let me inject a little Novocain around the cut, so you won't feel anything," he continued, reaching for the largest needle and syringe I had ever seen and retrieving a vial of anesthetic from the glass cabinet near the examining table.

After putting on his white doctor's coat, he shaved around the cut on top of my head, which hurt very little. A few minutes later, when he thought the Novocain should be taking effect, he began to insert his needle and thread. "Ouch," I exclaimed.

"Hmm...let me inject a little more. I only have these two vials but let's try another one. That should do it," he reassured me.

We waited a few more minutes and he tried to stitch again. "Wow, I can still feel that needle," I winced.

Thoughtfully scratching his chin, the doctor continued, "You know, this is twice the amount I should have given you. So I think that our Yemeni orderlies have been into the medicine cabinet again. They steal the drugs to sell or use themselves and fill the empty vials with water, hoping we will not notice."

Hmm, I thought, probably the same thing that happened at Alain's appendectomy. The doctor continued, "We need their assistance for our surgeries and find it difficult to watch them constantly and keep the supplies secured. I'm afraid I have nothing to deaden your pain. You'll just have to grit your teeth while I stitch."

So that's how I got five stitches in the top of my head, feeling every pierce of the needle. I kept telling myself this pain would be minor by comparison to labor in a few months. Among the stitches, the doctor inserted a piece of gauze that covered the top of my shaved spot. It perked up like a little bow tie. I felt like a poodle that had just been to the dog groomer. It would certainly generate conversation at all the holiday parties we were expected to attend.

Grateful for the antibiotic and pain pills the doctors found hidden in their stash, I soon headed home to sleep. Oh, how stiff and sore I was the next morning, mostly the muscles in my neck. I had not spent Christmas Day in bed since I had had measles at age five. It was a couple of days before I could get out of bed easily enough to even think of going to a party.

Not one to be laid up for long, I soon recovered. We celebrated our anniversary on the twenty-ninth with beef fondue prepared in the new Dansk fondue pot that David had bought at the PX to give me for Christmas. And, there I was for New Year's Eve in my paisley pants suit with a cute little bow on top of my long brown hair. The white gauze bow even matched the background in the print material, I remarked to all concerned.

Reflecting on that freakish accident over thirty years ago, I realize how fortunate it was that our guard did not shoot us and that I did not break my neck or lose the baby. That was by far the hardest fall I have ever suffered. X-rays today show a flat set of neck bones rather than the normal curved ones and osteoarthritis has crept in to remind me of my misadventure. But when we're young, the careless exuberance of the moment often impels us to actions we would not take at more rational times.

Starting a Family

Although David and I worked long hours at the Chancery and spent many evenings entertaining, we managed to find time for each other. Once we were settled into life in Sanaa, with most of the initial difficulties resolved, we were eager to begin a family. Fortunately we did not have to wait long. The birth of our first child, Lesley, came in June 1971, slightly over one year after our arrival. It was the highlight of our tour.

We believed we were safe enough in our physical surroundings to take on the challenge of parenthood. We would be in good hands provided my pregnancy was normal. Since this was our first child, I planned to go to Asmara a month before my due date. Traveling to the Jibla Baptist Hospital three hours away over a gravel road or delivering at one of the hospitals in Sanaa were not options I relished. However, Kagnew Station in Asmara had such a young military population the ob-gyn and his colleague were delivering a baby a day on average. We were thankful a good American military hospital was available relatively close to Yemen.

Going for periodic prenatal check-ups required some planning to dovetail with our periodic classified pouch runs. We made two trips to Taiz in the Land Rover to travel on Ethiopian Airlines to Asmara to see the doctor. The regional medical officer in Beirut, a traveling U.S. government nurse, and the doctors at Jibla Baptist Hospital also provided interim prenatal advice during their visits to Sanaa.

The pregnancy progressed normally, with my middle trimester being the most comfortable and satisfying. It proved to be a good time to make our R&R trip to visit friends at the embassy in Addis Ababa and to tour of Kenya.

The third trimester was much more challenging and cumbersome. The extra thirty pounds I had added were no fun. At eight and a half months, David and I carried the pouch from Sanaa to Asmara, via Jidda, Saudi Arabia, using newly opened Saudi Airlines. Since we had never visited Jidda, we stopped for two days with friends, David and Christa Newton, for a little R&R. We attended three dinner parties and a luncheon with British ambassador Willie Morris and his wife before we left. In the embassy's cabin cruiser, we toured Jidda's harbor, where the two Davids snorkeled twelve feet down while I admired the coral reefs from the boat deck above.

Flying from Jidda to Asmara, we stopped in Sudan at the old colonial town of Port Sudan, with its tile roofs and bougainvillea.

It was my first and only time in that country. There, we landed on a dirt runway and saw umbrellas and scruffy flowers trying to beat off the scorching sun.

In contrast, Asmara had a paved runway and a modern-looking airport I am sure had been influenced by years of Italian occupation and the American military presence. At Kagnew Station, David set me up in a room in the bachelor officers' quarters (BOQ) and left me to waddle around the base with the other pregnant women. During that month I made two new friends, one evacuated from Jidda and the other from Addis. Together we enjoyed hamburgers and milk shakes and took in all the new movies (including *Ring of Bright Water* and *Goodbye, Columbus*) at the base theater. It was the first baby for each of us, so we compared notes and made bets as to who would deliver first.

Marilyn Sobke delivered three weeks ahead of me. She and her husband returned to Jidda via Sanaa when their daughter Allison was only four days old. Finding themselves stranded at the airport waiting for a six-hour-delayed plane, they called David at the Chancery. He rushed to the airport and took them to our place for rest and some food rather than have them spend the afternoon at the inhospitable Sanaa airport with a new baby. They got home safely and now that baby has her own children.

Envious that Marilyn delivered first and eager to get to term myself, each week after seeing the doctor I asked the consulate in Asmara to send David a cable. Our plan called for David to carry the classified pouch out to Asmara—and thus get his ticket paid—when the doctor felt I was showing signs of delivery within the week. Finally, a month after David left me in Asmara he received the message to come. He arrived on a Thursday, but nothing happened for three days.

Then Sunday night we went to see the movie *Bob and Carol and Ted and Alice,* and all the wife-swapping and bed-hopping in the movie must have agitated me enough to jump-start labor. My first pains arrived at two a.m., and by five a.m. we were walking across the street to the base hospital. With the help of an epidural, the baby was born at 11:16 a.m. June 14, while David anxiously waited outside the delivery room. I asked the nurse not to tell him the gender of the baby when she carried it past him to the nursery. As I was wheeled to my room, I called out to him in the waiting room, "How do you like Lesley Karen?"

Of our team of three, I was the last to deliver, right on my due date. I set the record for the largest baby of the month, at 8 pounds, 11 ounces. Babies gestated at high altitudes like Sanaa and Asmara typically averaged less than seven pounds, according to the statisticians at Kagnew.

We waited in Asmara for ten days after the birth before we took Lesley and all kinds of baby paraphernalia back to Sanaa. I had hoped to nurse her to eliminate worries about bad water and powdered milk, but Lesley was never satisfied with what I had to offer. I remember middle-of-the-night foraging through the kitchen of Ambassador and Mrs. Nicholas Thatcher's house in Jidda on our return trip to Sanaa, looking for a pan to cook pablum in. Lesley did not like being at sea level, I guess, and she spent our two days in Jidda letting us know just how uncomfortable she was.

Delivering the baby in the relative comfort of an overseas American army base was a bit easier than the next seven months at post in Sanaa. As first-time parents we were nervous Nellies and worried about every unusual cough, cry, or potentially unhealthy visitor who came near our baby. Once in Sanaa, Lesley began to sleep a little better, but during the first three months she usually had colic each evening between five and seven. To help me, David came home early from work every day to pace the apartment with Lesley over his shoulder. My milk gave out after four months, and we resorted to USAID powdered milk that we could buy in the local market—the food aid that never made it into the starving villages in the Tihama. I began early supplementation with baby food and bottles of infant formula.

That same summer David's seven-year-old daughter Anna visited us from Greece. She met us in Jidda as we were transiting with newborn Lesley. During our stopover in that Saudi port city, we took Anna along on our visit to Hugh Leach's home where David went swimming with her and I tried to comfort Lesley. Apparently, I was spaced out enough with my new responsibilities that I remembered only vaguely the stress we encountered as we arrived at the old Jidda airport for our flight as a family of four back to Yemen.

Ambassador Newton has since reminded me that he accompanied the four of us to the airport. In those days, one had to send passports to the airport the day before a flight to be picked up at the check-in counter. When we arrived at the airport, Anna's passport was missing. We rushed to the next building to find the passport officer. I do remember the drawers of his metal desk bursting with passports. Newton added the punch line that I had forgotten: Anna's was not in the drawer. They looked down on the floor and saw it balancing the leg of the officer's wobbly desk!

Though stressed with a full schedule of office and representational work, I added two children to my life essentially overnight. On July 4 we attended a staff party at the O'Gradys' apartment one floor above ours. Although it was only a quick walk up a short flight of stairs, it took every ounce of energy I could muster to dry my tears and get dressed to put in an appearance. Overwhelmed

McClintocks at the O'Gradys' 4th of July party, 1971

by my new situation and major hormonal changes, I languished in a postpartum depression for only a day or two, as I remember, before external demands forced me to submerge it. I know that it affected me for several months because my comments on tape and in letters home were very different from the effusive enthusiasm I had espoused during the first part of our tour.

I heard my 28-year-old self make statements in a tired voice, such as: "We've had enough of this hardship post." "It's no place for a working wife with two children, including a newborn baby." "We will cancel our R&R plans and hope we can get out of here by the end of October." "We hope the State Department will give us an easier assignment next." By late fall—after Lesley was sleeping through the night, exhibiting all the benchmarks of precocious development and becoming a little person who could communicate with coos, gurgles and smiles—I began to sound like my old self again. Once we knew that our onward assignment would be Amman, it did not bother me that we could not leave Yemen until February. By then we were taking Lesley on excursions and seeing the world through her eyes. My hormones had leveled out and life could go on in the usual upbeat, optimistic way it always had.

Anna had a great summer. She was forced to learn to swim after our dog Fritz chewed up her water wings, which were not replaceable locally. She loved to have guests over. While we entertained the parents in the dining room, she hosted tea and supper parties for the children in her room, where they could make all the mess they wanted. At times she had difficulty sharing the limelight with Lesley, but generally she was quite attentive and loving toward her little sister, and Lesley adored Anna. In fact, we felt Anna communicated with Lesley better than David and I could. My biggest challenge was finding food that Anna would eat. Spaghetti, macaroni and cheese, and chocolate pudding were her early staples, but fortunately her diet included more veggies by the time she left.

One of Anna's favorite activities was playing around the compound with the several stray dogs we had adopted. Being softies, we fed every emaciated stray that came through the gates. The first dog we called Arwa, after the famous twelfth century queen in Jibla. She was noticeably pregnant and, amazingly, had not lost either of her ears in fights with other dogs. Arwa lapped up our powdered milk and hung around for more handouts.

The Yemeni staff were offended by the name Arwa, which means "queen" in Arabic, and called her Tonia. After she gave birth, we changed her name to Sheba. A week later two younger black dogs with markings similar to Sheba's arrived. We surmised they came from one of her prior litters. We promptly named them Solomon, Sheba's historic paramour, and Zenobia, the ancient queen of Palmyra.

By the time Anna arrived we had also taken in the urchin puppy Fritz. David built a doghouse made of plywood packing crates and plastic tarps when Fritz proved he was not trainable as a "house dog." After Fritz was finally able to hold his own during the daily food fray with the three bigger dogs, we left him outside.

Anna played with all of them, teaching our local employees not to fear dogs and how to pat them on the head and get them to roll over for tummy rubs. We thought Solomon was blind in one eye, but it seems he just had one light blue eye to complement its brown mate. One time Solomon found a pile of white gypsum powder (for making *guss*) to roll in during a rain shower. It dried on him like the plaster that it became when water was added. But, it was easier to clean up than the tar Anna got on her tennis shoes and shorts while hanging around the newly paved tennis court. The dogs—and Anna—were bright spots and provided humorous release to our often-frenetic days.

Our best story about Anna, who became an intrepid traveler over the years that followed, occurred at her departure in late August. A last-minute emergency came up, canceling David's plans to accompany Anna to Jidda with a diplomatic pouch. So, David arranged for Saudi Airlines to deliver her into the hands of the Bill Stoltzfuses, our friends in Jidda who had children Anna's age. They would keep her overnight and put her on the plane to Athens the next day.

As David sat working in his office late on the afternoon of her departure, he got an urgent telephone call from a British embassy diplomat whose son had been Anna's seatmate on the flight. "Saudi Airlines blew out a tire on landing in Hodeida and will not be departing for Jidda until tomorrow. Your daughter is being well cared for by an Australian UN family who lives on the beach," the gentleman tried to reassure David.

Despite the phone call, David was concerned about Anna's safety and needed to see for himself that she was all right. He waited until three a.m. before leaving with a driver for Hodeida. I could not go with him and take Lesley, because, after her rough time in Jidda, I was not sure how she would do in the heat at sea level. Without a landline in the house to receive a call, I waited anxiously for his return later that day.

David arrived in Hodeida by seven a.m. at the home of the Australian family. He found Anna playing ball on the beach with several children and a father supervising the little group. Totally nonchalant about the whole incident, Anna told her dad about the thirty-minute flight from Sanaa to Hodeida the day before: "Daddy, we had a pretty good flight yesterday." Although she had left Sanaa in a clean, cute little dress, it was a filthy mess when David found her because the airline had not allowed anyone access to their baggage. David put her on the replacement plane sent from Jidda about noon that day. She finally retrieved her overnight bag and some clean clothes at the Stoltzfuses' before arriving in Athens to meet her mother.

Anna (center) and friends at Sanaa airport

With Anna back in Athens for the school year, we settled into being a family of three for the remainder of our tour. Lesley accompanied me to the office each day so I could nurse her at my desk and she could nap in her small car bed. Before she learned to crawl, she often rolled around on a blanket on the carpeted floor of David's office, right next door to mine. When visitors were announced downstairs, I whisked her off the blanket and into my office so the guest would note the semblance of proper decorum in the chief of mission's office.

Lesley went with us to many a party, too, sleeping in her car bed in the host's bedroom unless something woke her to demand my attention. Although it probably would have been fine, we would not entrust Lesley to our Yemeni servant's care for more than an hour or two at a time and only when she was sleeping and we were nearby in the compound. Sue Koehnen and Peg O'Grady watched her a few times during the remaining seven months of our tour, but otherwise, childcare was David's and my responsibility 24/7.

Yemenis love children, especially babies, and our Yemeni friends gave Lesley many gifts, such as a brightly colored taffeta bonnet and an embroidered cloth to wrap her in. She still has Muhammad Abdul Ghani's gift of a small gold and black Qur'an bracelet charm that was meant to bring her good luck.

I had one promise to keep before we departed post and it took me several months to muster the courage to do it. Sheikh

Wedding dress from Bayt al-Faqih in the Tihama

Muhammad Zabara, the minister of public works, had given me a beautiful black tunic, embroidered with silver threads around the neckline and bodice as well as yellow and red diagonally-striped ribbon at the hemline and on the sleeves. Reportedly, it was a wedding dress typical of those used in his village of Bayt al-Faqih near Hodeida. Normally a full-length tunic on a Yemeni woman, on me it was only knee-length. I was very proud to own it and still wear it to parties with long pants underneath. However, his present had one condition: that, after I gave birth, I must hold a traditional tea party for my women friends.

Yemeni tradition requires a new mother to host a party for all of her women friends to honor herself forty days after the birth of her baby. At the party, she is the center of attention, often seated on a bed and decked out in all her jewelry and finest clothing. She receives many gifts, a well-deserved acknowledgement of her new status (and responsibilities it seemed to me) but a custom at odds with American practice.

For weeks after Lesley was born I agonized over the promise, trying to imagine myself being celebrated by my female friends. The fortieth day came and went. I simply could not picture me, the wife of the U.S. chief of mission, pretending I was a new Yemeni mother, sitting on a bed in front of all my friends. I felt that it would be a sacrilegious mocking of a tradition held in great esteem by Yemeni society. Yemeni women, although shy by nature, are proud of their wife-and-mother role and relish being the center of attention at marriage and especially after giving birth. Despite the Western tradition of baby showers, my pride and modesty would not allow others to fuss over me just for delivering a baby! Additionally, a hepatitis B scare circulated around Sanaa about forty days after Lesley was born, and I did not want to risk her health by having lots of strangers in our home.

I finally hosted the tea party when Lesley was ten weeks old, keeping my promise to the sheikh but, as a foreigner, doing it on my own terms. I invited forty women, Yemeni and others from the diplomatic community, late one afternoon and served tea and cookies. I showed off Lesley and hosted the party as any other Western woman would do. No presents and no qat chewing.

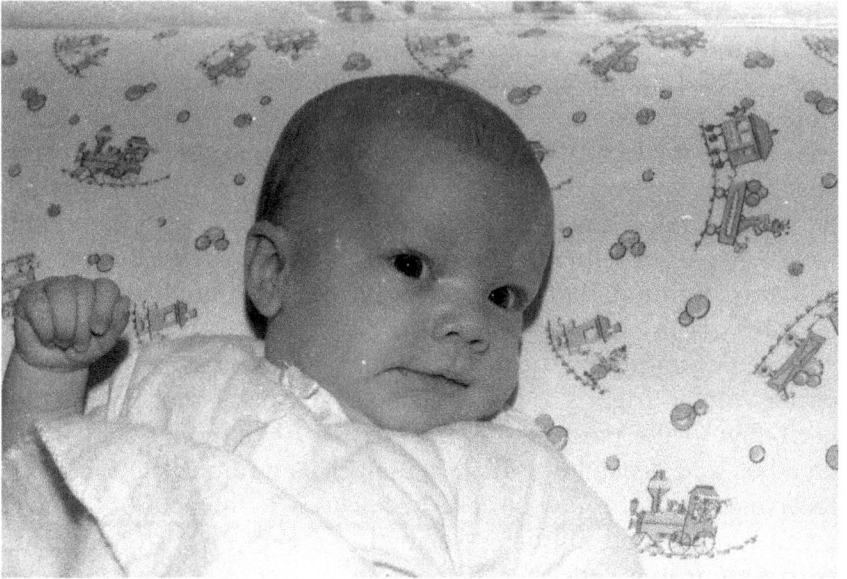

Baby Lesley

The next big event with our firstborn was Christmas. Even though we were far from home, experiencing the celebration with Lesley was extra special. Following the holidays, with the shipping of household effects and the farewell parties behind us, we returned to the States in early February 1972, our first home leave in two years. After visiting some eager grandparents in Texas and California, we spent a month in Ann Arbor. David had some research and writing to finish there so that he could complete his doctoral dissertation soon after our arrival in Amman.

Early in our Yemen tour, we had set up a room in the guest apartment in Sanaa for his thesis writing and my sewing. There David had spent about three weeks of vacation leave during the course of our tour in Sanaa, as well as countless hours in the evenings, to birth his own "baby." He interviewed people, researched, and later, during the last six months of our tour, drafted his thesis on the Yemeni foreign affairs elite, including forty or so leaders. He wanted to gauge how their study-abroad experiences ("transnational participation") prior to public service had affected their decision-making in foreign affairs. He found them more open to modernization and progressive ideas than what they had known growing up under the imam. However, implementing those Western values in an extremely conservative society had become their challenge upon return to Yemen.

We were due in Amman, Jordan, in May 1972. When we left Dulles airport on Pan American Airways en route to Amman, two tires blew out on take-off, a fact not disclosed to the passengers until we were about to land in London. When they announced we might have to evacuate the plane at the airport using emergency chutes (something that fortunately never occurred), David instructed me: "You take Lesley and I'll grab the thesis!"

Nurturing Our Mental Health

Maintaining our sanity and keeping morale high among the staff were major concerns, both for the State Department and for David and me. Our work was hard enough without worrying about disgruntled American employees. While David and I had many opportunities to get out of the compound and socialize—trying to balance our free time between Yemenis and the international community—the rest of the staff did not. Since we wanted to offer them as many of the comforts of home as possible, our initial priority for ensuring a happy post was to create Western-style recreational outlets for them to use in their free time. Travels away from our exotic environment for R&R were a second option. Both efforts gave all of us renewed energy for building a successful mission.

Our first initiative was the creation of a swimming pool. The only pool in Sanaa was at the Russian Embassy, which was off-limits to the Western bloc. With a little bit of American ingenuity, David converted our circular Persian fountain (*shadrawan*), the focal point of the large west patio of the Chancery, into a small swimming pool. A boon to us Americans, it was an ideal way to entertain our friends informally and for the American staff to relax.

The *shadrawan* had to be cleaned, repaired with epoxy, and waterproofed with a sealer before David could apply two coats of white primer and finally the blue-green marine paint that made it sparkle like a real pool. Fourteen feet square, the pool held about 5,000 gallons of water—enough for a 5'6" adult to be shoulder deep when standing on the bottom. The fountain mechanism, encased in a cement pillar, sat in the middle of the pool and no longer worked. Its large bulk forced divers to watch where they were going. The water registered about 60° Fahrenheit, painfully cold for adults, but the kids loved it.

Wanting to reactivate the fountain mechanism, David paid a visit to the National Repair Shop, a government-owned facility that looked like a factory out of Charles Dickens's time. Originally it had been an Ottoman Turkish horse stable, but it now had overhead drive shafts, leather belts, ancient lathes, and four or five American aircraft engines (550 horsepower each, taken from a wrecked aircraft) lying or hanging around everywhere.

David hoped to find a central squirting device that would make the water assume different patterns. He had heard that the Yemeni repair shop made something similar, one recently purchased by the Russian embassy, which attempted to mimic a 1,500-year-old Persian art form. The Yemenis gladly showed him a device made in two racks of pipes that was eighteen inches square. It had five brass birds attached. Each bird had wings that flapped and the whole thing turned as water ran through it under pressure. It was not quite what David had in mind. Fearing that the birds might fly off, he decided against the purchase.

Instead, he bought a small Italian pump for ninety dollars that recirculated and aerated the water by spraying it about fifteen feet into the air. He devised a really clever "reverse-flush-with-drainage filter system, using an old hot water heater tank and a little plastic screening stuffed with cotton and pushed down a pipe" [his words] to try to clean out the large amounts of dirt and sand that dropped in from the Sanaa plains. When that proved ineffective, he resorted to a vacuum cleaner with a 25-foot hose found in the storeroom to clean the bottom of the pool. Every two weeks or so, his Rube Goldberg system just completely failed, and he had to drain the pool and refill it, usually just before a big party was expected. He dumped six cups of Purex into the pool to prevent schistosomiasis (also called bilharzia), a disease endemic in Yemen caused by a fluke or flatworm that lives in the liver of a snail residing in still water.

One afternoon during the renovation of the *shadrawan*, when David was splattered from head to foot with marine paint, the

David painting the *shadrawan*

Yemeni chief of protocol, Hamami, arrived unannounced. Short, stocky and immaculately dressed in a suit and tie, he drove into the compound with a message: "The prime minister would like to see you as soon as possible about a matter of great urgency." David scrubbed up as best he could and threw on his suit and tie in record time.

The *shadrawan* also provided a venue for showing movies when friends or staff came over for an evening swim. The armed forces film circuit in Ethiopia and Turkey shipped us a variety of movies in unclassified pouches. We set up the projector inside the *mafraj* (the large sitting room behind the Chancery's French doors that overlooked the fountain outside) and opened the doors. We positioned the screen on the opposite side of the pool. This allowed everyone to sit around the *shadrawan* and watch the films, resting in bamboo patio chairs salvaged from the vacated American homes in Taiz. Despite the crude filtering system, we used the fountain and its surrounding patio for swimming, picnics, and movies throughout two summers.

A separate project, and our biggest entertainment achievement, was the conversion of a cavernous grain storage room on the second floor of the apartment building into a unique movie theater. With the help of Tom Seibert, David tore out the rock-and-mortar storage bins and replastered the walls before *gussing* the entire 15'x35' room and its 8'x10' entrance foyer. A curtain that hung around the screen just like in a real movie theater concealed two speakers on the wall behind the curtains. David and Tom placed one reconditioned 16 millimeter Victor sound projector (cannibalized from two others found in the warehouse) on a table in the back, and put up four lights painted red with Yemeni "hat baskets" over each one to create just the right atmosphere.

To soften the theater's stone-floor seating and reclining, we placed thin, single mattresses and back bolsters covered with bright striped Yemeni cloths along the walls, making the room similar to the *mafraj* in a Yemeni home. A few director's and card table chairs were placed here and there for those unable or unwilling to sit on the mattresses Yemeni-style. We wanted to create the nighttime feeling of a casbah (the older, traditional Arab core of a North African city with a suq, like Algiers) to entertain our guests.

Late one evening Alain and Marie Agnes Bertaud came over to help us decorate. David encouraged Alain to use his well-developed artistic talents, saying, "Please paint something very distinctive on the wall here so we can remember this unusual movie theater!" Plied with cognac, Alain painted murals all around the large room until well past midnight. Calling it an Arab theme "as seen from Baghdad," Alain outlined in firm strokes: a Saudi warrior with his *kafiyya* (checkered head scarf), dark glasses, and rifle; a Turkish wrestler with huge muscles standing on the dado and holding up the beamed ceiling; a Jewish money lender holding a cash box; a Bedouin tent; sheikhs in long robes; and scantily clad harem ladies dancing.

In the meantime, David tackled the entrance foyer and designed a 2'x3' mural to grab the attention of our moviegoers. You could not miss it as you stepped over the threshold and stooped through the short doorway into the casbah foyer. A wily fox, sitting on his haunches, operating a movie projector, greeted everyone who entered our theater, with a sign overhead appropriately naming it "11th Century Fox."

Speaking with affection and not disrespect, we Westerners used to laugh about how Yemen was rushing headlong into the eleventh century; hence the name of our theater. Coming out of the severe isolation imposed by the imamate, Yemen in the 1960s and 1970s was struggling heroically to modernize its infrastructure and become a respected, viable Middle Eastern nation. Their struggle had its ups and downs, some of which became amusing conversation topics. I fondly remember a dinner party David and I held at our home in Washington in the late 1970s. We invited four other couples who had also had "the Yemen Experience." We howled all evening, each trying to top the other with our Yemen stories. Pity anyone attending who had never been to Yemen! Some stories were so bizarre that unless you had visited Yemen, you would not believe they had happened.

Although we found eighty-five old USIS films in the storerooms, we mainly relied on movies shipped in from the armed forces film circuit. The State Department offered a "Hollywood Greats" series especially for hardship posts, but we did not qualify because our post was not big enough!

We showed movies to friends and the staff at least once a week. Oldies but goodies, such as *High Noon, Casablanca, Hud, Grapes of Wrath, East of Eden, Raisin in the Sun,* an older version of *My Friend Flicka,* Lone Ranger and Gene Autry westerns, Donald Duck and Road Runner cartoons, and TV shows like *Star Trek, Bonanza,* and *Markham* filled many an evening. Our 11th Century Fox theater provided a perfect although brief escape to the culture of our birth and a good venue for entertaining friends and staff, who also pined for some Western amenities. On rare occasions, we invited Yemenis married to Western women, who could better appreciate our casual brand of entertainment than Yemenis with Yemeni wives.

Building a tennis court was our next effort at making the compound feel more like home. There was just enough space between Bayt al-Hilali and the wall on the east side of the four-acre compound to accomplish such a feat. Since there were no tennis courts in Sanaa for us to use as a model, getting across the idea of what we were talking about to local workmen was a challenge. A German surveyor friend did a precise calculation and put in corner posts marked at the correct heights to lay a standard-size, level court.

Somehow we managed to put up a relatively high wire-mesh fence. Using David's trained eye, a level, and some advice from

Anna and Sheba on diesel roller

Alain, local workmen under Muhammad Abdul Ghani's tutelage laid out the court in a wooden-framed rectangle. They smoothed the soil with two-by-fours before having a contractor pour asphalt into the frame. The Ministry of Public Works sent over a Chinese-made diesel roller to smooth it out. Miraculously, they managed to get it reasonably flat. One UN official, upon hearing about our achievement, commented: "Here you can only strive for perfection. You never achieve it." But we came close enough.

For various reasons, we did not complete construction of the court until late spring, a year after our arrival at post. When finished, the tennis court became another venue for diplomacy, although we found no Yemenis who knew how to play. David and the German ambassador had weekly meetings on the court prior to the Vestrings' departure in September 1971. Other Western friends came over to play. Not much of a tennis player, I still rallied frequently with David, giving each of us plenty of exercise chasing my misplaced balls around the court. Many balls purchased at the PX in Asmara were lost over the compound wall, but that was a small price to pay for good fun and exercise.

David and I requisitioned the second tomblike storeroom in Bayt-al-Hilali for a darkroom. The windowless room had two huge stone laundry sinks with water faucets, perfect for washing photos after developing them. My parents shipped via APO all the equipment needed to set up the photo lab. David commandeered the one electrical outlet in the room to rig up a photo light over his work area.

After Lesley's birth, working in the photo lab became an obsession for both of us. Our parents were clamoring for photos of their new grandchild. We put Lesley in her little car bed and carried her down the stairs into the darkroom many an evening after supper. With Lesley asleep, we could work until late at night using the enlarger to capture her first seven months in black and white prints. During Anna's summer visit she helped her dad transfer the prints from bath to bath.

Among David's many interests was astronomy, but he had never had the opportunity to study the stars. Without the interference of bright streetlights, Sanaa's skies were so black and the stars so brilliant it was the perfect place to stargaze. I was eager to learn, too, and before Lesley was born, I accompanied David to the Chancery rooftop on clear evenings. Stepping out onto the third-floor roof, we had a magnificent 360-degree view over the rooftops of Sanaa, with only the hint of light through nearby residence windows to interfere. If there was a moon out, we could see the silhouette of the mountains to the east and southeast and once again capture for ourselves that magical feeling of being in an exotic land.

David created a small observatory on the rooftop using an old lift van that had arrived carrying the belongings of our communicator and his wife. He hinged one side of the crate to create a door and stapled plastic to the walls inside to cover the cracks and prevent moisture or sand from seeping in. There he could store his Sears telescope, star maps, and everything he needed to become possibly Sanaa's only rooftop astronomer. He delighted in sharing the stars with staff and a few interested friends and in taking Anna up to the rooftop—at seven she was very curious about everything and loved to do things alone with her Daddy.

Periodic R&R trips generally relieved our stress as well. We rotated pouch runs so that everyone had an opportunity to get away every few months to either Asmara or Jidda. Travel over the rugged gravel road getting home from the airline in Taiz proved an adventure on our last R&R to Asmara, when Lesley was five months old. We left Taiz at 12:30 p.m. for the return to Sanaa in the Land Rover, with Abdul Kadir driving. We stopped briefly at the famous Janad mosque from the year 638 CE, one of the oldest mosques in Islam, before beginning the climb up through the mountains. Lesley did fine with all of the bouncing in her car bed. About an hour south of Sanaa, a taxi driver passed us, pointing to our left rear tire. Discovering that three of five bolts had sheered off the wheel, we felt very lucky we had not flipped and rolled down the mountainside.

Accompanying us in the Land Rover were three FSNs returning from their Ramadan holiday. We paid $20 baksheesh to the taxi driver to take one FSN on to Sanaa to get Sam Case, our new administrative officer, who could bring another vehicle out to retrieve us. I managed to change, feed, and bed down Lesley as the sun was setting. It was pitch black by 6:30 and the FSNs built a fire beside the road while we waited. Soon an empty taxi stopped, and we paid the driver $18 to haul us all back to Sanaa. We met Sam on the road and all got home safely by 8 p.m.

Someone went out early the next morning with a truck to retrieve the damaged Land Rover—the wheel was an oval, no longer round, and totally ruined, and the brake drum was missing! After that we sent our classified pouches out through Jidda on Saudi Airlines from Sanaa and bought a motorcycle for the FSNs to run errands around Sanaa. Consequently, we made few overland trips to Taiz while waiting for the West Germans to pave the road between Taiz and Sanaa.

When it was our turn for R&R, we got safely overland to the airplane, as we always did except for the above scare, and went to Kagnew Station in Asmara. There we did medical checks and loaded up on PX items and American food. We could stay at the BOQ for $2 a night and eat a full dinner at the officers club for $1.50.

Susan and Fran McConnell in Asmara

A doctor's appointment cost $1.75. Sundaes were 30 cents, and beer 20 cents. You could not beat the prices.

Besides enjoying the army base's American pleasures, we ventured into Asmara's marketplace, eating such things as *doro wot* (a national dish of chicken stewed in hot pepper *zigani* sauce), *injera* (moist, spongy-like bread made of *teff*, a grain from lovegrass, similar to millet but smaller in size), and *yebeg wot*, freshly made lamb stew served with *injera*. We rode horses and partied with consulate families and some of the international community. Once we waved at the Ethiopian emperor, Haile Selassie, as he rode by in an open-air convertible and later visited the royal lions and baboons at his Asmara palace grounds.

On one of our early trips to Asmara, we visited Massawa on Ethiopia's Red Sea coast. Because Ethiopia and Eritrea had been Italian colonies, Mussolini had the opportunity to build a fine port at Massawa. There we spent the weekend at the Red Sea rest center run by the U. S. Army, staying in the VIP annex for the modest fee of two dollars a night. In the early 1970s the Eritrean People's Liberation Front (EPLF, or ELF for short) was very active in the countryside. So we decided to fly rather than ride down in a time-consuming military-escorted convoy. Even the convoys proved unsafe. One Marine, carrying a mail pouch between Asmara and Massawa about three months after our visit, was pulled from his car and murdered.

Our holiday in Massawa was lovely until David ate squid at the seafood buffet of the new Red Sea Hotel restaurant. An allergic reaction forced him to spend the rest of the weekend in bed, giving him plenty of time to recall a similar episode on a trip to Spain twenty years earlier. However, I salvaged the holiday for myself by wandering the beach and eating things like broiled red snapper and oysters on the half shell. Even though David was miserable much of the time, we liked Massawa but never returned because of the ELF tension.

During a typical two-year tour, the State Department gave each family at a Middle East hardship post a one-month R&R trip to Europe or some nearby place. Since ours was only an eighteen-month tour that was extended to twenty-one months, we had to pay for our midtour vacation ourselves when I was six months pregnant. We chose to go to Kenya in February, their summer, with a stop in Addis Ababa, following the advice of a British friend in Sanaa who helped plan our trip. He had grown up in Kenya and had wonderful memories of leisurely car trips through Kenya's backcountry.

Addis was delightful. We stayed with the Robert Yosts, David's old friends from the Philippines, and had dinner with Dick Petree, a former colleague of mine on the Japan desk, and his wife. We visited Africa Hall, the university and national museums, and Koka Dam, which had been built in the late 1950s on the Awash River forty-five miles south of Addis. We also bought a Coptic scroll containing a prayer written by a priest 150 years earlier.

The Norfolk Inn in Nairobi was luxurious and our night at Treetops, a hotel on stilts for folks on safari, surpassed our expectations. After weeks of no elephants showing up at Treetops to impress the tourists, we had thirty-seven come to the watering hole for us! After that, the trip went downhill. At that time in Kenya, we soon discovered, you either went first class or no class. The British travel agent in Nairobi had booked us into off-the-beaten-track motels that our British friend had remembered as exceptional places twenty years earlier. The only case of bed bugs I have ever had in all

Elephants at Treetops

my travels occurred in a dilapidated cabin at Thompson Falls. We tried to change our routing and go to the beach at Mombassa, but all the hotels were filled for the summer holidays.

We did manage to reschedule a night at Lake Naivasha, with its graceful cranes and flamingos. Having turned in our rental car in Nairobi before going to the lake, we shared a cab with a chatty Indian Sikh businessman in a Peugeot 504 taxi.

On our return to Nairobi, the taxi station wagon was filled with locals. Sitting in the far back seat of this very crowded vehicle, I marveled at the long looped earlobe of a Masai in front of me. During the entire return trip to Nairobi he twisted and pulled on the elongated skin as if it were a piece of putty to stretch and mold. A nervous habit similar to chewing fingernails, I guess, but it was mesmerizing to watch.

We got back to Nairobi five days earlier than planned, staying in luxury at the Intercontinental Hotel overnight before catching a plane back to Asmara and its American military base. Kagnew Station allowed me to indulge in all the creature comforts my pregnant body craved. We decided that for future trips we would make sure recommendations were based on current information and pay whatever price was required in order to cash in on the true meaning of R&R.

Back to the routine of life in Sanaa, we kept up with the outside world through various media. We heard haunting Arabic music on Sanaa radio and picked up Paris radio and the BBC news five to seven times a day on our shortwave. The news always discussed international issues, offering a markedly different slant from the Americocentric coverage we were used to in the States. We eventually received *Time, Newsweek,* and the *New York Herald Tribune,* where we first began to learn about something called Watergate.

An old Grundig phonograph found in the warehouse played our classical collection and the records of Elvis, Simon and Garfunkel, and Frankie Avalon. Unfortunately, we had little time to read from the large library of USIS books that had been shipped to the post in the early 1960s to feed the minds of isolated Americans.

In addition to the pool and tennis court outside, the photo lab and movie theater inside, and the rooftop observatory, David and I had guitars for group folk singing and a badminton set. The rest of the staff indulged in some of our activities and also spent free time polishing rocks with kits sent from the States, listening to ham radios, and spelunking in volcanic caves north of town, where they crawled on their bellies through underground rooms the length of a city block. We all played table tennis. The guys built a Ping-Pong table after finding boxed table tennis sets (balls, paddles, and a net) in the suq that were made in Shanghai.

Adding these activities to our travels, parties, and Yemeni and international friends, we found plenty to keep us busy in the few "off" hours we had. Although some of the enthusiasm for the challenges of Yemen had waned by the end of our twenty-one months, particularly because of our worries about caring for a new baby, our life as Americans in a very foreign land was full, and never dull or boring. For that, we felt most fortunate, even if it might sound to an outsider that we focused more on entertaining ourselves than socializing with Yemenis.

5

Diplomacy at Work

A Parade of History and Culture

Along with the other diplomats in Sanaa in 1970, David and I had front-row seats in the covered grandstands for the 26th of September independence day parade. Held at Maydan al-Tahrir, the large public square near our compound, the parade marched many colorful groups in front of the reviewing stand. They were celebrating the overthrow of the imamate in 1962 and the end of centuries of unprogressive theocratic rule.

Thousands of people brimming with national pride jammed the square. All the hotels in town were booked, and police had to work hard to keep the crowds out of the parade path. To get a better view, spectators clamored onto the tops of nearby buildings and the large public *hammam*. For David, it was a joy to see an all-Yemeni celebration, without the Egyptian military presence that had dominated his previous tour in Sanaa.

Military men marched in various types of service uniforms. Men in Western khaki shirts and pants and men in traditional dress, many carrying rifles or *janbiyyas*, paraded enthusiastically before us. Among the traditionally dressed men I noticed a *hajji* with a beard, bright red with henna, which proclaimed he had been on a pilgrimage (*hajj*) to Mecca. Russian-made MIG and Ilyushin aircraft of the Yemeni air force flew overhead. Antiquated Russian T34 tanks belching gray smoke paraded by, with Prime Minister al-Aini riding in a jeep and waving to the crowd. Turbaned President al-Iryani sat regally in the grandstand reviewing the troops as they passed by.

People on top of *hammam* watching parade

Yemen Airlines DC3s dropped bags of candy from the sky, which landed with force, banging a few people on the head. Musicians, sword-bearers, and tribesmen dancing with daggers or riding in open trucks contributed their magic. Fierce-looking men in teargas facemasks decked the bed of a truck. They were crop sprayers for an agricultural project, who wore their masks for the sake of the parade to show the spectators how they did their work. Until the women's float appeared at the end of the parade there were no women participants, only spectators. All presented an impressive and colorful display of nationalistic fervor.

One noticeable feature at the parade was the huge contingent of Chinese officials, both men and women, in their gray pantsuits, the women with their hair in short bobs. Before the China "thaw" in 1973, they ignored Americans completely and did so at the parade. On the other hand, the Soviets, who were also in the grandstands, were always polite to us, although we did not see them socially.

Joy, passion, exuberance—how had this marvelous event, a symbolic culmination of Yemen's impressive history and culture, come

Men wearing gas masks in parade

to pass? During the five hours we watched the parade, I had time to reflect on this question. Yemen's origins went back to the Old Testament and Qahtan, the Biblical Joctan, a descendant of Shem, the first son of Noah. Supposedly, Qahtan was the son of the Prophet Hud and the great, great grandson of Shem. Whatever the truth of his ancestry, Qahtan was the legendary forefather of all the tribes of South Arabia through his twenty-four sons. To the Greeks and Romans, the ancient South Arabian civilization was known as Arabia Felix, Fortunate Arabia, or Arabia the Blessed. Yemen's scenery was breathtaking for sure, but that day I could truly understand why its people, culture, and history were also special.

Kingdoms and empires had risen and fallen for more than 3,000 years in South Arabia. The heart of Yemen's ancient South Arabian culture was Marib, located 100 miles to the east of Sanaa. Just as Sanaa was originally named Azal for one of Qahtan's sons, Marib was reportedly founded by a descendant of another of Qahtan's sons named Saba (Sheba in Hebrew) long before the legendary Queen of Sheba (Saba), or Queen of the South as she is called in the Old Testament, ruled the area in the tenth century BCE. The queen reputedly carried treasures from South Arabia by camel to Jerusalem to visit Solomon. Stories of Solomon and Sheba later became major themes in Islamic art and literature. Over the centuries the Sabaeans jockeyed for power with the nearby Himyar, Qataban, Hadramawt, Awsan, and Ma'in civilizations.

Economically, Marib entered its heyday in the seventh century BCE, during the time when Sabaean monarchs were building the Marib dam, a huge project that took many decades to complete. Although traveling there was off limits in 1970, I had long heard about the huge earthen dam (estimated at somewhere between 2,000 and 2,500 feet wide and 50-to-60 feet high) with a large bastion on each end. It had a vast hydraulic system that could irrigate 25,000 acres in this desert terrain. Despite the fact it collapsed and had to be rebuilt three times over the next thousand years, the dam must have been a significant engineering feat for its day, over 2,500 years ago.

Marib straddled an immensely prosperous caravan trade route for such exotic items as the resins of frankincense and myrrh. The route extended from the Indian Ocean through Arabia, Egypt, and other parts of the Middle East to Greece, and Rome. Writer Caroline Singer states that South Arabia (broader Yemen, which included the YAR and PDRY) and Oman were two of the only areas in the world where frankincense and myrrh trees grew naturally and that it was impossible to cultivate them. According to author Tim Mackintosh-Smith, the South Arabians exported approximately 3,000 tons of incense and 600 tons of the more expensive myrrh each year, both probably as precious to its buyers as our petroleum oil is today. Legend has it that the three wise men left from somewhere in South Arabia for Bethlehem to see the Christ child and present their gifts of frankincense and myrrh (commodities then more expensive than gold.)

The ancient world used the priceless resins extracted from these gnarly trees in worship, for mummification and funerals, and for medicine. These rare items joined the silks, spices, and fragrant woods that came from the Far East through the Indian Ocean by dhow (a wooden sailing vessel), then overland on caravans headed for Mediterranean ports, Egypt, and Mesopotamia. The South Arabians were thus able to exact heavy tolls on pain of death for these coveted commodities as they passed through Marib, and even

The Treasury at Petra

through Sanaa for a time, en route to trading centers like Mecca in Saudi Arabia and Petra in Jordan. The highly prized nature of frankincense and myrrh was something hard for me to imagine centuries later, since I was able to buy these items in the Sanaa suq for only a few riyals to burn as incense.

The South Arabian economy declined dramatically following the development of seaborne trade by the Romans. Other causes of the decline included the rising prominence of the "silk road" from the Far East through Persia as a competitor to the "gold and incense road of Arabia Felix" (in the view of writer Fritz Peipenberg); the Christian church's campaign against the use of incense; and the final collapse of Marib's dam around 570 CE, which led to the emigration of South Arabians northward and eastward. Yemen entered a lengthy era of poverty and isolation from which it emerged only briefly in the seventeenth century to satisfy Europe's demand for coffee, which flourished in Yemen's mild climate. Several European countries and Egypt even opened offices on the Red Sea coast to oversee their trading interests at a time when Yemeni coffee was being consumed by royalty and in wealthy homes all over Europe.

David and I visited Mocha, on the Red Sea Coast south of Hodeida, which had been the center of this coffee trade four centuries earlier. However, in 1970 when we passed through and saw sand dunes covering old building ruins, I found Mocha to be only a sleepy fishing village. It was hard to imagine that Mocha had been one of the busiest ports in the world until other countries with mild climates began to supply Europe with coffee grown from stock they had obtained from Yemen.

Yemen's political history, with its blending of religion and politics, was as rich as its cultural and economic past. The dichotomy between uniforms and traditional dress parading in front of me triggered thoughts of the religious as well as the modernist-traditionalist split in the country.

The ancient Sabaean kingdom collapsed in the mid-second-century CE, leaving rival dynasties, both local and foreign, including Abyssinia (Ethiopia) and Persia (Iran), to compete for power in Yemen over the next 500 years. By 300 CE the Himyar had emerged as leaders, with Himyar kings converting to Christianity and later Judaism, two religions that had gained small followings in Yemen. For a while in the sixth century, Yemen was ruled by a cruel, heavy-handed Jewish king of Himyar descent who massacred hundreds of Christians at the Najran oasis in 525 CE. The Aksumites of Ethiopia invaded five years later in response to the persecution of Christians but were pushed out around 570 CE by the Sassanian Persians, who were in turn defeated by Muslim armies in 638 CE.

The Prophet Muhammad was born in 570 CE. According to the tenets of Islam, God first spoke to Muhammad in 610 and revealed the Qur'an over the next twenty-plus years. In about 612, the Prophet began spreading Islam from its capital in Medina (Saudi

Arabia) through other parts of the Middle East. South Arabia was one of the first areas to be influenced by the expansion of Islam, with a Yemenite follower of the Prophet converting the Yemenis, as well as the Persian governor of Sanaa, to Islam in 628 CE. Muhammad's father, according to several references, had traveled to Yemen prior to his son's birth. In the early Islamic period, Yemenis served in the Islamic conquering armies all over the Middle East, and Yemenis populated new cities in Syria and Iraq, as well as Sudan, Tunisia, and as far away as Spain and Bordeaux, France.

Following the Prophet Muhammad's death in 632 CE, his close followers began a line of caliphs that was contested by 'Ali ibn Abi Talib, the Prophet's cousin and son-in-law. 'Ali's followers assassinated the 3rd caliph and made 'Ali their leader and 4th caliph from 656 until 'Ali himself was assassinated in 661 CE. The Ummayad dynasty, loyal to the tradition of the first three caliphs, emerged as leaders of the majority of Muslims known as Sunnis. Followers of 'Ali, through his son Hussein, established the Shi'a line, thus inaugurating the Sunni-Shi'a split we see in Islam today. Representing a microcosm of this split, Yemen was a battleground for the two opposing sects for the next 650-plus years.

After the Prophet Muhammad converted the sheikh of the al-Asha'er tribe in Medina, the sheikh established an Islamic settlement in his homeland of Wadi Zabid in the Tihama as early as 630 CE. 'Ali himself came to northern Yemen to convert the Hamdan tribes. Muslim missionaries were sent to build the Janad mosque near Taiz and the Great Mosque in Sanaa, which still stand today. The al-Asha'er University, established as a prominent center of Sunni learning in Zabid in 819 CE and continued as such for over 500 years, allegedly employed the man who developed Algebra (originally called al-Jabr). Al-Asha'er provided some of the early teachers for the famous al-Azhar University in Cairo that opened in 971AD and continues as a foremost center of Sunni learning today.

Sunni Muslims in Yemen subscribed to the Shafi'i interpretation of Islamic law, one of the four schools of Islamic Sunni law that are found in the various regions of the Muslim world. The Shafi'is, larger in number than their Shi'a rivals, settled at an early date in the coastal plains and southern highlands. They always formed the commercial and business class. Their descendants were the many Yemeni-Americans who visited us at the chancery or sent remittances to their families from other parts of the Middle East where they found employment.

Rival Shi'a peoples called Zaydis, named for Zayid, the great-grandson of 'Ali, reached Yemen about 897 CE. Led by Imam al-Hadi ila 'l-Haqq Yahya ibn al-Hussein from Medina, they were invited to Yemen to resolve a fractious conflict among the Hamdan tribe and settled in the northern mountain areas around Saada. Tribal warfare between the Shafi'is and Zaydis continued until 1323 CE, when the Zaydis emerged as the victors and established themselves as rulers of the mountainous interior, and at times throughout all of Yemen.

The Zaydi imams and their sayyid administrators ruled Yemen for more than 600 years until the Republican Revolution of 1962. Outsiders interrupted their dominance only for a few brief periods of control (most notably the Ottoman Turks in the 16th and 19th centuries). These imams used their theocratic power to build a tightly knit oligarchic society. Shifting tribal allegiances and what military power the imams could garner determined the territorial limits of their rule.

The conservative Zaydi imams allied themselves politically, though not religiously, with Ismailis (a Shi'ite sect based near Manakha), who espouse an esoteric philosophy that believes in the Hidden Imam. These Zaydi imams lived in the highlands, using Sanaa as their capital.

To ensure their power they regularly imprisoned several hundred boys, typically the sons of rival tribal leaders, as hostages. They extracted taxes from the Shafi'is in the southern part of Yemen centered near Taiz and further south into the Hadramawt. Distrusting foreigners, they fought hard to keep Yemen in isolation and free of modern influences during their years of rule through the first half of the twentieth century. The Sunni Shafi'is, by contrast, reached out to the world, became merchants and tradesmen, and took jobs abroad.

Imam Yahya, founder of the fourth and last Zaydi dynasty, was assassinated in 1948 by rivals, who were members of the "free-Yemeni" movement organized by Yemeni exiles in Aden. Yahya's son, Imam Ahmad, quickly overpowered them and moved the capital from Sanaa to Taiz for security reasons. Imam Ahmad also survived several assassination attempts during his fourteen-year reign.

Bill Stoltzfus, deputy chief of mission at the U.S. embassy in Jidda, visited us in 1970 and told this story about Imam Ahmad: When Bill was working at the American legation in Taiz in the late fifties, he flew with a Yemeni pilot in an Aero-Commander to Asmara to pick up an X-ray machine for use in looking for bullets to be extracted from the imam's posterior following an assassination attempt. Imam Ahmad used to fly Stoltzfus up to Sanaa to show movies to the imam and his harem (or his "extended family") when he spent time there away from Taiz. One time Bill's visit dragged out several days. The imam loved *Seven Brides for Seven Brothers* so much he demanded Bill show it to him and his entourage seven times!

Regardless of his love for movies, Imam Ahmad wanted to stem the tide of Western influence and sought weapons from Eastern bloc countries to fight the tribes in the north, who were independent and unruly. Those countries later turned against him and supported the moderate Yemeni Republicans when they overthrew newly crowned Imam Badr on September 26, 1962, five days after his father Ahmad's death. Badr led the Royalists in the northern part of Yemen during the 1960s and retired to London following the 1970 peace treaty between the Republicans and Royalists.

This brought me full circle to the parade marching before us. With the overthrow of the imamate, civil war raged between the Royalists, primarily Zaydis under Badr, and the Egyptian-backed Yemeni moderates (both Shafi'is and Zaydis). Funded by the Saudis, Iran, and even Jordan for a while, the Royalists based themselves in the northern highlands.

Because of the tremendous tension and distrust between Gamal Abdel Nasser and King Faisal over the issue of Yemen, U.S. President John F. Kennedy in April 1963 sent in Ambassador Ellsworth Bunker, who carefully brokered a peace agreement between Saudi Arabia and the United Arab Republic (dominated by Egypt). The agreement had eight points, including the gradual withdrawal of UAR troops from Yemen along with Saudi withdrawal of support for the Royalists, the halt to UAR bombing of the Saudi-Yemeni border, the insertion of UN peacekeepers, and creation of a no-fly zone between the two countries.

Although tensions eased between Saudi Arabia and Egypt, the UN was slow in implementing the agreement on the ground in Yemen. It was only with the UAR's defeat in the six-day 1967 Arab-Israeli war that the Egyptians, who had dominated the independence parade during David's earlier mid-1960s tour, finally withdrew their troops (50,000 men) from Yemen. Once the Egyptians withdrew, the Saudis eventually stopped funding the Royalists.

Between 1962 and 1970, Republican leaders in Yemen rotated into power, engaged in a civil war with the Royalists, and worked to consolidate the fledgling moderate government. At the same time they were attempting to achieve legitimacy externally. The YAR opened up diplomatic missions with both the East and West, except with the United Kingdom, which still regarded the deposed imam as the legitimate ruler of Yemen and vehemently protested President Kennedy's decision to support the Republicans.

The Jidda agreement officially ending Yemen's civil war was finally signed in March 1970 by Yemen's prime minister Muhsin al-Aini, the very same man who was waving to us from his jeep in the parade. With the exception of the imam and his Hamid al-Din family, the agreement allowed the Royalists and other Yemeni exiles to return to Sanaa. It also gave them two added seats on the Republican Council and twelve on the newly expanded National Council, three ministerial portfolios, and two governorships. Yemen's first permanent constitution was passed in December 1970 with a three-man plural executive, creating a consultative parliamentary government.

The jubilation all around me was thus a celebration of Yemen's emergence as a legitimate player on the world stage. The procession passing in front of us was a fitting climax to an incredibly rich, if conflicted, parade of history. With peace at last between Royalists and Republicans, a civilian government firmly in control, and the capital back in Sanaa, the YAR was able to celebrate its independence for the first time. Yemen had finally overcome its isolation and subjugation, putting on an excellent show of nationalistic pride for its citizens as well as its new foreign friends, from both the East and West. We were honored to share that historic event with them.

As a footnote to this big event, a year later, on September 30, 1971, Nasser's death followed on the heels of Yemen's national day celebrations. Despite their love of independence, the Yemenis still admired Nasser and declared three days of mourning, staged a parade in his honor, and sent an entourage of sixty people on the Russian-made presidential plane to his funeral. Nasser had not only helped the Yemenis succeed in their 1962 revolution but had also been a good mediator with the Israelis. His death created concern worldwide and caused David and me to contemplate its possible consequences upon the Middle East peace process.

Cold War Politics and U.S.-Yemeni Relations

With the Republican success in the 1962 revolution, Yemen could at last open its doors to the world. The country required major infrastructure development: roads, water systems, airports, a military force, telecommunications, a deepwater harbor, and medical facilities. The major Cold War powers were eager to oblige because of their interest in Yemen's strategic control of the Bab al-Mandeb straits, the southern entrance to the Red Sea. Some had already been active during the last few years of the imam's reign, each trying to maintain some sort of presence with the imam and increase its sphere of influence. Other countries and international organizations, such as the UNDP, Hungary, Italy, Kuwait, and India, established diplomatic missions or contributed various aid projects.

While the United States had completed a road and a water project before leaving during the 1967 Arab-Israeli war, the UNDP, the Soviet Union, China, the West Germans (FRG), and the East Germans (DDR) were all sponsoring large aid projects when David and I arrived in spring 1970. The United Kingdom finally dropped its loyalty to the Royalists and opened an embassy in North Yemen by the summer of 1970, giving their resident ambassador in Jidda accreditation to Sanaa. While each bloc tried to outdo the other, the YARG carefully courted both sides and offered the world its own display of East-West competition.

The biggest example of Cold War rivalry came in the form of three primary roads constructed in the 1960s. USAID built a gravel road from Mocha through Taiz to Sanaa, connecting Yemen's two main cities via the Sumarra pass and high mountain range. The Russians developed and paved a road between Hodeida and Mocha. The Chinese constructed a paved road between Sanaa and

Hodeida and another from Sanaa to Saada in the north of Yemen. The latter road was completed as far as Amran during our tenure, finally making it possible to drive our Land Rover there to visit Sheikh al-Sa'r, who had befriended David during his first tour.

The Eastern bloc countries were extremely active. The East Germans had a telecommunications project to replace the old landline from Ottoman Turkish days. When we drove from Taiz to Sanaa, we saw leaning wooden poles made from small tree trunks not much taller than a fence. A single line that paralleled the road connected the poles and reminded me of my grandmother's backyard clothesline. It was the most antiquated phone line we had ever seen. Communication between the two cities had occurred over this landline since 1902, so it definitely needed updating!

The Russians and the Hungarians each built a medical facility in Sanaa. These were our two main choices for emergency services unless we wanted to try our luck at the Yemeni hospitals or at the Kuwaiti-built military hospital. In addition, the Soviets constructed a new harbor in Hodeida and the Chinese built a textile mill in Bajil in the Tihama.

France signed a contract to build the first television station in Sanaa in the spring of 1971, taking almost two years to complete it. West Germany (FRG), also a major Western bloc contributor, modernized Yemen's telephone system. During the 1970s the FRG paved the U.S.-built gravel road between Taiz and Sanaa and improved some of the feeder roads ignored by the United States, Soviets, and Chinese.

The FRG also expanded the Sanaa airport, adding another twenty meters to the old runway and deepening the one built by the Russians. Until the upgrades were completed and the airport dedicated in May 1971, it was not possible for commercial jets to land in Yemen, except at the Russian military airport in Hodeida. David attended the dedication for laying the four cornerstones of the new Sanaa airport terminal. President Abdul Rahman al-Iryani was on hand to commemorate the occasion. However, he found himself standing on a stage facing the *back* of the bleachers rather than the audience in the grandstand. This faux pas had to be quickly corrected before the ceremonies could proceed. David and his Western colleagues shook their heads and lamented, "Only in Yemen."

Prime Minister al-Aini waving from jeep

Airport lighting came sometime later. Once Saudi Airlines began using the new airport, car headlights had to rescue landings made late in the day or at night. Sometimes there was a quick turnaround and the Saudi plane had to find its way out in the twilight.

FSN Abdul Kadir was at the airport when U.S. Secretary of State Rogers arrived on July 4, 1972, to re-establish full relations. USINT staff, and apparently some local tribesmen, lit flares and lined up all the vehicles at the airport with their lights beamed at the runway to accommodate a nighttime landing. According to FSO David Newton, also on the ground waiting, Rogers was late because the two USAF C-130s prepositioned at Hodeida airport had engine trouble on final warm-up. So, Rogers commandeered an old C-47 (DC-3) belonging to the U.S. Military Training Mission in Dhahran, which was bringing in Marine security guards. Rogers left behind the wives, as a trip up through the mountains was risky.

By the time he landed, it was too dark for him to read his arrival statement. But, this did not seem to matter. When he departed the next day, the streets were lined with cheering Yemenis. Rogers said the Yemenis were sophisticated because they did not ask anything of him. Although one of the five poorest countries in the world, they merely requested he put in a good word for them with the World Bank, the IMF, and the UNDP.

On one occasion David and I personally got caught up in Cold War one-upmanship. Late in our tour, we received an invitation from the Yemeni chief of protocol's office to the dedication of a new Chinese school. Even though we assumed it to be a mistake, given that in 1971 we had not yet resumed diplomatic relations with China, David decided we should go anyway. Perhaps the invitation was some indication of a thaw in relations, and if not, it would be interesting to see how we would be treated.

Dressed in appropriate business attire, we asked our driver to deliver us to the school close to the ceremony's ten a.m. starting time. We instructed him to hide our "getaway" VW van behind a nearby building and wait for us. Many Eastern bloc and United Nations diplomats who had gathered were facing the steps of the school where the Chinese ambassador stood, waiting to address his audience.

As we approached the group, the ambassador became noticeably agitated and quickly summoned the Yemeni chief of protocol, Hamami. Soon Hamami came rushing toward us, wringing his hands. We showed him our invitation. Nervously but apologetically, he stated it had been a mistake and that it would be a great embarrassment if we stayed. Not wanting to prolong his misery, we graciously turned away and found our car so that the ambassador could begin his ceremony. That was the closest we ever came to being declared persona non grata, though we were only asked to leave a small piece of foreign territory, not the whole country. I suspect some careless Yemeni official regretted that mistake.

Other than a few small incidents in Yemen in the early 1970s, we had only one other reminder that we were part of the Cold War era. On a regular basis the Russian courier plane swooped low over our compound, presumably just to let us know the Russians were alive and well and probably to do a little aerial reconnaissance. We found it amusing rather than irritating.

Bilateral U.S.-Yemeni relations date to 1946 when the U.S. consul in Aden made his first trip to Yemen to call on the imam. The United States sought a presence there in order to "thwart what the United States saw as USSR and 'Chicom' [Chinese Communist] mischief in the area," according to retired FSO Robert (Ted) Curran, who served in Taiz with the U.S. Information Service (USIS) in 1962-64. To track Soviet-Chinese activities and to meet with Yemen's sole decision-maker during the 1950s, FSOs assigned to the U.S. consulate in Aden traveled 10–12 hours by jeep to Taiz (a hundred miles away over rugged terrain).

As recounted in their oral history interviews conducted by the Association for Diplomatic Studies and Training (ADST), these FSOs spent ten-to-fifteen days each month in Taiz, taking up their own food and staying in one of the imam's guesthouses, since there were no commercial hotels. Although the guesthouse in Taiz had an ornate central courtyard with a fountain and balconies, the sleeping quarters consisted of two floors of crowded dorm rooms with no toilet facilities. They called on Imam Ahmad or traveled to Sanaa to see Prince Badr and other ministers to accomplish their business, including bringing in some PL-480 wheat during a late-1950s famine. In the meantime, the U.S. ambassador to Jidda was making yearly public relations forays into Yemen to amplify the efforts of the consulate in Aden. As a result of the prolonged, monthly communication efforts by all these FSOs visiting Yemen, the United States finally obtained an agreement with the imam in 1959 to open a legation in Taiz, attached initially to the U.S. embassy in Jidda and later to Cairo.

A few of the FSOs lived in Taiz and worked at the new legation prior to the 1962 revolution. Several described Taiz as a medieval city whose gates were locked at sundown each night. There was no running water or sanitation, no police force, few cars or roads, no banks, a pre–World War II communications system, no paved airfields, little modern housing, and a primitive government system.

There was no electricity, except for a few hours in the evening from the ancient town generator, or if one purchased a connection to a small generator that an Italian had set up to run as a private enterprise. They had to use kerosene-powered refrigerators, some of which were always smoking and/or having their wicks burn out.

Because they initially had no communications gear, the officers had to use "one-time pads" to transmit encrypted messages from Taiz's telegraph office to Washington, fly to Asmara, or drive to the Aden Consulate to send classified messages.

There was no paper currency either. Bill Wolle remembers signing a lease on two buildings for the new legation in Taiz and paying with a whole jeepful of wooden crates containing Maria Theresa silver thalers (large Austrian coins brought to Yemen by the Turks). Because the landlord physically counted each thaler, it took several hours to transfer the money. Additionally, 500 Yemenis who had served in the U.S. merchant marine had returned home, and Ted Curran had to hand out U.S. social security payments to these men, driving to villages with jeeploads of silver thalers to settle their accounts.

Despite their hardships, Bill Stoltzfus spoke in his 1994 ADST oral history interview about his relationship with the Yemenis and his time at the legation in Taiz this way: "Yemenis are the nicest, most friendly, hospitable people I have ever known....Yemen was beyond the beyonds....It was the 13ᵗʰ century in the 1950s. We were Connecticut Yankees in King Arthur's Court. The Cold War was in full swing and Egypt was plotting the overthrow of Imam Ahmad. Yet all of us foreigners felt a kinship, a tolerance and fellowship totally outside politics and the normal outlook on life."

The imam in those days personally approved all property leases, food imports, and travel permits. A large, reclusive, fierce-looking character, he held audiences every Friday in the central square to receive petitions from citizens and to oversee public executions, which were broadcast by town criers whenever one was scheduled. He only permitted schools where boys memorized the Qur'an and learned little else.

Other than the handful of Yemeni students he allowed to study in Italy in the 1940s because he felt they posed no threat to the monarchy, the imam generally refused to let Yemeni youth study abroad. Abdullah al-Sallal and Hassan al-Amri were exceptions; and after 1962 both would serve as Republican leaders. The Yemenis who did study abroad during those years were exiles living in Aden. When they joined the Republicans after the revolution, many became cabinet ministers in the new government.

As the imams had for centuries, Imam Ahmad kept his population well isolated and trusted few outsiders. Ambassador Marshall Wiley's first Foreign Service assignment had been to Taiz in 1958, and he remembers receiving the 67th visa ever issued to a foreigner by North Yemen!

Crown Prince Badr saw little of his father and lived in Sanaa, where the Russians and other East bloc missions resided. More moderate and personable than his father, Badr was known as the "Red Prince." Besides obtaining extensive military and technical assistance from Eastern Europe, Badr, not Ahmad, agreed to Yemen's membership in the short-lived UAS (United Arab States) with Egypt and Syria in 1958, while his father was away in Italy getting treatment for his morphine addiction.

Paralleling his son's interest in the outside world, the imam in the late 1950s began to welcome aid projects into Yemen to finance the much-needed infrastructure development, since he had few funds in his own coffers. Ted Curran, who arrived two months before Ahmad's death, may have been one of the last FSOs to meet with the imam. He and colleague Isa Sabbagh made arrangements with the ruler to expand the antiquated Sanaa radio station.

The imam had doctors from both the East and the West who treated him for his arthritis and various other maladies. The American doctor was on duty the night the imam died. Dr. Foster told his retainers the imam was sleeping and not to disturb him until morning. He ran home, packed his family into the car, took his prearranged exit visa, and fled to Aden.

By 1962 the U.S. mission had 140 people in Taiz, either at the legation or working on the road and water projects. Living conditions for Americans had improved considerably. They were comfortable, adequately supported, and included a primary school and a small Piper Aztec plane, with a pilot for necessary flights to Asmara or Aden. By late 1963 they even had an American doctor.

In January 1963, following the September revolution, the United States secured *agrément* (approval or consent) to open an embassy in Taiz and assigned a chargé d'affaires. The USG also opened a small branch office in Sanaa, where David served as deputy to the officer-in-charge on his first tour in Yemen from 1964 to 1966. The embassy moved from Taiz to Sanaa in August 1966.

Along with the establishment of a diplomatic presence, the United States contributed significantly to Yemen's development between 1961 and 1967 with economic aid and cultural exchanges. In addition to the big Mocha-Taiz-Sanaa road project, USAID directed the Kennedy water project in Taiz. Before the 1967 war, USAID employed numerous Yemenis, training them in road construction and the operation of the regional water purification and distribution system. USIS offered scholarships and exchange programs for professionals and other visitors to encourage positive U.S.-Yemeni relationships. By April 1963, barely six months after the imam's death, there were sixty Yemeni students studying in the United States.

The YAR canceled the USAID agreement in the spring of 1967 after an incident in which two USAID officers were arrested and charged with a rocket launcher attack against the Egyptian army. Claiming the charges were trumped up, the United States withdrew all USAID personnel. As tensions mounted, the State Department removed all nonessential USG personnel a month prior to the June 1967 Arab-Israeli war, because the YARG could no longer guarantee their safety. When the Yemenis broke off relations, the last six FS personnel left Yemen on June 9. They had only twenty-four hours to shred, burn, and destroy everything that might compromise U.S. security if discovered. They also had to pack a few essential personal items. The United States did not return officially until David and I reopened the post as an interests section in late April 1970.

Setting up USINT within the Italian embassy was part of an informal system that some of us termed "gray diplomacy." However, when queried in recent years, neither Ambassador David Newsom (editor of *Diplomacy Under a Foreign Flag*), nor Ambassador David Newton (former ambassador to Iraq and Yemen), nor Ambassador William Eagleton (chief of USINT Algiers and USINT Baghdad and Ambassador to Syria) had ever heard of the expression.

The phrase may have been my husband David's personal concoction, and he used it frequently in informal discussions with colleagues. This policy by whatever name has been a common tool used by the United States over the years when full diplomatic relations have been broken, to maintain a low-profile presence in an uneasy or tension-filled relationship with another country, such as with Cuba today. Since 1977, the United States and Cuba have conducted bilateral affairs within the Swiss Embassy in each other's capitals.

Forced to close a number of our Middle Eastern embassies as a result of the 1967 Arab-Israeli war, the United States established interests sections within European embassies in Syria, Yemen, Iraq, Egypt, Algeria, Libya, and Sudan. Lebanon, Saudi Arabia, Morocco, Tunisia, Kuwait, Jordan, and Iran did not sever relations.

By sending minimal representation, the United States remained less visible while testing the waters before resuming full relations. This third-party representation offered us the opportunity to conduct business as usual, yet keep a low profile by flying another country's flag. It helped Middle Eastern governments who wanted our aid and support to save face with their Arab colleagues and the rest of the world. It gave both sides the ability to have their cake and eat it too.

In 1967 when Egypt, Sudan, and Algeria broke diplomatic relations with the United States, they retained their consular relationship so that the United States could continue to issue visas to their citizens. In Egypt, a handful of U.S. consular officials who were not forced to leave formed the nucleus of the first U.S. interests section in the Middle East following the war. Our "ambassador" to Cairo, Donald Bergus, had the official, working title of "chief of mission or principal officer" of USINT Cairo and the diplomatic title of "minister" to the Embassy of Spain. A Spanish flag on his automobile and calling cards indicating his position with the Spanish embassy were two symbols of his official status in Egypt.

The Yemen Arab Republic hosted the fourth interests section to be established in the Middle East following the 1967 war. It was the first country, however, that had broken both consular and diplomatic relations to allow an interests section to be opened under the protection of a foreign embassy.

David's new title became "chief of the Political Section" and "first secretary" of the American interests section of the Italian embassy in the YAR. His first secretary title, as opposed to the higher rank of minister given to Bergus in Cairo, reflected several things. First, there was the lengthy history of U.S.-Egyptian relations and the greater importance of Egypt to the United States in the worldwide scheme

David, President Iryani, and Ahmad Nu'man with moon rocks

of things. Second, Cairo required a much larger staff than USINT Sanaa, and Bergus was a more senior member of the U.S. Foreign Service than David. Finally, we had sent ambassadors to Egypt, but there had never been a resident U.S. ambassador assigned to our embassy in Sanaa because our agreement with Yemen stated that the United States would accredit to Yemen its ambassador residing in Cairo or Jidda. American chiefs of mission actually residing in the YAR in the early 1960s were referred to by the title of chargé d'affaires. Even if he did not have the title of ambassador, David was delighted to have his own post at the relatively young age of thirty-eight.

In addition to scholarships for Yemeni students, which the United States resumed awarding upon our return, and famine re-lief aid, David continued the spirit of helpfulness the United States had shown Yemen in the past. On one occasion he presented to the minister of health some surplus dental surgical equipment that the U.S. Army in Asmara had given us. Worth only about $750, it was nonetheless useful in Yemen.

Perhaps the most symbolic highlight of David's tour as chief of USINT Sanaa was to present President Abdul Rahman al-Iryani and the YAR a gold-wrapped box with a sample of the moon rocks from the 1969 landing, the 5"x7" Yemeni flag astronaut Neil Armstrong had carried to the moon, and an inscribed brass plaque. President Richard Nixon wanted every nation with whom we had diplomatic ties to have a piece of the moon as a token of friendship and goodwill. David was thrilled to spend thirty minutes speaking Arabic with the famous president, one of the grand old men of Yemeni politics. We taped the presentation, which was broadcast over Sanaa radio, and sent it home to our parents.

Our little outpost laid the groundwork for a much bigger operation. In July 1972, six months after our departure, Yemen resumed full diplomatic relations with the United States, a couple of years ahead of Sudan, Egypt, Algeria, and Syria. Secretary of State William Rogers personally visited Sanaa to raise the American flag over our embassy compound. With the elevation of USINT Sanaa to a full embassy, William Crawford became the first American diplomat to arrive at post with the title of ambassador. By 1974, a staff of up to eighty-five people had arrived in Sanaa, including the Peace Corps and USAID.

Ah, the Diplomatic Life . . .

In the United States the phrase "diplomatic life" often brings to mind a poorly informed, erroneous stereotype born of a long-standing anti-elitism. Diplomats are frequently portrayed as leading lives of luxury characterized by large houses, servants, glamorous dinner parties, exotic places to travel, and hobnobbing with important host-country officials and personalities. What the stereotype rarely considers is that the majority of diplomatic posts outside of Western capitals like London, Paris, and Rome entail a great deal of hardship and risk.

Today, as in the 1970s, there are three different classes of diplomatic posts: modern countries and capitals, industrializing countries, and countries still clearly underdeveloped and often facing some sort of crisis. The hardship pay received for service in this last category—where climatic factors, political insecurity, health hazards, isolation, and lack of modern amenities and support services make living both difficult and dangerous—is more than fully earned by diplomats and their families.

Yemen in 1970 was definitely a hardship post. The State Department gave us the maximum amount of hardship pay (40 percent over David's normal salary) to compensate for our discomforts. The department did not know we found the life, at least after the first few months of struggle, great fun despite the inconveniences. Calling it our "Peace Corps tour," we relished the adventures that were so different from anything back home. We loved the friendly Yemenis, who were eager to learn more about Western ways and to share their customs and resources with us.

Naturally, the State Department has many expectations of its employees in exchange for diplomatic service, whether in Paris or Sanaa. In the 1970s it had expectations for wives, too. The attitude was "two for the price of one." Wives had to carry out social and diplomatic functions, because we would be evaluated in our husband's annual Foreign Service officer efficiency report (OER). The OER was the vehicle used for recommending promotions to the next higher officer rank.

In Washington young Foreign Service wives, or "dependents" as we were called, received a two-week course called "The Wives Seminar," which focused on life overseas and the ins and outs of protocol and entertaining. There was no time in Washington for me to get the training. Instead, when we headed to Beirut for two months before going to Yemen, I grabbed a copy of the thin letter-size standard booklet *Social Usage in the Foreign Service*.

Because we were on temporary duty in Beirut and living in a furnished one-bedroom hotel apartment, no one expected us to entertain. Rather, I observed how others practiced their best etiquette and precise diplomatic protocol. I learned that the highest-ranking official always sits on the right in the back seat of the car so that he or she can alight from the car at the curb. In representational situations we always addressed our seniors by their official titles and last names. There was no use of first names unless we happened to be good friends already—and certainly not in public.

Since there was a protocol for visiting, I ordered calling cards and informal folded notes with "Mrs. David McClintock" on the front panel. I needed to be able to leave my card (usually in a little silver tray on a table in the entrance hall) when calling on another higher-ranking diplomatic or host-country wife. I was expected to use the informal notes to reply to teas and send thank-you's. To introduce myself in Beirut I first called on the wife of U.S. ambassador Dwight Porter at her home. I developed enough courage from that encounter to begin calling on other wives, staying no more than the recommended fifteen-to-thirty minutes. Through this prescribed procedure, not far different from today's informal networking outside the home, I met many interesting people. In this way I began doing my part to help my husband succeed at his job. I was also plugging into the time-honored way of making new friends, both American and foreign, so I would more quickly feel at ease in my new home.

We purchased two hundred printed "Mr. and Mrs. David Mc-Clintock cordially invite you to attend...." blank cards so that I could fill in the type of event (dinner, luncheon, reception) and the date and time. Since we had to pay for these invitations ourselves, we were delighted to find in the chancery in Sanaa an additional supply of blank white invitations embossed with an eagle, which we promptly put to use. David had carried along his official State Department cards but in Beirut he had to order a card designating him as first secretary of the Italian embassy with our address in Sanaa.

David William McClintock
First Secretary
Embassy of Italy

Sanaa

David's calling card

I was agog at the fine china, silver, table décor, and servants that our peers in the Foreign Service were using to entertain in Beirut. We did not own anything as nice, so I was immensely thankful that Yemen was to be a fully furnished post, supposedly complete with the ambassadorial china and silver left over from the previous chargé. Also, being in a hardship post, I knew we would not be expected to display the latest and best in accoutrements for our guests. There would be time to accumulate these before we arrived at our next post after Yemen.

At the end of our Beirut sojourn we traveled to Tehran, where we met and dined with all of our State Department seniors at the chiefs of mission conference. After that experience I waltzed off to Yemen feeling much more confident about what lay ahead but was caught off guard by what we did not have when we arrived at post. We discovered some of the twenty-four place settings of ambassadorial china and stemware used by the previous chargé, but many pieces had been broken, lost, or perhaps stolen. Because David did not have the rank of ambassador, the State Department would not send out any new official china or silver, telling us to "make do" and supplement what we had with purchases at the PX in Asmara.

We had no soupspoons, no dinner knives, and no sugar and creamer set. Since there was little fish available locally, we had to apologize to our guests each time we offered silver fish knives to cut a fillet of tenderloin served from the kitchen. Lacking everyday dishes, we resorted to feeding our adopted dogs on the ambassadorial platters outside the apartment building's front door. We managed to entertain adequately, though not elegantly, with the pots and pans we found in apartments that had been hastily evacuated in 1967, augmented by purchases at the Kagnew Station PX. All of our visitors were very polite and seemed to understand.

The State Department and its officers in the field always had one primary purpose for putting on an official function: to facilitate communication and promote U.S. interests among the key players living and working in the host country. When embassy personnel entertained, they included among the invitees officers and their wives new to the post so that the newcomers could meet important officials and participants in the local community. Following the initial whirlwind of parties, the department presumed the officer would then be able to schedule future, more informal conversations with these new contacts in order to report back to Washington on local happenings that affected U.S. interests and the local government. The host and hostess often used special seating arrangements at dinner parties to ensure that the newly arrived couple talked with the "right" people. After a brief time, the couple was expected to continue the tradition of official entertaining to expand their circle of contacts. David and I were no exception and eagerly jumped into the game. In Yemen we had to rely on the diplomatic community, especially the Italians, to introduce us to key players.

Reciprocally, the State Department's insistence on all the entertaining had its payoffs for the wives too. In those days most wives (today, referred to as spouses, since many are men) did not have gainful employment at post, unless it was teaching at an international school. Mandatory entertaining forced us to meet people, and even the shyest wife would have difficulty claiming she felt isolated and friendless or that the post was inhospitable. Since two years was the average length of a tour, the State Department expected us to arrive at post, unpack our lift van, hang pictures, and settle into our new life in record time. This unwritten expectation effectively facilitated the new arrivals' rapid adjustment to post, both physically and psychologically.

The first party we hosted was spontaneous, a surprise house-warming the evening the painters finished. Italian Ambassador Massa-Bernucci brought the Spanish ambassador, who was resident in Cairo but also accredited to Yemen, up from Taiz for a couple of days and dropped by unexpectedly at 6:30 while we were still organizing our home after the mess of painting. Fortunately, we had a supply of whiskey and wine and a cook on hand to whip up hors d'oeuvres. On another evening that week Ambassador Massa Bernucci held a cocktail party for the Spanish ambassador at his Sanaa residence, where we met all forty or fifty Westerners in the entire country.

Two months after arriving we hosted a cocktail party for fifty-five people (fifteen nationalities) in honor of the visiting International Monetary Fund team. Planning for everything to come together at the right time was my responsibility, but I relied on the servants to implement the plan.

This first big effort at diplomatic entertaining proved to be a nerve-racking photo finish. After invitations went out, Abdullah disappeared for his hemorrhoid operation. We then had to rely on the cooks of two of our staff members to make the hors d'oeuvres and to serve. David's last-minute drought research trip to the Tihama with the prime minister had caused him to arrive home exhausted just a few hours before the party. Meanwhile, I spent the day recovering from food poisoning the night before and worrying whether everything would come together in time.

Liquid supplies (of an alcoholic nature) for our parties arrived from Asmara in unclassified pouch shipments. We served hard liquor, beer, and wine, as well as plenty of soft drinks, which many of the Yemenis preferred to liquor because of their Muslim religion. Several of our male Yemeni friends who had traveled widely were happy to imbibe, especially because they only had access to alcohol available on the black market at high prices.

During most weeks we entertained or were entertained at least two or three times, sometimes as many as five or six times, depending

(l to r) Wife of Iraqi ambassador, Mrs. Livadiotti, the Ambassador of Iraq, Susan McClintock, Irish woman married to Yemeni

on who was in town. Ladies' teas, dinner parties, luncheons, cocktail parties, an occasional potluck around the pool, and receptions were the norm among the American and international communities. A few turned into dancing parties with records or live musicians. Some lasted until one or two in the morning. One time we sent out invitations to a dinner party for twenty, and Deputy Prime Minister Yahya Jaghman—who had studied at Boston University and had an MA from Columbia—arrived a full week ahead of the appointed time. We always had to be flexible and, in this case, operated on the spur of the moment, pulling out some refreshments for our friend. He returned again the following week.

Yemenis usually entertained us with ten-course lunches and afternoon teas, though at least once we had an evening meal in mixed company. That special night we ate dinner at Prime Minister and Mrs. al-Aini's home to honor Monsignor Harnett of CRS, who was back in Yemen to evaluate the famine relief food distribution in the Tihama. A typical Yemeni multicourse meal, followed by Turkish coffee in the *mafraj*, it was a sit-down dinner, not buffet-style, for the ten or twelve people who attended.

Monsignor Harnett in Hodeida

The largest party we ever hosted was a New Year's Day brunch in 1972, inviting the entire diplomatic community, which by that time amounted to about 120 people. As I recall, the Russians and Hungarians attended, but the Chinese did not. Some of our Eastern friends were suffering from New Year's Eve party hangovers and our Bloody Marys, chipped beef on toast, and ham and eggs allegedly provided a welcome cure.

Who and when we entertained was often dictated by the arrival of outsiders, guests who came to Yemen for commercial, governmental, nonprofit humanitarian, or other purposes. We invited Yemenis as well as local members of the international community to meet our traveling visitors.

In order to be reimbursed for entertaining our guests (except U.S. staff members), we had to file monthly purchase orders called representation vouchers. As vendor, we collected anywhere from a dollar a head for tea, soft drinks, and light snacks, to $3.00 per person for luncheons at which alcohol was served and $4.75 per head for an elaborate buffet or formal dinner with alcoholic drinks and several courses. Only because I still have copies of those representation vouchers do I know that over the course of twenty-one months we made claims for entertaining 901 people. And that did not include U.S.-staff-only parties. That's a lot of planning and preparation for someone who had never done quantity cooking or served elaborate meals!

Richard Murphy, director of Arabian Peninsula Affairs in the State Department and David's boss, came to visit us in March, when I was six-months pregnant. He stayed in the guest apartment but took his meals with us. I planned menus and gave detailed instructions to our cook, anxiously trying to vary our usual fare to impress him—or at least to appear sophisticated in the ways of the Foreign Service, even if we were in a remote, hardship post.

We hosted a dinner party for Murphy the first evening and an unprecedented 50 percent of the Yemeni officials' wives attended with their husbands. The economics and health ministers came, and the last guest did not leave until 1:15 a.m. The next day the Yemenis held a luncheon for Murphy at the imam's old palace in Rawdah, not far from Sanaa, and that evening the Italian ambassador hosted a dinner party. On the third and final evening of his visit to

Sanaa we had a large cocktail reception attended by many Yemeni officials that lasted until 11 p.m. Wearing the long turquoise and blue Kenyan dress I had recently purchased on our R&R trip, I felt quite proud of myself that evening. There I was, barely beyond a graduate student, orchestrating several servants and a lively reception that the prime minister attended.

During his visit we introduced Murphy to Alain Bertaud, who believed Murphy had helped him get out of jail in Aleppo, Syria. Alain had been hitchhiking from Beirut to Chandigarh (India) and was put in jail during the February 1963 revolution that brought the Ba'ath regime to power in Syria. The French consul would not help him, but Murphy, as the American consul, came to rescue him and four Americans incarcerated with him. A grateful Alain had last seen Murphy at the Turkish border. Murphy vaguely recalled the incident, having rescued countless American students from arbitrary arrest and remembered once helping a non-American.

Murphy was to leave Yemen for Jidda on Saudi Airlines from Hodeida, so on his last day we packed the Land Rover and escorted

Mountaintop village as seen from above (photo by Peggy Crawford)

him to the coast. It was a long and bouncy trip that played havoc with my bladder, due to my state of advanced pregnancy. Two or three times I had to plead for understanding: "Are there any villages where I might find some sort of public restroom? If not, can we please stop by the side of the road?" I was desperate to relieve myself. On one mountainous stretch, abandoning all modesty, I remember squatting to the right side of the vehicle while the men politely turned their backs. Glancing up at the rocky cliffs, I was surprised to see the bright pink bare bottoms of several baboons that lived there. I guess they thought I was mooning them so they mooned me back!

We had no servants with us, and so it was up to me to ensure that domestic chores were done when we reached the cement-block building the YARG gave us to use as an overnight guesthouse at the beach in Hodeida. I swept the salty, sandy floors, changed the sheets, and brought out food that had mostly been prepared in Sanaa for our supper. That evening we waded in the surf as I made first use of my maternity bathing suit. A couple of CRS staff members came by with two motor scooters and we went riding down the beach. At last I was able to relax.

Always a gentleman, Dick Murphy was friendly and put me at ease. I had felt nervous during his visit for I knew he would evaluate me as "wife" in David's yearly OER. Thankfully, when the report arrived the following summer, Murphy gave both of us stellar reviews. In the last paragraph, devoted to David's wife, he said: "I would like to put in a special note of praise for Mrs. McClintock. At the time of my own visit to Yemen she was, in addition to working as classified secretary to the office, carrying on an active, productive social life as the principal officer's wife. She was also shortly expecting their first baby, a prospect that appeared to slow her down not one bit as she traveled with us by Land Rover from Sanaa to Hodeida and back. The McClintocks make a fine representational team." Because the women's movement in the United States was beginning to make itself felt in the practice of U.S. diplomacy worldwide, 1971 was the last year that efficiency reports could contain any mention of the wives.

Apparently, while swimming together in the Red Sea at Hodeida at the end of his trip, Murphy (who later became a distinguished career ambassador serving in several key posts) told David that in all his fifteen or more years in the Foreign Service he had never seen any wife so well adjusted as I was to the career and life at a hardship post. Over thirty years later, hearing that statement, which David had recorded on tape, affirmed for me that I had learned quickly and played my role well, even though a novice. Perhaps my teenage summers at Girl Scout camp sleeping in hammocks in the woods and cooking over fire pits had helped prepare me for life at a hardship post. Both adventures certainly taught me to be self-sufficient and resourceful.

The International Community and Mixed Marriages

With its isolated culture, evolving political structure and climate, and relatively safe physical environment, Yemen was a magnet for adventurous travelers. We found this "stew" of diverse backgrounds, cultures, politics, and careers fascinating and were eager to meet the many citizens of the world we encountered. Some were memorable characters and a few became friends.

Yann and Veronique Bertaud
in Yemen, 1972

Alain and Marie Agnes Bertaud were our closest friends. Alain was the son of a French seaman who had traveled the world before settling down in the south of France to become an engineer and raise a family. Alain had graduated from the École Nationale Supérieure des Beaux-Arts in Paris and was an accomplished architect and urban planner.

Marie Agnes grew up in Algeria in a French *pied noir* military family. She began her career as a teacher before majoring in architecture and art history in college. She oversaw the building of a few houses in Yemen and later became an urban planner in Washington.

Their two young children Yann and Veronique were Anna's playmates when she visited. We bought Veronique her first baby shoes at the PX in Asmara when she was two years old, already walking everywhere in her bare feet or wearing velvet booties made by her mother. They could not find baby shoes locally, since young Yemeni children mostly went barefoot.

As an urban planner with the UNDP in Yemen, Alain spent most of his time designing and laying out the new streets of Sanaa, in particular the first ring road around the city. He also designed new homes for Yemenis, built with local materials for $300-$1,000 each. He later developed a computer model that could be adapted to other countries so the residents could build low-cost housing using their own designs and materials.

Alain put his plans to the test and proved that they worked. When his greedy landlord kept raising the rent (initially $500 a month) with each new improvement that Alain made to his rented house, Alain simply built his own home. A Yemeni friend at UNDP "loaned" him a piece of land to build on with the condition that at the end of Alain's tenure in Sanaa the house (including water heaters, pumps, and other fixtures) would revert to the friend.

In only one month Alain built a traditional Yemeni house for $3,000, borrowing an advance on his salary from the UNDP. A walking tour of his new home, as well as a model he built for other Yemeni houses, revealed a one-story, four-or-five-room structure, made of basalt stone (for the foundation and an 18" base wall), a cement floor, stained glass windows, a water well with electric pump, a flush toilet, running water, and electricity, amenities many Yemeni families did not have. The roof was made of wooden beams

Courtyard in the Bertauds' Yemeni house

Bertaud living room

covered with twigs, then mud. The owner of the land—remember, he was to inherit the house upon Alain's departure—was disappointed that Alain did not use stone and baked bricks, because the cheaper mud (adobe) building was considered a "peasant" rather than a "city" house.

What amazed us about the Bertauds was that, unlike most of the expatriate community including ourselves, they lived off the local economy as much as possible and decorated in the local fashion. They put narrow mattresses covered with bright cloths on the floor to create a living room, just like the Yemeni *mafraj*. They slept on pallets on the floor. No need for much furniture, though I do recall they had a table made of two sawhorses and a door to eat on. They continued this tradition, never taking many possessions with them, wherever they were posted: El Salvador, Haiti, Thailand, and finally Washington, D.C.

Over the next thirty years, when we visited them back in Washington, we took our shoes off upon entering their spacious condo apartment in Chevy Chase and sat on single-bed-size mattresses, bolsters at the back, around a low coffee table. A week or so after they arrived in Washington, a condo staff member asked them when they were going to need the service elevator to move in their furniture. "Oh, we won't need it. We're already moved in," Alain explained to the dumbfounded concierge. The Bertauds have retired to a small town in New Jersey, near two of their children. Jokingly they say it is the most exotic place they have ever lived!

Another friend, Aimé Percque, a Belgian with the UNDP, served in many posts around the world. We became acquainted with him during the 1970 famine relief effort. A Belgian-in-exile in the British navy during World War II, he trained for months to assume the identity of a captured German sailor and then infiltrated into Germany. He spent the war in the Nazi navy, pouring sugar in gas tanks and sand in gears when no one was looking. At one point, he was on the ground hand-signaling Allied bombers to target areas. After the war he was with the United Nations in Port-au-Prince, Haiti. On the side he ran a swanky restaurant, until Papa Doc took charge and ousted him for his friendship with the previous president.

It is no wonder that Aimé found Yemen just another uncommon adventure that kept his adrenaline going. He was sent to Bangladesh after Yemen to run the emergency relief effort until he was accused of corruption and left the U.N. The Bertauds last saw him in 1974 in Haiti, where he was running a mushroom farm with his new Haitian wife.

Edward Polansky, the UNDP resident representative, became another good friend, whom I visited and stayed in touch with until his death in May 2004. Born in Holland of Czech and Slovenian ancestry, he received a graduate degree at the Australian National University in Canberra. A bachelor and inveterate traveler, Edward was fluent in English, German, Dutch, French, and Bahasa-Indonesian. After Yemen he worked in New York with the UNDP, where he displayed on his apartment wall a detailed map of Manhattan. He drew a red line over each street along which he had walked. By the time his tour ended, he had walked every street in the city. Likewise, in his apartment in Innsbruck, Austria, after he retired from the UN International Atomic Energy Agency, he kept a large world map on the wall marked with red pins for every country he had visited—193 as of 2004! So, finding him in Yemen when we were there was no big surprise.

Ed and his map with Susan in Innsbruck, 1999

Ed's balcony

Edward lived in a lovely Yemeni house with an intricately carved Indian-style wooden balcony, more like the architecture of Hodeida than Sanaa. Invited there one evening for dinner, we were surprised to find the East German ambassador as the only other guest. Since the United States did not recognize East Germany, we were intrigued to have one-on-one time with an individual who was normally off-limits to us. Not one to let Cold War politics influence his choice of friends, Edward delighted, I'm sure, in getting two adversaries talking with each other over some of his delicious Czech food.

Alfred and Ulrike Vestring became special friends as well. Yemen was Alfred's first posting as ambassador for the West German government, having been sent there when Yemen resumed relations with the FRG in the summer of 1969. A couple of years older than David, Alfred had once been an aide to former FRG Chancellor Willie Brandt. The Vestrings had three children close to Anna's age. I still have a poster they gave us of the ill-fated 1972 Munich Olympic games. We were sorry to see them leave for their new posting in Mauritius several months before our own departure.

Ambassador Vestring and family at airport with Anna

A Google search reveals they are still active in Germany, but I have not been able to communicate directly with them.

Helmut and Jutta Schreyer were neighbors within walking distance of our compound, which made casual visits possible. Helmut worked with the FRG telecommunications aid project and Jutta was an artist. They loved to bring their young son Kai to swim. We enjoyed time with them on our Fridays off, including playing darts in their basement recreation room. Helmut had access to a horse and brought it over for Anna to ride and enjoy. After one of their parties, we brought twenty-one of their guests back with us to swim in our tiny *shadrawan!* There are many Helmut Schreyers in Germany today, and I have not been able to locate them.

Dr. Mario Livadiotti we called Yemen's answer to Albert Schweitzer. He ministered to everyone. Dr. Mario handled routine problems well, was friendly and had a good bedside manner. He and his wife and two sons arrived in Yemen in 1961, a year before an Italian legation opened in Taiz. Working at Sanaa's only hospital, the Mutawakkil, later known as the Republican Hospital, Dr. Mario also attended to the needs of Crown Prince Badr and the royal court. He left for Tanzania in 1965 but returned to the Republican Hospital in 1967 and was working there when we knew him. Dr. Mario was a prominent member of the Italian and diplomatic communities and Westerners as well as Yemenis sought his advice.

In a 2000 *Yemen Times* interview, Dr. Mario described how he rode a horse to the hospital each day and was greeted ceremoniously by a guard playing a trumpet, which signaled the gates to swing open and allow him to enter. He mentioned that his wife Jana was the first woman to drive a car in Sanaa and went on to recount his fortuitous escape the night Imam Badr was overthrown in 1962. The car that was supposed to have picked him up to drive to the palace to attend to the new imam's ill wife never appeared. Instead, he went to an Italian gathering where the partygoers experienced a sudden blackout and heard gunfire. The coup was on, and a number of Mario's friends were killed. Badr escaped, but many members of the royal family were murdered. Mario, now retired in Rome, and I have been in touch by mail and through his son, Marco, who lives in Sanaa and runs a travel agency.

The other Italians in Sanaa had such impressive-sounding names they need to be mentioned if for no other reason. On hand to welcome us to Yemen, Fausto Pennacchio and Ambassador Romualdo Massa-Bernucci were friendly and comported themselves like Italian aristocrats, whether they were or not. Ambassador Baracchi-Tua, who was a count and his wife a Romanian countess, replaced Massa-Bernucci. Baracchi-Tua spoke French, German, Russian, English, and Italian, and was a member of the Knights of Malta, something that really impressed David. The couple were most generous and agreeable, definitely not aloof, as their heritage might have suggested.

Dr. Claudie Fayein, a French medical doctor, was one of only three foreigners in Yemen in 1950. Hired by Imam Ahmad to come to Sanaa for six months to care for his harem, she took the job on the condition she be allowed to tend to all the women in his household. Claudie was so successful the imam persuaded her to stay a year

Dr. Claudie Fayein, 1984
(photo by Peggy Crawford)

and a half. Accompanied at times by her husband, who was also a physician, and her family, she lived and traveled in Yemen off and on over the next forty years. *A French Doctor in the Yemen* offers her description of the poor state of healthcare there in the early 1950s. Regarding the tiny women and their small pelvic areas, Claudie stated that often, to save the mother, she had to deliver a stillborn child piece by piece. Claudie was granted Yemeni citizenship in 1992, perhaps the only foreign woman ever to receive it.

We met Claudie through the Bertauds when she was in Sanaa under a UNESCO grant to preserve Yemen's antiquities. She had a marvelous collection of costumes and dresses for her ethnology museum. Claudie found a colleague after her own heart in Dr. Paola Costa. An archeologist sent by the Italian government, Dr. Costa helped the department of antiquities organize Yemen's treasures, stored in warehouses, and set up the national museum of Sanaa.

Claudie and Costa invited us to visit temporary exhibits in a warehouse-like building where they had displayed a huge cache of artifacts in several rooms—the beginnings of the new museum. Antiquities, most of which had been discovered during expeditions of American archeologist Wendell Phillips in the early to mid-1900s, were lying in piles on the floor. There were bronzes from the time of Christ, including a duplicate of the leg of a horse, the original of which is housed at Dumbarton Oaks in Washington, D.C., with a copy in the British Museum, or vice versa. Stone carvings from Marib in 1200 BCE featured images of women and children.

Their exhibits included the famous bronze statue of Dhamar Ali (50 CE), a ruler of Yemen. Reportedly, when Imam Yahya saw the statue of Dhamar Ali on a dig in 1929, he bashed in its face because the statue was bigger than he was. The department of antiquities told us they had the nose and planned to put it back on the statue's face. It was otherwise in perfect condition when it was found on the plain of Dhamar south of Sanaa. In addition to the nose bashing, the statue had its shoulder broken while workers were trying to get it to Sanaa. Today the Dar al-Shukr, a palace Imam Yahya built in 1938 at Tahrir Square, houses the public museum and its fine collection.

Other interesting personalities we met—some you might describe as "characters"—were either posted to Yemen or were simply adventurers passing through. Mathias T. Oppersdorff, a college roommate of CRS Director Michael Sheehan, was a tall, lanky professional photographer who trekked all over Yemen and other parts of the Middle East decked out in a pith helmet.

Himyar carving in alabaster

His distinguished-sounding name suited him. Mathias also visited David and me in Jordan. I tracked down both Mathias and Michael in 2008, and we shared our stories and information about acquaintances. Mathias's passion for his adventures in the deserts of the Middle East shines through his 2001 tabletop book of black and white photographs, mentioned in the bibliography.

Hugh Leach, a British diplomat, single and posted in Jidda, fascinated us with stories about trekking in the Hindu Kush. Milan Kubik was a *Newsweek* correspondent who stopped by to interview David as we were busy cleaning the place during our first month in the country. Lee Griggs with *Time* magazine entertained us with stories of growing up in Hyannisport, Massachusetts, and playing touch football with the Kennedys. Once folks made it as far as remote Yemen, we felt we had a great deal in common with these adventurous souls and enjoyed their company in our isolated post.

Western couples were treated with respect, but also as great curiosities in Yemen. In the newer parts of Sanaa, a Western woman could get away with wearing her usual knee-length skirts and dresses, as long as they were not revealing. However, I always wore long sleeves, jeans, or a skirt, and sometimes a trench coat when I went shopping, especially in the old city, where I even donned a scarf. I did not want to offend anyone or get too many stares.

The foreign-born wife of a well-educated, well-traveled Yemeni with a prominent position in society was usually allowed more freedom than the wife of a traditional Yemeni. For instance, the European wife of one of the cabinet ministers met her Yemeni husband in London. She had rebelled against the veil soon after her arrival six years earlier and made a compromise with her husband. When she went out in public, she wore only a trench coat, dark glasses, and a nondescript scarf. She was somewhat circumscribed by the Yemeni system, for she could go to women's parties alone but to a mixed party only if mostly Europeans attended.

Several times during our tour, I met up with one American girl married to a Yemeni. I will call her Ruth. She had only been in the country nine months when she came to visit me for afternoon tea soon after we arrived. Ruth had met her husband at a large university in the United States. With her husband and three-year-old daughter, she lived in a four-room house along with nine of his relatives, including his parents and several of their young children. The house rented for just under twenty dollars a month. They had only a bed, a table, and a few odd chairs, so most of their living was done on the floor Yemeni-style.

Even though she held a college degree, Ruth felt fortunate to hold a clerk's job with an international organization. Because she was a woman, it was unlikely she would ever be able to put her degree to use in her adopted home. Initially, she was quite philosophical about her situation and fascinated by Yemen despite the many hardships.

Over the months, I noticed that Ruth had bites all over her legs and arms when she arrived at afternoon tea parties. "We have no window screens, and the bugs get me at night," she explained. Colleagues where she worked reported seeing bruises over her exposed body, once she got to work and took off her *sharshaf*. We all feared physical abuse, but she was proud and probably fearful for her daughter's safety. She would not admit to it when questioned. Fortunately, her husband worked for a company that sent its employees abroad, and Ruth managed to escape from the marriage with her daughter when they were living in a European city, as I learned years later.

Ruth's story was not unusual. Western women married to Yemenis had my sympathy and concern. The lives of most were far more circumscribed in Yemen than they had been led to believe they would be prior to their arrival. The Yemeni male living abroad adamantly proclaimed his liberated view of women and made promises to his intended that he would protect her rights once they returned. Unfortunately, the proclamation made abroad was often squelched by family pressure once they set up housekeeping back in Yemen.

Generally living in close proximity to her extended family, often in one house, the Western woman soon succumbed to her situation, although she attempted to make compromises with the system. She fully covered her body and at least her hair, went out only in the daytime and never in mixed company unless with a relative. She often lived under the control of her mother-in-law. Western couples in the international community were relatively free to do as they pleased, whereas the fate of the Western woman married to a Yemeni was determined primarily by her unique family situation.

Famine Relief

When we arrived in 1970, Yemen had a population of five and a half million and the Tihama region on the Red Sea coast was in the midst of an unrelenting drought. There had been no rain for four years. In June, after only a month in Sanaa, we entertained a Mr. Stanissis from the League of Red Cross Societies in Geneva. He had received an urgent appeal from Yemen for help and spent eight days in the country surveying the situation. He mobilized the international community, organizing shipments of food to relieve the nearly two million starving people (60 percent of them children).

The United States was eager to participate. In the absence of full diplomatic relations with Yemen, however, congressional legislation prevented direct country-to-country aid. But U.S. law did permit third-party intermediaries to distribute relief supplies on behalf of the U.S. government. Catholic Relief Services (CRS), based in Rome with a New York office, could legally serve as the distribution conduit for U.S. food aid.

Before committing food aid, the State Department requested that David make an inspection trip to the famine area with the CRS representative from New York, Monsignor Harnett, and report his findings. A tall, stout, gray-haired man, appealing in his clerical collar and with a twinkle in his eye, the monsignor dined with us in Yemen a time or two.

Putting the trip together in great haste, Prime Minister Muhsin al-Aini and the Yemeni army orchestrated the group's survey activities. The entourage left at 6 a.m. on a Friday morning in late June 1970. Led by PM al-Aini and various YAR officials and escorted by Yemeni army contingents, Harnett and David were joined by Aimé Percque, our Belgian friend with the UNDP in Sanaa.

They traveled 450 miles in three days over hard terrain, with much regalia and fanfare. The army escort carried rocket launchers and up to eight soldiers in each Russian-made jeep. There were no traffic signals to stop them. The PM's brother-in-law and the governor of Hodeida, Sheikh Sinan Abu Luhum, rode in the first jeep and led the group through towns and villages.

Men and women with African features inhabited the small villages dotted with beehive-shaped houses made of adobe walls and grass roofs. All of the villagers were struggling to locate food for their malnourished children and mobbed the cars as the PM's entourage passed through the villages. The visitors found people steaming twigs broken off trees and eating the bark for food. Any food held in storage had disappeared after four years of drought. Cows of skin and bones were dropping in their tracks. On top of that, it was 120°F–130° F along the Tihama coast at that time of year.

At lunch and dinner on the second day of the trip, the group dined in the former imam's palace in Hodeida overlooking the Red Sea. Gilded wooden furniture with upholstery adorned the room. The group ate on the former ruler's dishes. Because of the heat, the minister of the interior dined in his undershirt. David napped on the imam's bed, sharing it with Percque, both of them

Cows emaciated by Tihama's drought

finally stripping to their undershirts too. In the heat and humidity, protocol and etiquette be damned!

To avoid drinking the local water, David gulped one sugary soda pop after another to quench his thirst, downing twenty-four bottles during the three-day trip. While sitting around chatting in the imam's palace, he watched one Yemeni in the group take off his dirty sock and wipe the mouth of his soda bottle. So much for hygiene, David thought, relieved he did not have to share that soda pop. The Yemenis obviously had more antibodies than David had built up during his two short months in the country, and he wanted to be careful.

The prime minister commented on what a nice resort this palace would make and how Club Med could start bringing tours to Yemen. Although once elegant, the place needed repairs. Keeping his thoughts to himself, David did not feel as optimistic as the PM did about the palace's prospects, at least for the near future.

The PM's group saw firsthand that something needed to be done quickly and arranged for approximately 70,000 tons of Yemen food relief—from the UN's World Food Program, the European Common Market, the Soviet Union, and other governments and entities. Washington sent 72,500 tons, partly in outright gifts but mostly in credit sales. David worked many hours with CRS's Michael Sheehan to oversee the distribution. I spent some time helping Michael's wife get acclimated. She was an Iranian-born, naturalized U.S. citizen. Yemen was not like any other Middle Eastern country the couple had visited.

It was one thing to get the food into the port at Hodeida and quite another to get it to the starving people. Yemen simply did not have the transportation infrastructure to distribute the foodstuffs to remote villages in large trucks over marginal dirt tracks. Hence, a lot of the food aid ended up a year later in the local markets of the main cities, never reaching some of the neediest people. I learned from British ambassador Willie Morris where in the Sanaa suq to buy some of this food aid, notably forty-pound sacks of American powdered milk, which the ambassador used to feed his dog and I bought for Lesley.

The famine occurred before West Germany upgraded and lengthened Sanaa's airport. The tarmac was only twenty

Luftwaffe cargo plane bound for Djibouti

centimeters thick, and the high altitude made the runway too short for large planes, something the German pilots did not know when they first brought in relief supplies. When three of their 707s carrying food aid tried to land after dark in Sanaa, numerous cars, as typically happened in such cases, lined up their headlights so the pilots could see well enough to land. The first plane blew two tires as it set down on the runway, endangering its engines with flying rocks and gravel. The other two, forewarned, flew back to Djibouti overnight, unloaded, and the next day ferried in the food on smaller planes.

After their first unfortunate incident trying to land a large plane in Sanaa, the FRG used Djibouti in the French Territory of Afars and Issas as the staging ground to airlift many tons of food aid into Sanaa. They made runs across the Red Sea every other day for several weeks in a Luftwaffe cargo plane (equivalent to the C-130). The most memorable part of the famine relief effort for me was a trip in August 1970 to Djibouti on one of the West German cargo planes. FRG ambassador Vestring invited David and me to join the Percques as passengers. We flew over empty and returned loaded with foodstuffs, including sacks of wheat and dried milk.

I had never flown on anything but a commercial airliner. Strapped to jump seats that dropped down from the walls of the cavernous aircraft, I anxiously waited for the gigantic plane to take off. Once we were in the air, I eventually mustered the courage to get up and walk around. After we crossed the Red Sea, the pilot invited me into the cockpit. By then my fears had vanished and I was eager to stand right behind him, where I could see everything.

Holding tightly onto the back of his seat, I felt my stomach do somersaults as he swooped low and made hairpin curves over the deep coral reefs in the waters of the Gulf of Taburja. That was much more exciting than the roller coaster ride I had once taken at Six Flags. Hovering only fifty feet above the water, we could see giant manta rays with eight-foot wingspans floating in the crystal-clear water. Then we raced above the beach at the same altitude, feeling as if we could touch the tall grasses and white sand dunes as they disappeared under the nose of the plane.

Once on the ground at the airport, we exchanged some currency and hopped into a taxi to the French colonial town of Djibouti. Walking amidst drooping tropical trees, we admired the two-story buildings whose wooden balconies reminded us of New Orleans. The marketplace was alive with women in colorful African clothing, a marked contrast to the more somber colors seen in the Sanaa suq. We were startled to see so many Peugeots and small, modern European cars lining the streets and found it a treat to glimpse our first railroad track in several months.

We spent the night at a classy air-conditioned seaside hotel, swimming at the beach and eating a gourmet dinner that included crab thermidor, steak flambé, frog legs, cheeses, French wines, and Calvados. There were no signs of famine in that hotel! We returned to Yemen the next day, the cargo area loaded with food aid, our small group, and some souvenirs, including Somalian avocados, and ten 10-liter bottles of Spanish red table wine contained in hemp baskets. The Yemenis allowed diplomats to import a maximum of ten bottles of wine at one time, but failed to designate how big the

Djibouti hotel

bottles could be! We drank that wine for months, serving it at all our dinner parties. I still have one of the bottles and the baskets were great for trash.

In late October, four months after his survey with the prime minister, David took a four-day trip along the Red Sea coast to the northern Tihama to investigate rumors that the food distribution had broken down. Along with Tom Seibert of CRS, Abdul Kadir from our staff, and several other CRS workers, he packed dozens of gallons of water and emergency gasoline into a long-base Land Rover. They bounced along on "multinational" tires: one English, one North Korean, and two Japanese. Formerly owned by the Kenya territorial police, the vehicle had 88,000 miles on it and had survived some rough terrain. Since only dirt camel tracks ran into that northern coastal region, it took the party twelve hours to cover one eighty-mile stretch. It was plain to see why the distribution system had broken down.

　　I wanted to go with them, but because I was early in my pregnancy, my Asmara doctor recommended I not go bouncing over a

CRS trip through Tihama (Abdul Kadir and Tom Seibert in center)

lot of unimproved dirt tracks. Upon his return, David agreed those roads would have really tested my stamina. Bringing a healthy full-term baby into the world was more important than forcing myself to endure hardships simply for the sake of adventure.

Accompanied by a Yemeni general, the group left Hodeida, waiting until three p.m. to cross the Tihama desert. They passed grass huts and tumbledown Turkish forts along the way. They reached a wadi—dry riverbed—and climbed up some cliffs to camp in a small Yemeni army outpost, where they slept under the stars on Russian cots. The next morning they made their way down a cliff and through the wadi to find green sorghum fields, signs that the drought might be coming to an end.

On the way up the coast, the group maneuvered to the town of Luhayya over salt flats, which, except for the Arab dhows, reminded David of approaching Mont St. Michel on the coast of France. Founded in the eighth century CE, Luhayya resembled a ghost

Two CRS workers with Tihama villagers

Hosts in Luhayya

town because of the recent drought. They feasted on a grand lunch given by the governor of the town. The scrumptious meal showed no evidence of the recent drought.

Dining Arab-style in the countryside throughout the Middle East usually meant sitting around a cloth on the ground or floor with the soles of the feel or shoes turned outwards, since it is considered rude to show dirty feet. One ate with the fingers of the right hand only. The left hand was reserved for ablutions and cleaning oneself. Some Arab hosts, generally in the cities, offered forks or spoons to Westerners, but in rural areas of Yemen, eating with fingers was required.

Although David disliked touching food with his hands, he apparently overlooked his preference for cutlery and enjoyed the meal anyway. In a letter to his father describing the Luhayya luncheon, he wrote, "The roasted fish and chicken, along with about twenty other courses, were delicious, and my three enterovioform (anti-diarrhea) tablets carried me through without trouble. The hosts prepared the twenty-inch fish by gutting its cavity and filling it with coarse-ground pepper and curry powder. It was closed and roasted, giving it a delicious flavor."

The guests drank Pepsis while servants stood at both ends of the tablecloth whacking at flies. Yemenis do not talk much while they eat. The only way the Westerners knew the meal had ended was when servants arrived with soap and water. Whether David was dining in the desert or in a home, the servants typically poured water over his food-covered hands as he left the table, offering him soap to wash and a towel to dry them.

Leaving Luhayya, on the way to Midi, they drove on the huge salt flat up the coast where it was easy to get stuck because the sea had washed in. They had to put pieces of wood under their wheels and use several of the sixteen different speeds available in a four-wheel drive to move forward. When they discovered they were on the wrong track, they turned back to Luhayya and soon ran into a camel caravan, whose driver showed them how to get to higher ground. They finally arrived after dark at the old Turkish governor's house, now a military fort. The Westerners in the group excused themselves to sleep on the roof under the stars rather than in the musty, dirty fort. Everyone stayed up late playing radios and watching for the new moon to signal the month of Ramadan. Before the group continued their trip north, their hosts provided a breakfast of fried eggs with *ful* (broad beans), bread and tea. Traveling on past Midi, David and his group came within two thousand yards of the Saudi frontier at Harad. There they saw enormous Mercedes trucks checking in after crossing into Yemen from Saudi Arabia.

On tape and in a letter to our parents, David commented when he returned:

> Swimming in Maydi [sic] was paradise. We went into the channel there, a Red Sea dhow harbor, about twenty feet deep and about 100 feet wide, protected by a sandbar the sides of which were hard-packed at a forty-five degree angle. The incoming tide made the water cool and nice, not like the pea-soup swimming I've done around Hodeida. Some sailors unloading a nearby dhow asked me to take their picture, and then asked if I was a Russian. I replied, "No, American." They nodded and murmured approval, yet another example of how friendly the average Yemeni is toward America at this time. We got back to Hodeida late that night. The next day Michael Sheehan sent me home with three fishes, each three feet long and fifteen pounds, plus frozen shrimp from the Kuwaiti captain of an American fishing boat. I had to borrow a huge freezer to carry all of it back to Sanaa.
>
> Driving through the Tihama involved a bouncy, rough, pitching motion that threw dust all through the vehicles. It's a wonder any food got distributed to the people. But, this trip, four months after our first one, revealed that the food situation is much better. All the farmers are happy with recent rains. The people in the Tihama are of African stock and not inclined to raids and warfare like some of the mountain peoples of Yemen. They are good farmers, and all they want is rain and peace. Indeed, we could learn many new farming techniques from them.

On his return David decided he would continue to recommend the powdered milk food aid for the nursing mothers and preschool children, as the young ones still showed signs of malnutrition. Whether the rains or foreign aid came, or both, the famine ended by the following summer.

6

Social Life With Yemenis

Yemeni Hospitality

In some countries where I traveled before and after Yemen, the tourist influx had created among the local population a jaded wariness and greediness that felt threatening to me. At times it seemed that all I represented to the host-country residents was a dollar sign or that they viewed me as the gauche, ugly American tourist with camera and tennis shoes. In contrast to my previous experiences, the genuine friendliness and openness of the Yemenis toward me were refreshing. Their warmth encouraged my trust, which helped me feel safe and accepted in Yemen, even more so than in other Middle Eastern countries. My trust paralleled that of others who found Yemenis uniquely personable.

Whether they had known David and me awhile or we were total strangers, Yemenis were hospitable and welcoming. Possibly because we were fair-skinned curiosities or simply because we were foreigners, they were always gracious. Or perhaps, since average Yemenis had had so little exposure to Westerners in 1970, they did not have the same negative preconceptions of Western ideas as did other nationalities. Maybe it was merely their nature and culture. Whatever the reason, Yemenis were eager to befriend us and share their resources, whether modest or abundant.

The following are just a few stories of Yemenis we encountered during our posting. I selected them from my experiences to illustrate their genuine friendliness and authenticity. They had no pretensions. They were who they were, and proud of it.

One Friday early in our tour we spent the Muslim holy day with Yemenis in a neighboring town. It was a welcome relief following many days of nonstop work at the office. Rick Rauh, David, and I drove to the village of Hadda, about five miles or thirty minutes south of Sanaa. Maneuvering over the dirt road through rocky terrain, we were pleasantly surprised to find Hadda lush and green like an oasis, with walnut, apricot, peach, and other fruit trees in bloom. We cracked the green-hulled nuts of the almond trees to get to the meat. Water rushed down from green, terraced mountains through ancient rock channels to the town's water reservoir.

Climbing up a rocky hillside we encountered a turbaned farmer, who was pleased to see us. He invited us to picnic in the shade of his orchard of budding fruit trees. Dressed in a man's suit jacket over a long-sleeved shirt and a *futa* of striped cotton, he cinched in his clothing with a wide embroidered belt that held his *janbiyya*. Greeting us with vigorous handshakes, *Ahlan wa saahlan's* (welcomes), and *As-salaam 'alaykum's* (peace be unto you), he quickly brought blankets from his house and laid them out on the dusty ground for us to sit on.

We chatted over lunch and shared our tea. He introduced us to his wife, who shyly held a head cloth across her face to reveal only her dark eyes rimmed in kohl. Intricate henna decorations on her hands against her black clothing caught our attention. Their two barefoot young daughters had curly tangled hair, dark eyes, bright faces, and colorful dresses. They giggled and hid behind their mother's black *sharshaf*, frequently peeking at us.

The best way we knew to thank them for their hospitality was to put the old Polaroid camera to use. We had found it in our apartment building's storeroom and figured it would come in handy at some point. The farmer said he did not have many family photos and was delighted with our instant images.

On several occasions during our tour, we showed visitors the imam's summer palace, an eight-mile journey of forty-five minutes northwest of Sanaa in the small village of Wadi Dhahr. Coming out of the mountains and dropping into a picturesque wadi, we found the dry river valley lush with cultivation, including various kinds of fruit orchards such as grapes, apricots, and pomegranates. Constructed on top of older ruins in the 1920s by Imam Yahya, Dar

Imam's summer palace in Wadi Dhahr

al-Hajar (the Rock Palace) was a six-story traditional tower house. It was spectacularly situated on top of a massive 120-foot-high solid-rock boulder that reached skyward from the floor of the valley and took center stage among the village's other two- and three-story houses. We had to climb carefully up some footholds carved into the rocks to reach the palace.

On our first visit we were guests of Sheikh al-Sa'r of Hamdan, a village not far from Sanaa near Wadi Dhahr. The sheikh had befriended David during his first tour. Once when the Egyptians were staging a riot in front of David's house and banging on his door, Sheikh al-Sa'r scaled David's back wall to give him a gun, which fortunately he did not need to use before the mob dispersed.

After eating sweet ripe pears in his orchard, the sheikh, David, and I met up with a guide from the Department of Antiquities. He escorted us to the top floor *mafraj*, where we saw thick pallets covered with colorful striped cloth lining the walls, an inviting place for men to sit, chew qat, and smoke their nargileh. Moving our eyes from the pallets up the walls, we saw the tall, clear glass windows that could be covered from the outside with the attached carved wooden shutters. Above these, stained glass windows in brilliant reds, greens, blues, and yellows, similar to those we had in Sanaa, created a fan-shaped light of colors cast across the floor by the sun shining through.

Awestruck by the view, we sat with Pepsi Colas listening to the sheikh as we gazed out the windows at the magnificent 180-degree-plus panorama below. From the top of the palace we could see alluvial fans created by rushing water when it coursed through the valley below during its wet season. The rugged, jagged cliffs in the distance could have been anywhere in the American Southwest. The imam must have loved to retreat to the top floor of his fortress. He could see for miles, and probably easily pick off any approaching enemies!

Next, we descended the palace's external stairs and wandered through the narrow dusty paths of the village, comprising both mud brick and stone houses. We came upon about ten exuberant men, dressed in turbans and khaki, olive, and gray skirts and jackets. Dancing in circles down the tree-lined dirt path, they played flutes and waved their *janbiyyas* in the air. Russian-made, ominous-looking Kalashnikovs were slung over their shoulders.

As they jumped around energetically, we moved quickly out of their way. David and I were both petrified that the rifles might accidentally go off into the crowd while they were doing their whirling dances. Reportedly, the Russians were training them to be fighters with modern weaponry and the dancers were obviously very proud of their rifles.

Dagger dancers

David told me several stories about dining with Yemenis, always men, who provided hospitality a bit different than that offered to mixed company. Like the meals I had experienced, they always had the lavish multicourse lunch. However, David was not usually offered silverware, as I was, and thus ate with his hands.

Having lunch with one powerful Yemeni sheikh in his home, David received a graphic lesson in meal etiquette. Speaking not a word during the meal, the sheikh finished his lunch, let out a big belch, got up from the table, kicked over his chair, and headed to the *mafraj* for after-dinner conversation, coffee, and smoking the nargileh. When David saw the chair being kicked over, he gulped down the bite he was chewing, even though he was not finished with his meal, and quickly followed his host into the *mafraj* after washing his hands.

After the Chinese road was completed to Amran, we accepted another invitation from Sheikh al 'Sa'r. He wanted to take the Bertauds and us to visit his family home about thirty miles or so north of Sanaa on the road to Saada. The trip to Amran over the newly paved thoroughfare was a real treat for David. He had not been able to travel there during the mid-1960s civil war for security reasons and also because the old rocky track was impassable for ordinary vehicles.

Sheikh al-Sa'r and friends

The open fields of green followed by desert terrain disappeared the farther north we went, exposing us to incredible amounts of lava rock on both sides of the highway. It seemed as though we were traveling through a moonscape or some other forbidding place. Upon arriving in the small village, the sheikh took us to the *mafraj*, the reception area in his two-story home, and gave us tea and Pepsis, introducing us to his children and others in his family. We were allowed to photograph the males and enjoyed a walk around the village to see interesting Himyaritic carvings before we returned to Sanaa.

Muhammad Nu'man, a Western-educated Yemeni diplomat from a prominent family and political adviser to President Iryani, befriended us early in our tour. During his career he also served as Yemen's ambassador to Paris and Bonn. As an exile in Aden during the 1950s, he was Consul William Crawford's "threadbare" Arabic teacher, who loved to eat corn flakes when visiting his American friend. When serving as foreign minister in 1972, according to Crawford, Nu'man requested that Crawford be appointed the first U.S. ambassador to Yemen.

Azziza Nu'man allowed me to photograph her with her children and
baby Lesley in my home

When Nu'man and his wife, Azziza, resided in Europe in the Yemeni diplomatic service, they sent their two daughters to school in Switzerland. The girls, Assia and Maha, spoke good English and were attending school in Sanaa when we met them. We exchanged occasional visits while they lived in Yemen and were not away at school. Unlike their mother, who had grown up in Sanaa and spoke little English, it must have been difficult for them to return to the traditional role of being a woman in a strict Muslim environment.

The girls and their mother would come to my house in their *sharshafs* and take them off inside, revealing knee-length Western-style dresses. Once when I went to visit them, they brought out their grandmother's wedding dress to show me. Assia modeled this marvelous red creation and allowed me to photograph her in it up on the family's rooftop. Another time they invited some local singers in to entertain us at their home. The singers, both male and female, were from the Tihama. Unlike most women from Sanaa, these coastal women were from a different social class and usually did not mind having their faces photographed.

One day while visiting the girls and their mother, I was granted the privilege of sitting in the *mafraj* with them and their famous grandfather, Ahmad Nu'man, who was then serving on the three-man Republican Council. He had also served as prime minister and held other important posts. It was late afternoon following tea and he was relaxing cross-legged on his pallet. Dressed in a long blue and white striped cotton *zinna*, he was not, as I recall wearing a turban. In very witty form, Mr. Nu'man spoke broken English and made jokes in Arabic, which the girls translated for me. He entertained us with stories about his life and Yemen in the imam's days.

Time was ticking by and it was getting dark. I knew David would be worried that I had not returned home. The Nu'mans lived close enough to our embassy compound that I had walked there earlier in the afternoon. Because we had no phone in our apartment I knew I could not reach my husband to tell him of my delay. But I stayed as long as I dared, until twilight, hanging onto Mr. Nu'man's every word. I knew it was a rare audience that I, a Western woman, had been granted. I felt like a schoolgirl in awe of a famous movie star, which is probably the reason I cannot recall any of his stories. Though David had become quite concerned by the time I finally

Assia poses for me in her grandmother's wedding dress

got home, he easily understood my delay when he learned where I had been.

I last heard from Assia in 1975. The girls' father, Muhammad, was assigned as ambassador to Paris toward the end of our tour in Sanaa and then to Lebanon. In 1974, while we were in Jordan, Muhammad was assassinated in Beirut. I learned from Ambassador David Newton and from reading Ambassador William Crawford's oral history that Yemen's president had sent Muhammad on a YAR government mission to Baghdad to protest to the Iraqi government its interference in trying to overthrow Yemen's government. The story at the time was that the YARG had found documents in a house fire in Taiz implicating the Ba'ath Party of Yemen and Iraq in a coup attempt. Nu'man was carrying the proof with him to Baghdad. Iraq denied the accusation and retaliated by having Muhammad murdered by the Arab Liberation Front (ALF), an Iraqi-controlled Palestinian group.

We were shocked and saddened to learn of Muhammad's death. I sent a letter of condolence and this was Assia's response some time later, in her own words:

23 October 1975
Dear Mrs. Mr. McClintock,

I received your kind words, which make me happy that you still remember the Noman family. It's very kind from you.

We left Beirut after the accident directly to Cairo. We stayed one year. This year I'm staying in Yemen, studying to have the baccalaria.

I received also the nice pictures. Nathan looks like his mother, "he is lucky" he is very sweet. Lesely, I remember her when she was a baby, she has nice smile in this picture. I would like that you visit Sana'a again. You are welcome in our house.

My best Greetings,
        Assia Noman
N.B. My kisses to Nathan and Lesely

I have had no word from the Nu'man family since. I learned at the Yemen symposium in 2003 that Mrs. Nu'man and one of the girls are living in Cairo and the other daughter in Saudi Arabia. I have tried to send messages to them via people who thought they knew how to find them, but so far have had no response. I wonder how they are doing and what their lives are like today.

Mrs. al-Aini's Women's Group

My introduction to Mrs. al-Aini's women's group occurred on the unlikely occasion of the 26th of September independence day parade in 1970. After sitting for more than four hours through the colorful display of enthusiastic nationalism, David and I were surprised to see a flatbed truck pass in front of us filled with at least ten women, fully veiled, dressed in long, black *sharshafs*. A sign in Arabic indicated this was the "women's lib" float, proclaiming women's literacy and work outside the home. Several women sat trundling away behind sewing machines, seemingly oblivious to the watching crowds. Three other women sat on chairs at the edge of the flatbed facing the spectators. They were reading books, which they held on their laps and gazed at through the mesh of their veils.

The irony of the scene struck me enough to begin asking questions. I learned that the group of women who had paraded in front of us did so under the tutelage of Prime Minister al-Aini's wife, Azziza. I was fascinated and wanted to learn more about her work with them.

As a Western woman, I was privileged to meet and socialize with Yemeni women, something my husband was not allowed to do. So I took the opportunity to call upon Mrs. al-Aini, a meeting

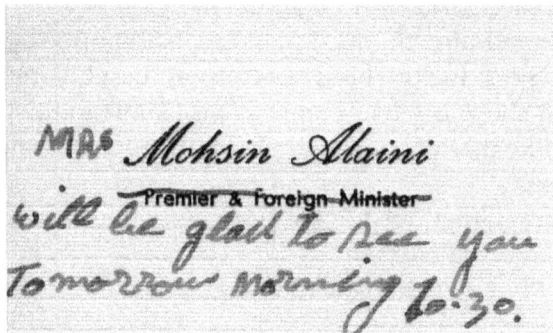

Azziza al-Aini's calling card

easily arranged by our two husbands. Soon after my arrival at their family home not far from mine, Azziza told me in English, "We meet regularly in the afternoons to improve our [Arabic] literacy, do volunteer projects to benefit other women, and attempt to increase our knowledge of the world. After all, Yemeni women receive little formal education and this group is my effort to teach them about life outside their home and family." Azziza's primary focus, besides fulfilling her role as wife of the prime minister and mother, was to develop and promote the "consciousness raising" (the term we used in the United States at that time) of this group of Yemeni women.

Listening to her, I realized that such a group could have been organized only under the mentorship of someone of her unusual background and prominent position in Yemen's conservative society. Azziza was indeed an anomaly among Yemeni women. The sister of powerful Sheikh Sinan Abu Luhum, who was governor of Hodeida in 1970, she had married young to Muhsin al-Aini, one of the few Western-educated members of the political elite in the 1950s and '60s. Muhsin, an orphan who received scholarships for his education, rose fast in the Yemeni government hierarchy. He took his young bride and her mother with him when he was appointed ambassador to the United States in the mid-1960s. They had returned to Yemen some months before we reopened the U.S. mission in 1970.

Friends tell me this previously shy woman with little education learned the ways of the West quite rapidly. Although I have not found an archival photo to verify the rumor, I heard that at one point during their tour Azziza was pictured in the *Washington Post*'s Style section dancing with President Lyndon Johnson! Outwardly she appeared confident and spoke fairly fluent English in Washington diplomatic circles. She told me, however, of her trepidation when making the required protocol visit to Mrs. William Rogers, wife of the secretary of state. No doubt this admission was designed to put me at ease during my initial visit to her home.

Although I suspect she found returning to Yemen a challenge after experiencing the freedoms that Western women enjoyed, she was in a position to pick and choose among Eastern and Western customs those that best suited her needs. For example, Azziza

Azziza al-Aini, 1997
(photo by Peggy Crawford)

delighted in hiding her public profile behind the veil, using it as her mask of freedom. She confided, "With my husband out of the house frequently and my young son cared for by the maid, I enjoy putting on my *sharshaf*, jumping into our old family sedan, and driving unnoticed around town to visit my friends." Unlike Saudi women, Yemeni women obtained the right to drive sometime between 1964, when Ted and Marcia Curran left, and 1970 when I arrived. I had a driver's license but chose not to use it.

One evening while my husband and I were attending a dinner at the al-Ainis' home, I invited Azziza's group to tea at my house. I was eager to meet her women friends, though it took a couple of months to set a time and work out the details. "Expect about fifteen women," she informed me a few days before the meeting.

My cook Abdul made some cakes and cookies and handled all the advance preparations but left before the tea party began. Since men in the Sanaa region were not allowed to view women's faces, his presence would have prevented them from removing their veils. And I wanted to see the lovely faces and colorful dresses that I knew were hidden under the black cloaks.

To make this an educational outing for them, I planned to show three short USIS movies about women's work lives in other parts of the developing world. I hoped they could understand what opportunities women were finding in other countries. Because no male could be in attendance, my husband taught me how to run the movie projector. Fearing that I would not be able to change the reels fast enough, I opted to line up three projectors side by side, each loaded with a separate film. Pushing a button to start each reel was the only mechanical skill I would need.

In midafternoon on the appointed day, over forty-five women showed up for the twenty-five straight-back chairs I had assembled in my living room from all four American apartments. Azziza was not as surprised at the numbers as I. "They are all very curious to see how an American lives," she commented. Unlike most Yemeni homes, however, where people sit on floor cushions all around the room, our Western home was furnished with two or more different brands of durable government-issue furniture, nothing special to us but unfamiliar to these women. That did not stop the Yemeni women, who are quite petite. They simply sat two to a chair! A few sat on the floor.

While they were removing their veils and getting comfortable, Azziza, Diane Cole, and I scurried around my kitchen, making extra tea and putting out more cakes for this larger-than-expected crowd. Azziza surprised me, given her privileged position in society, and I was most appreciative of her willingness to pitch in and help. After tea, the women pulled qat leaves out of their bags and stuffed them into their mouths, relaxing and chatting among themselves, waiting to see what would happen next.

Finally, Azziza and I decided it was time to begin the movies, all in English, two with Arabic subtitles. We started with a colorful fifteen-minute animated film based in a Central American country. Its message was about hygiene and cleanliness: "It is important to keep animals out of the kitchen, to sweep the floors, wash the fresh foods, use the outhouse, and keep it clean." They loved that cartoon and laughed uproariously. Next came a movie of Lebanese women, working as ballerinas, musicians, office workers, and teachers— what we would call traditional jobs for women in the developed world. This was harder for them to understand but not impossible. The final film featured Egyptian women working in professional and nontraditional jobs, including one driving a tractor on a farm and another as a hardhat civil engineer working on a road project. This last film was incomprehensible to them.

By 5:30 or 6:00 p.m., they all veiled up, put on their *sharshafs,* and headed en masse down the stairs and out into the courtyard.

Our three unruly dogs greeted them outside the apartment building's front door by barking and chasing the black-draped figures all the way out of the compound amidst screams and running feet. Meanwhile, I swept up the remnants of the qat leaves, reveling in this privileged glimpse of Yemeni women. It had been fascinating to watch their curiosity and reactions to Western culture in my home.

Chewing Qat and Celebrating Births

Qat chewing was a major pastime in Yemen during our time there. The country's high altitude, mild climate, two rainy seasons, and terraced mountainsides covered with rich volcanic soil were ideal for cultivation of qat leaves. Unlike most of the rest of the Middle East, Yemen's climate and terrain were similar to the highlands of Ethiopia, where the mildly stimulant plant originated. It is still chewed in Yemen, as well as in parts of Ethiopia and Somalia just across the Red Sea.

Some maintained that Yemenis spent more money on qat than they did on food. An appetite suppressant and very dehydrating, qat reportedly stimulates mental activity and concentration. It supposedly enhances one's perception but does not alter it. After achieving the altered state of *kayf* toward the end of a good qat chew, indulgers say they can sit still and be introspective, increase their attention span, and solve problems better.

In the 1970s both men and women chewed the leaves, though the women never chewed in public. Bought fresh every day, qat leaves came in varying grades and prices. Every time I ventured outside the compound I saw men, especially in the old city, chewing on huge wads of qat leaves stuffed in one side of the mouth. On late afternoons in the suq I occasionally saw men with bulging cheeks sitting in their merchant stalls, staring out with glazed eyes like zombies. I wondered if they were in a state of *kayf*.

The almost daily custom after the 1:00 p.m.–2:00 p.m. lunch hour was a men's gathering at which friends engaged in social discourse. They sat on the floor in the *mafraj* of someone's house, chewing qat and smoking the nargileh into late afternoon or early evening. At intervals during the afternoon some may have eaten pieces of peppermint to mellow the bittersweet flavor. Whether people were "addicted" to the qat or simply enjoyed the afternoon

Antiques merchant in suq chewing qat

social camaraderie, nearly everyone chewed and had probably spent years developing a taste and tolerance for the bitter leaves.

Rick Rauh told me how he felt after chewing qat during long afternoons with his Yemeni cronies: "When you are done, your mouth is shriveled and you feel agitated, as if you had smoked twenty packs of cigarettes." Then, he warned, "The only antidote for the inevitable constipation that ensues is grapes. Always follow a lengthy chewing party with grapes."

For better or worse, qat chewing was simply a way of life in Yemen. Although in the suq they chewed while they worked, most businesses simply came to a halt before lunch each day. Only some followed the pattern of the Spanish siesta and reopened by late afternoon. The habit put a huge damper on national productivity.

While qat chewing was a custom in its own right, it also played an integral part in other social gatherings. One such occasion focused on a father's celebration of his baby son's circumcision and occurred seven days after the birth. While the men feasted and celebrated, the women of the house prepared and served a huge meal for the proud father and his guests.

Muhammed Qassim, USINT Sanaa's forty-eight-year-old administrative assistant, invited David and me to the circumcision party for his new son. His sixteen-year-old wife gave birth in late June 1970 to their first child—a boy—which made the Yemeni family proud. By tradition, the local barber performed the ritual cutting of the foreskin early in the morning—in this case, on the Muslim holy day—before the guests arrived around noon.

At Muhammed's house in the old Turkish *bustan,* or garden quarter, of Sanaa, we took off our shoes and climbed up the narrow stone stairs to reach the third-floor *diwan,* a reception area, which in this case was also used as a bedroom. The only woman in the room, I joined about twelve-to-fifteen men. Many were turbaned and dressed in traditional *zinna* and *janbiyya* with a suit jacket. Some were in Western attire. All were sitting on narrow mattresses (similar to futons) that lined the walls of the room. The barber as well as one of the prime minister's brothers joined us.

Photographs of assorted people, three delicate handbags with silver threads woven through them, and small silver good luck charms for the new baby decorated the walls. Many pictures of relatives hung interspersed with photos of American and Arab movie stars. A double bed with a new cloth on it, in one corner of the room, was the only piece of furniture. Opened glass windows, hinged, dual-paned, and unscreened, gave us a wonderful view of the green gardens and trees below. Flies flew all around, but in Yemen we learned to be oblivious to such annoyances.

Leaving the *diwan* temporarily, I went upstairs to see the baby. Tightly swaddled in a small blanket, he was lying on his back by himself on a pallet on the floor in an unfurnished room. His forehead was marked with ashes and his head was encircled with a wreath of small green leaves. An expressionless face with deep brown eyes stared up at the ceiling. There was no indication of the pain he had suffered earlier that day.

I noticed five or six veiled women in an adjoining room peeking at me from around the doorjamb. Walking into their dark kitchen, smoke-blackened by the open clay cylinder-shaped *tannur* (oven), I gave them my heartfelt greetings in Arabic. The few expressions I knew—for example, *marhaba* (hello), *sabaah al-khair* (good morning), *kayf halik?* (how are you?), *aysh ismak?* (what is your name?), *ismi* (my name is..), and *mabruk* (congratulations)—made me feel most inadequate. I tried to make up for the missing words with nods, hand gestures, and smiles.

The women were all busy cooking. Muhammed's mother-in-law and his wife's sisters were among them, but his wife was not present. She was presumably secluded in another room to bask in her traditional period of recuperation and freedom from household chores. I do not know whether this occurred for Muhammed's wife, but according to R. B. Searjeant and Ronald Lewcock (1983), typically, on the seventh day after giving birth, a new mother goes to the *hammam*. There her female friends sprinkle incense around her to ward off the bad spirits or jinn. Also, to ensure fertility, they break an egg at the door when she enters the bath and again when she returns to the entrance door of her own home.

I knew this would be my only chance to see these women, all of whom were thin and much shorter than I. Most wore scarves and either black or long dull-colored, flowered dresses. As a woman, I was allowed to gaze into their brown eyes and lined faces that spoke to me of their hard lives, despite the young ages of all but Muhammed's mother. After exhausting all I could remember of "kitchen Arabic" (the minimal amount we learned to communicate with household help), I told them goodbye, only to see them later in their veils as they served our luncheon.

It was not long after returning from the kitchen before several of us sitting in the *diwan* were led down a half-flight of stairs to the tiny dining room. I recall no more than two windows, unscreened and open, in the room. Because the room was so small, we ate in three shifts. Everyone sat around a plastic cloth on the floor that served as the table. It was overflowing with dishes of food. Although we were given a fork and spoon to use, David and I joined the majority by eating with our right hand and making sure the soles of our feet were turned away from the table.

The luncheon menu was typical of an elaborate multicourse meal for guests served as the main meal of the day. There was *hilba*, a yellowish-green dipping sauce used throughout the meal. (*Hilba* is made from ground fenugreek seeds mixed with water and whipped by hand to a frothy consistency.) Another dish called *shafut* was made of pounded and chopped leek tops, mixed with

Susan McClintock and John Cole at typical Yemeni lunch table

buttermilk, mint and spices. These were served with *lahuh,* thin flat sourdough millet pancakes of Ethiopian origin, with sponge-like holes in them. The pièce de résistance of the dinner was a bread-like item made of honey, butter and flour called *bint al-sahn* (daughter's cake—literally, daughter of the pan) served in the middle of the meal. Then came small pieces of lamb or goat mutton cooked in a cilantro-flavored broth, dipped in the *hilba,* and wrapped in Yemeni homemade bread (*khubz*). As a last course, to aid digestion just before dessert, we dipped bread into a paste called *salta,* made from beef broth, egg, rice, and peppers and seasoned with cumin, coriander, fenugreek, and leeks.

While these particular dishes are the same foods written about in books six hundred years ago, other items were likely inspired by more recent European fare. These included: ground beef and cheese pasta; baked chicken with French fries; a Russian salad with green peas, carrots, and tomatoes; green spinach in small square patties; peppered rice; radishes; boiled okra (*bamiya*); potatoes cooked with paprika; egg turnip soufflé in small cakes; and *salatah* of tomato, red onion, and lettuce leaves.

Tea flavored with ginger and cinnamon (*shai*), fruit such as oranges and bananas, and/or a large bowl of white custard flavored with rose water for all to share completed the meal. The latter we ate with spoons.

After we finished, the second group of men was ushered in to eat. The last to eat were the women, who got the leftovers, just like mother lions after they feed their families.

Moving back to the *mafraj*, we were offered either *qishr* or a café *bunn*. The *qishr* was made by boiling the ground husks of the coffee bean with ginger and other spices to create an infusion (known in Yemen as a drink for poor folks and women). The *bunn* was made from roasted coffee beans minus the *qishr* and was similar to Turkish coffee. These two drinks were followed by more *shai.*

Finally, the nargileh with its mouthpiece and long hose was placed in the middle of the room. Each guest took deep puffs of smoke drawn through the mouthpiece before passing the hose to his neighbor. Out of politeness, I tried it, managing not to embarrass myself by coughing with the inhalation. Smoking tobacco through the nargileh did not give me any physical sensation or high, as I had heard chewing qat did. Smoking the nargileh may be just another way to celebrate community and friendship.

At 2:30 we bade adieu, leaving the Yemeni men to their afternoon qat chewing. As I reflected on the special celebration that day, I realized that as an honored Western woman in 1970 Yemen I could travel between the male and the female worlds, unlike the men. Because of my limited Arabic, I unfortunately spent far less time in the kitchen with the women than I would have liked. However, I got to enjoy the conversation of the Yemeni men, many of whom spoke some English.

Circumcision party given by Muhammad Qassim
(white shirt, center, behind boy with nargileh)

I'm sure the men were curious to see the exposed face and legs, covered only by a knee-length A-line skirt, the Western fashion at the time, of a fair-skinned Caucasian woman as she sat on the floor trying to keep as much covered as possible. I had chosen to wear a long-sleeved blouse with a skirt rather than pants, because, in those days before pantsuits, we "dressed up" in skirts, which I thought the occasion deserved. I would have been a lot more comfortable in pants, as I can still feel the stares of the men, who sat around the room listening to the few men, including my husband, who led the conversation.

Just as the proud Yemeni father holds a party to celebrate the circumcision of his new son, the female family members throw a *tafritah*, a big invitational party, or *haflah*, for the new mother on the fortieth day after the birth of a son or a daughter. In fact, the party is the culmination of a forty-day highly prescribed diet and ritual that new mothers traditionally observe.

Searjeant and Lewcock state that the new mother's diet includes drinking raw eggs and eating two-week-old baby chickens for fifteen days, beginning right after the birth. Presumably the added protein helps her regain strength. Eating special bread dishes with lots of honey, ghee, and fresh dates, as well as drinking spiced coffee each morning for seven days, is designed to make the menstrual cycle return. She also has fresh bread baked for her daily. The husband's family provides this special diet for the first week and then the mother's family takes over for the remaining thirty-three days.

In addition to the food, there are congratulatory visits in the morning throughout the forty days from family members on both sides, who bring coffee, ground flour, eggs with ghee and honey, and chickens, as well as clothing and blankets for the baby. All bring leaves of aromatic rue to ward off the bad jinn. Beginning on the seventh day in the birth room, there are afternoon women's parties with dancing and singing, in which paid women singers perform.

A two-day feast begins on the fortieth day and is the grand finale to which many outsiders are invited. I attended several during our tour. A slaughtered animal is generally cooked as part of the feast. These parties often involve qat chewing as well as singing and dancing. Such birth celebrations are frequently more expensive than weddings.

Typically, we arrived at the home to find the large *mafraj* filled with colorfully dressed Yemeni women, some with babies. At one party there must have been a hundred squeezed into the room, sitting on the floor around a four-poster bed upon which the new mother lounged. Under the *sharshafs* and black veils the guests arrived in, the women wore knee-length satiny dresses decorated with gold or silver braid on a fitted bodice and a skirt gathered at the waist, usually with elbow-length sleeves. Pregnant women simply hiked the gathered skirt up over their tummies. Married women wore little pillbox hats on top of their *lithma* (scarves), while unmarried women simply wore their *lithma*, which they usually did not remove from their heads, and showed their faces.

In some cases the women had lined their eyes and decorated their faces for this grand occasion. They used black kohl and drew a thick line from under the nose to the bottom of the chin. Some also put three dots on each cheek.

Propped up by mountains of lacy pillows, one new mother I remember sat elegantly in the middle of the bed. Elaborate henna-colored patterns decorated her hands. Gold bracelets covered her

Women singers and young boy at a party

arms while numerous gold necklaces adorned the bodice of her turquoise satin, brocaded dress. Her smile revealed a few gold teeth
as well. Short black curls framed her face. Kohl rimmed her eyes,
and her face gleamed for all her friends to admire. A number of
feminine gifts such as scarves, perfumes, and decorated handbags
covered the remainder of the bed. This was her biggest day of celebration for a job well done.

I had heard that during its first few days, the baby was essentially ignored, wrapped in swaddling clothes, supposedly to make
it feel secure, and left alone on a floor mat. Like the baby boy at
the circumcision party, this woman's baby was not displayed to her
audience. However, guests often brought their babies to the parties.

At this particular event, the music consisted of women beating
a piece of steel on the bottom of a tin pan and singing. One member of the group had a knack for ululating with her tongue (like
yodeling). Done by women from the rooftops for the men parading
through the streets, ululating and drumming on metal were common at wedding processions as well.

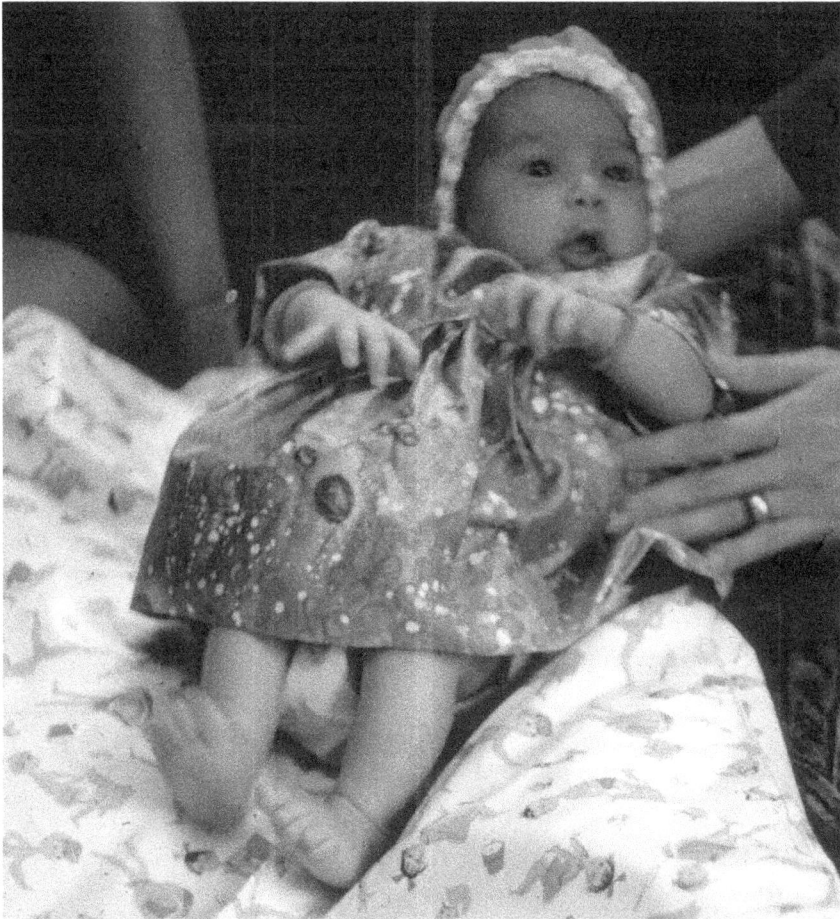

Baby girl brought by guest to a party

After ginger *shai* and too many sweets, cakes, and cookies, the qat chewing began. Some of the older women had been at it from the very beginning, chewing and using not-so-discreet spittoons. As a guest and not the hostess this time, I felt free to indulge. What a bitter taste I experienced—not the bitter sweetness I had been told to expect—as I crunched down on the quarter-sized leaves. It did not take long before my palate had had enough of the tannic acid to make my mouth pucker. Since I feared my teeth might turn green, I politely refused the next round of leaves offered.

When the brief experiment was over, my mouth simply felt dry and raw. I felt no change in mental state, no buzz or high—just the awful taste in my mouth—and like I had drunk too much coffee. I guess I was supposed to work harder, to stuff one cheek full and really chew for several more hours to release that bitter juice and get the full effect! No thanks. I'm glad I did not indulge very long, based on Lealan Swanson's comments. She once had a bad anxiety attack, feeling as if the sky were falling, that could only have been explained by the lengthy qat chew that preceded it.

Glancing around the room at the qat-induced animation of the women in their multiple conversations, I noticed the smiling mother enjoying the revelry of her party. This might be the biggest event in her life, more than her wedding had been, I thought to myself. Here she was free to be herself, among her peers and female family members, the center of attention. She had produced a son for her husband and his family's posterity, the ultimate gift a Yemeni woman can offer to the world.

7

Climbing Nabi Shu'ayb

On a crisp, clear Friday in early October during our first autumn in Sanaa, David and I struck out at about 9:00 a.m. with Alain Bertaud. On our day off, we were eager to locate and climb the highest mountain in Arabia, Jebel Nabi Shu'ayb, about 3,760 meters high, or 12,368 feet. In addition to some architectural sites and a village along the way, we hoped to visit the Yemeni military fort on top of the mountain, built by the Turks in the nineteenth century.

Leaving the embassy compound in the Land Rover, David headed our vehicle west over the road toward Hodeida. About fifteen miles and forty-five minutes later we came to the small village of Matna, where we inquired about how to reach our destination.

Abdullah, a fiftyish, turbaned tribesman who lived in a village higher on the mountain in question, volunteered to accompany us on the hike and jumped into the Land Rover. His feet clad in sandals made from the treads of old tires, Abdullah led us to a rugged dirt road.

As we were winding our way up the washed-out road, a Yemeni guard at a military fort located in the foothills of the mountain stopped us. After some conversation with both David and Abdullah, he granted us permission to proceed to Abdullah's ancestral village. The road, also built by the Turks, was so rocky we soon parked the vehicle at 9,000 feet and began the long, tedious foot journey.

Our guide Abdullah in his village on Nabi Shu'ayb

Wearing sturdy shoes, we each carried a light jacket, food packs, and cameras on our backs. We wandered across numerous small terraces planted with wheat and over jagged volcanic rocks. We made our way slowly up the mountainside, definitely challenged trying to follow the confident, too-quick stride of our guide. Barely keeping up with him, we finally had to ask him to slow down. Some barefoot boys, who had been helping to harvest the wheat on one of the terraces, began to accompany us and leapt across the rocks like little mountain goats.

Spectacular scenery, breathtaking for its beauty as well as its physical challenge, greeted us everywhere we turned. The distance up the mountain over the well-worn short-cut trails of the tribesmen seemed endless. We snapped photos of the huge gray boulders and smaller igneous rock formations, interspersed with patches of green.

Several clifftop villages hidden from the road emerged into view from crevices and ravines as we made our way upward. The first major village we came to was full of curious inhabitants. The women were veiled and showed the same Turkish influence as in Sanaa. We noticed simple, yet unusual, stone architecture,

Interior of mosque near Abdullah's village

Soldiers pose on top of Nabi Shu'ayb

including a lovely old mosque with a minaret, carved pictures, and inscriptions that David and Alain thought might be pre-Islamic, perhaps Sabaean or Himyar.

Having left the car at 11:00 a.m., we finally staggered into the Yemeni military fort on top of the mountain at 2:30 p.m. About twenty Yemeni soldiers greeted us excitedly. To their knowledge we were the first foreigners (except the Turks) ever to visit the fort in recent times, which meant David and I were undoubtedly the first Americans. "Some Russians visited the village about an hour below the peak, but never came to the top," stated one soldier in Arabic to David. "Your wife is probably the first foreign woman to visit the fort," he continued.

The lieutenant in charge of the fort invited us into his small six-foot-square cubicle of a room to rest and drink some hot, sugary *shai*. I was exhausted, and, at his invitation, collapsed onto his cot to rest my weary body. That steamy sweet concoction was honestly the best *shai* I had ever tasted, and I lavished *tammams* (good) and *shukrans* on the friendly soldier. The sugar gave all three of us a much-needed energy boost. For some reason, David and Alain were not as exhausted as I by the high altitude. Perhaps my tiredness

Alain (top left), David and Abdullah (center), with soldiers
near tomb at top of Nabi Shu'ayb

was attributable to the fact, as I learned only later, that I was in my
first month of pregnancy with Lesley.

After regaining our strength, we joined our soldier friends on
a tour of the fort. Surprisingly, they invited us to take pictures. We
were fascinated to find an old mosque and reportedly the tomb of
the Prophet (*Nabi*) Shu'ayb, something we had not anticipated. The
Shorter Encyclopedia of Islam lists the prophet as a contemporary
of Lot. One story we heard is that Shu'ayb's legend accompanied
'Ali, Prophet Muhammad's son-in-law, when he and his followers
founded the first Muslim mosques in Yemen and allegedly discovered Shu'ayb's tomb.

David exclaimed to Alain and me, "The mosque is so old, these
worn-down places on the wooden pillars supporting the ceiling
were probably made by Muslim pilgrims who came to visit Nabi
Shu'ayb's tomb." We felt privileged that the soldiers allowed us
non-Muslims to explore this holy place.

From this highest point in Arabia, we could almost see Sanaa
over the distant mountains. What a spectacular view of the green

terraces and valleys below! The air was thin (we had been panting all the way up the mountainside), and most certainly unpolluted.

About 3:30 p.m. our guide decided it was time to leave if we wanted to reach the car before sundown. We found the descent much easier than the breathless climb up. Walking down the mountainside for about thirty minutes, we stopped on an unplanted terrace to have our long-overdue lunch of bread, Danish blue cheese, and carrot sticks. We had not wanted to eat on the mountaintop because we did not have enough to share with the soldiers. As we sat basking in the sun and enjoying our lunch, we were startled to hear the strains of Arab music from a transistor radio. Looking up, we saw one of the soldiers running down the mountainside and waving at us.

What could he want? Did we leave something behind? We checked our cameras and hiking gear. A bit breathless, the soldier proudly presented three paper cups we had brought with us and used for drinking water at their fort. We had left them in the lieutenant's quarters rather than stashing them in our backpacks for the return journey. In today's more environmentally savvy world, we would have felt guilt-ridden for not carrying out our trash. What seemed like a precious modern keepsake to these soldiers was merely rubbish to us Westerners. Shaking his hand and giving him a cookie, we thanked him profusely for his kindness. We carefully put the used paper cups back into our packs for the trip down the mountainside and said our goodbyes. Touched by the soldier's depth of sincerity, Alain exclaimed to David and me, "Only in Yemen would something like this happen."

As our guide Abdullah scampered down the mountainside, he insisted authoritatively in Arabic that he would accompany us all the way to the car. We tried several times to get him to stop off at his village, but he would hear nothing of it. In his culture I suspect his honor was at stake lest anything happen to these guests he had befriended. It was probably fortunate he stayed with us so we could find the right trail and locate the car again before dark.

Thanks to Abdullah's expertise, we reached the Land Rover at 5:30 p.m., with plenty of time to spare before sundown. We found a military man guarding the Land Rover. He had voluntarily come up the mountain from the lower fort to watch our vehicle. He would accept no payment for his all-day services. "*Maalesh* (never mind, it's nothing)," he assured us with a downward wave of his hand. Our guide, we were pleased, accepted five riyals (about one dollar) for his day's labor.

David wearily maneuvered the car down the rugged mountain road. Soldiers stopped us at the lower fort to ask if we had any food left over. We did and gladly gave it to them. At that time we did not realize how poorly the YARG provided for its soldiers, either in food or clothing. A few years later, we learned that during a rare Yemeni snowstorm a number of soldiers froze to death atop Nabi Shu'ayb.

Giving him a cheery and thankful farewell, we dropped Abdullah off in Matna, the same village where we had met him in the morning. Two soldiers who had spent the holy day in their nearby villages asked to hitch a ride with us, and the five of us headed back to Sanaa. Three of us at least were eager to see our beds that evening. Nursing sore muscles the next morning was small payment for the tremendous view and unanticipated hospitality we found at the top of Arabia. I basked in the knowledge that I was probably the first foreign woman to reach the summit of Nabi Shu'ayb!

Epilogue

As I was completing the first draft of this manuscript in December 2005, my writer friend Kathleen Anderson presented me with a CD of Yemeni music as a Christmas gift. The music is haunting and a fond reminder of my time there, much like listening to the audiotapes I recorded years ago. Hearing the familiar singing and instrumentation left me wondering whether the dream I had in 1998 about a return to Yemen was a portent of things to come.

David and I always said we would have to write about these experiences someday. That is what I have done—told our story—and doing so has brought closure for me on that incredible experience. However, my research for the book's Part Two, about Yemen today, as well as contacts with Yemenis and others who have visited the country recently, rouse my curiosity and make me eager to return to see the changes for myself.

In October 2007, I was visited by one last dream about Yemen:

David and I are back in Yemen as equal partners, not married but good friends. We are reopening a large embassy building that is in need of many repairs. There is a big hole in the floor of a basement room, through which I can see the ground. That will need closing. There are beautiful red and black Bukhara-style Persian carpets hanging on the walls and big doors in the main entrance/reception room. As I go through that room into a huge sitting room, where we plan to hold an organizational meeting, I see water leaking from the roof and add that to my list of repairs. It is an ornately decorated room, and I worry that furniture will be damaged by the water. Through its large windows I can see a busy street with cars and trucks passing by. I realize we are no longer at Bayt al-Hilali, but perhaps in the new embassy building built in the 1980s.

A group of friends, many Westerners as well as Yemenis, have come to greet us. Three, including my good friend Judy, have flown out from Baltimore for the occasion. We are calling everyone to a meeting to discuss how we will make the repairs and get the embassy operational. Some people in the group lived here earlier and are now leaving. I have agreed to store a few boxes of books and clothing for a college student but not his pet snake and armadillo, which he has disguised in costume to make me think they are stuffed animals. As hoards of people I have invited to this first planning meeting begin to arrive at the Embassy by crossing a wooden bridge, the bridge begins to collapse. I run out and try to help people across before they fall. I wake up—before people have found their places and the meeting has begun.

Despite the somewhat ominous ending, this dream makes me believe I will someday go back to visit Yemen. The bridge collapse warns me of the varied, daunting, and urgent issues confronting Yemen today and suggests it will not be an easy journey. I may take some friends with me, at least through story and photos, perhaps those of you who have read this book and been introduced to this magical country in a remote corner of Arabia.

My recent encounters with people who care about Yemen, my readings, even my dreams, remind me that Yemenis are good people, inquisitive and kind, who are now simply unwitting pawns in a game of world politics, with little control over their country's future. However, I have hope for Yemen's survival.

Following the two world wars, many Middle Eastern states were created with arbitrary boundaries containing diverse ethnic and religious groups, most notably Iraq and Lebanon, both of which struggle for survival today. In contrast, Yemen's nation-state has grown out of an ancient civilization with a strong ethnic and cultural identity. That fact alone should provide some of the underpinnings for the strength and cohesion the country needs to face the pressing challenges that lie ahead. *Inshallah* (God willing).

PART TWO

Yemen Today

8

Friends Compare Yemen Then and Now

Serendipity has shaped the course of my life countless times. In fall 2004, while attending a political rally in Bernalillo, New Mexico, I took a seat at a table with a gentleman and his wife. She was wearing a colorful Palestinian shawl over her shoulders. I commented on its origin and beauty. The man, Lew Reade, said he had been US-AID director in Amman, Jordan, in the late 1980s. When I told him I was writing a memoir about living in Yemen in the early 1970s, his face lit up as he explained, "I visited Yemen in 1958 and actually met the imam. Then I almost went back as AID director in 1980."

"Tell me about meeting Imam Ahmad!" I couldn't believe I was sitting beside someone in New Mexico who had actually visited with the imam. Although I had read oral history accounts, I had never heard anyone speak about a personal meeting with this historic figure, who, in my mind, occupies mythical status.

Lew then began what turned out to be an almost incomprehensible tale about his journey to Yemen only twelve years before I arrived:

> I was working for Westinghouse in Rome in 1958. Our New York headquarters wanted to develop business in the Near East and North Africa. They were particularly eager to compete for business that would normally go to British General Electric (GEC), which had a small operation in Aden. As an adventurous young engineer, I gladly volunteered to visit these Muslim countries.

While in Cairo, I hooked up with a local Westinghouse firm eager to open up business in Yemen. I went by car with an Egyptian named Khalid as my translator to Port Said, where we picked up a small coastal freighter and crossed the Red Sea to Hodeida, Yemen. In Hodeida we tried to hire a car and driver to get to Sanaa but discovered there was no paved road, and anyone who might rent us a vehicle would charge an outrageous fee. Declining that, we learned a camel caravan would be leaving in two days. The caravan, which we joined, took eight days to reach Sanaa. We stopped in the villages of Bajil and Manakha along the way and slept in small black tents or the occasional caravansary, all of which were filthy.

In Sanaa we got quarters in a sort of makeshift hotel. It took a couple of days and plenty of baksheesh to get an audience with the imam, who normally lived in Taiz but was in Sanaa on this occasion.

Bill Stoltzfus and camel caravan on Sanaa-Taiz trail in 1961—probably similar to what Lew Reade experienced on his Hodeida-Sanaa camel trek

We had the audience with Imam Ahmad in an old palace. I remember the gas-driven sound of the generator, which people in the palace told Khalid was a five-kilowatt Honda. I saw only a single light bulb hanging overhead in the room where we met the imam. There may have been other lights in the building, and indeed in Sanaa, but we didn't see any. There certainly wasn't electricity in the sense of a municipal grid, or we would have spotted it.

I made a big pitch that a significant electrical-power-generating station with associated distribution would be good for development in Yemen, helping men, women, and children. The imam whispered to his attendant, who then whispered to my Egyptian friend, giving the following reply, translated into English from Arabic: "The men in Yemen have enough work to do now, the children learn their Qur'an by rote, the girls don't need to learn anything, and the women stay at home. We don't need your American power plants and their electricity, so please get out of my country."

Whether his retort had political or economic motives, I don't know. He might have had some relationship with British GEC in Aden, because I learned later that Taiz had electricity by the mid-fifties. With that definitive answer, I left Sanaa, again taking eight days by camel caravan to return to Hodeida. I did not return to Yemen until 1980, when I visited the John F. Kennedy Waterworks in Taiz and was amazed at the changes I found.

As Lew Reade ended his story, I found myself staring at him in amazement, my mouth wide open, but also feeling puzzled. I knew David had had electricity when he served in Sanaa from 1964 to 1966, and it was hard for me to believe that no one in Sanaa except the imam had electricity as late as 1958! However, I had read the transcription of Ambassador Marshall Wiley's oral history, stating that electricity in less-isolated Taiz in 1958 was available only via a small generator owned by an Italian, who sold people a connection to it. By 1970, only twelve years later, both Sanaa and Taiz were fully electrified, although our electricity frequently went out and some homes in the old city still relied on their alabaster oil lamps in the evenings.

Also, in 1970 we were able to travel from Sanaa to Hodeida by Land Rover over paved road in less than four hours. I cannot imagine what it would have been like spending eight days on a camel to travel between the two cities.

Apparently, in barely more than a decade after Lew's memorable visit to Sanaa, Yemen had performed miracles to reach the level of development it had achieved by the time I arrived, a fact I did not fully appreciate until I heard Lew's story and learned of the monumental differences between Yemen in the 1950s and Yemen in the early 1970s.

The Republican revolutionary government that overthrew the imam made incredible leaps in only ten years and deserves credit for its rapid buildup of Yemen's infrastructure through its careful East-West juggling act. We should also admire their seductive courting of both the Egyptians and the Russians, from whom they got the majority of their military equipment and training in the early days of their republic.

Lew's story prompted me to think about Yemenophile friends who had made multiple trips to Yemen over the years since I had left the country. I wondered what changes they might describe between their times in Yemen in the 1960s and 1970s and what they had observed in more recent years. Three in particular—David Newton, Lealan Swanson, and Marjorie Ransom—came to mind. The insights they willingly provided reflect the tremendous changes, some good, some troublesome, that they see in contemporary Yemen, some difficult for me to imagine, just as Lew Reade's story was.

Ambassador David Newton, who served three tours in Yemen with the U.S. Foreign Service (1966–67, 1972–75, and, as ambassador, 1994–97), offered these comments:

> Yemenis have always been sure of their identity, being part of a real and ancient country. Their culture endures, as Yemenis are proud of it, unlike many other peoples in developing countries. They are also a pragmatic people, perhaps because they are a nation of farmers, even though some have been radicalized in Afghanistan or by Wahhabis

coming from Saudi Arabia. In 1966, when Yemen was almost totally undeveloped, I found them very civilized and hospitable people. Even when most were illiterate, they were famous for their love of oral poetry.

Yemenis today (and even Yemen itself) look much the same as in the 1960s, but the traditional mentality has largely disappeared with the growth of education and exposure to the world. The civil society has evolved fairly impressively, but democracy is still tentative, despite the average Yemeni's strong sense of independence, which makes governance hard. The tribal system has consequently weakened, with the loss of authority of major sheikhs, who have become "citified."

Qat use has grown tremendously: what was a weekend event is now daily, and women and even children have their own afternoon sessions. Cities have grown and spread enormously, with serious urban problems. Modernization has brought other problems, especially rapid population growth, unemployment, poverty, and a critical water shortage in the highlands. Corruption is a fact of life . . . and often causes resentment.

I wondered how his comments would compare with those of my other two friends. Dr. Lealan Swanson, retired professor of Art History at Mississippi's Jackson State University, now teaching part-time at the University of Oregon in Eugene, lived from 1974 to 1975 in Taiz, where she taught school, and from 1982 to 1984 in Sanaa, where she worked as director of the American Institute for Yemeni Studies (AIYS). She returned for a few weeks in the summer of 2001 on a National Endowment for the Humanities grant to conduct research for a comparative study of the architecture of Sanaa, Fez (Morocco), and Timbuktu (Mali). Lealan pointed out the changes she saw with some very personal illustrations:

When I returned in 2001, the changes I witnessed were monumental. The simple matter of refrigeration, which most North Americans take for granted, is an interesting example. In 1974, we had two small children with us. For the first six months, we had no refrigeration. Cooking was

Lealan in *sitara* and *moghmuq*

done on a two-burner gas tabletop stove in a small pressure cooker that could be re-pressurized to save food for the next day. Milk was made by boiling water to mix with a powder. After nine months in Taiz, we finally bought a small refrigerator that allowed us to keep butter, milk, eggs, and leftovers. Even so, the electricity couldn't be trusted to run at the proper levels all the time. Sometimes it ran low, and sometimes it quit altogether.

By 1982, on our second trip to Yemen, we lived in the capital at Sanaa, and our refrigerator was a large one with a proper freezer. We sometimes made ice cream or frozen desserts and enjoyed cold drinks. Imported frozen meat and butter were luxuries. The situation with electricity (to run the machines) was much more stable by then, and many Yemenis also had refrigerators. There were some small shops and push-wagons that sold ice cream on the streets, which we were reluctant to try.

I was, therefore, pleasantly surprised to go with my [Yemeni] friend and her four small children to a real ice cream parlor in 2001. The menu boasted sundaes, parfaits, whipped cream, chocolate syrup, and many flavors of ice cream. Wonderful! It was a really lively scene, where families indulged small children, who raced up and down the aisles. . . . The contrast was enormous. . . . In the twenty-seven years since I had first visited the country, they had gone from few appliances and unreliable electricity to a European-style ice cream *gelateria* or *konditeri*, which made a delightful place for family outings.

In contrast, or perhaps in echo of the children crowding the ice cream facility, were the overburdened streets. In 1974, Sanaa closed its gates at ten every night and let out the dogs. My first memory of Sanaa is of dark city streets, deserted except for packs of dogs. The new Sanaa a quarter century later is crowded with people and cars even at one in the morning. Donkeys, cattle, and camels are gone from the streets. There are still a few dogs. The downtown is a roar of frantic activity, and the city has grown far beyond the Turkish brick kilns and the German experimental farm that then formed the outskirts of a rather small, dusty town.

Lurking under the patina of this shiny new progress, however, is underemployment, pervaded by a new kind of religious intensity. Mosques in Sanaa, which used to simply give the call to prayer, now singe the airwaves with sermons denouncing many ills in the society, especially those of their sisters, wives, and mothers. I wonder what the owners of these fervent voices think about ice cream parlors for their new generation.

Marjorie Ransom, a retired Foreign Service officer and Arabic specialist who served in several Middle Eastern posts, is the only one of the three to visit Yemen in the post-9/11 era. She lived in Yemen with her FSO husband, Ambassador David Ransom, in 1966–67 and 1975–78. Following her husband's death, Marjorie returned to Yemen in fall 2004 on an AIYS grant to research traditional Yemeni jewelry. She sent the following by email during her trip:

Right now I am overwhelmed by the growth and change in Sanaa. There is an explosion of hotels in every part of town and offices in almost every block, where you can make local and long distance calls. There are many restaurants and a large number of stores selling consumer goods. The demand for Internet access is extraordinary and the cybercafes are often full, with people waiting to log on, . . . mostly young Yemeni males, but not entirely. In Taiz, when I had difficulty logging on, a veiled young woman was there to help. I have asked about the reason for the increase in economic activity since 1998 when I was in Yemen on State Department business, and I am told it is because of the number of Yemeni Americans who have returned from the United States and invest in houses and small businesses. I have no way of testing this.

The majority of women are veiled, but many women are working in offices either veiled or in what I call *sharshaf*, the veil wrapped tightly around the face. Yemenis are as friendly and inquisitive as I remember. Even taxi drivers want to know where you are from, your marital status, and how many children you have. I have been invited for many *iftars* [after-sunset dinners during Ramadan] with Yemeni families, thanks to my female gender and single status. I have been struck by the depth of the religious beliefs of all the Yemenis I have met and worked with in this holy month of Ramadan. More than I remember anywhere, the men pray five times a day and the women seem to do so as well, in the privacy of their homes. Yet they are friendly to outsiders and never forget to offer water and tea, even during the hours of their fast. I compromise by fasting after breakfast!

People complain that corruption is rampant and worse than ever, but I have not been in a position to judge. . . .

Since I have not returned to Yemen, I must rely on my friends' comments about how things have changed. In the final chapter, I shall add the perspectives of journalists and historians as well as the comments of two educated Yemeni women who grew up there and have traveled abroad. Between the two sets of perspectives, I hope to identify the challenges that face Yemen today, as it sits near the epicenter of Middle Eastern tensions and global economic and terrorism realities.

9

Yemen's Challenges Today

The Fort Hood killings in September 2009 by a U.S. Army psychiatrist and the failed Christmas Day attempt by a Nigerian man trained by AQAP (al-Qaeda in the Arabian Peninsula) to blow up an airliner over U.S. soil thrust the Republic of Yemen squarely into America's face. Both the attacker at Ft. Hood and the would-be suicide bomber had been in contact with a radical Yemeni-American cleric, Anwar al-Aulaqi, who is now on the U.S.'s short list of militants "targeted for killing or capture." According to Dana Priest of the *Washington Post*, since December 2009 U.S. military teams and intelligence agencies have been heavily involved in clandestine joint operations with Yemeni troops in locating and killing suspected terrorists. The American advisers have reportedly shared intelligence, helped plan operations, developed tactics, and provided weapons, but they have not been involved in the execution of the raids on terrorist strongholds. This stepped-up joint counterterrorism activity presumably inspired the Christmas Day retaliation by AQAP.

The bombing of the USS *Cole* in 2000 put Yemen on the world's radar screen. However, events during the past two years, many instigated by AQAP, have pushed Yemen to the foreground in the war on terror. As a growing training ground for Islamic militants, Yemen is but one of several fragile countries where al-Qaeda has decentralized its operations far away from the Afghanistan-Pakistan theater. Already faced with multiple, interconnected challenges threatening its survival, the weak Yemeni government is fighting for its life under enormous pressure from increasingly bold activity by militant radicals operating within its borders. If not handled successfully, these challenges could bring down the government, plunging the country into chaos, and creating not only increased regional instability but also expanded opportunity for radical Islam to flourish and pose threats in the broader world. Despite diverse efforts by the government of Yemen (GOY) and its concerned donor allies to confront these obstacles, much more needs to be done—and quickly—before Yemen's 2013 presidential elections, when a leadership crisis is likely to occur.

In a September 2009 report of the Carnegie Endowment for International Peace (CEIP), Christopher Boucek delineated three broad categories for Yemen's interlocking challenges—economic, demographic, and domestic security—that are useful here. Boucek and others, including those attending the January 2010 London summit on Yemen, have also made specific recommendations cited at the end of this chapter for helping Yemen solve its many problems.

Economic Challenges

Yemen was already considered the poorest country in the Middle East before the global economic crisis. World Bank 2009 figures estimated an annual per capita income of only $870. At the top of the list of Yemen's economic challenges is the major depletion of both its hydrocarbon and water reserves. Increased qat production and a poor agricultural infrastructure threaten food security. A downturn in remittances from Yemenis working abroad, a decline in tourism, the global recession, inflation, and a substantial drop in oil prices and thus hard currency have all significantly reduced Yemen's resources for paying its bills.

Depletion of Oil and Gas Reserves. In early 2009 Yemen's oil production, which represents 75 percent of its economy, had dropped to only 62 percent of its peak in 2003—far less than its oil-rich neighbors. Although the French Total project in Aden began producing liquefied natural gas in mid-2009, that production cannot make up for the loss in oil revenues. While Total projects $50 billion in revenue for Yemen over the next twenty-five years, the World Bank estimates less than half that amount. The World Bank also maintains that Yemen's oil and gas reserves will continue to plummet and be depleted by 2017. At least one energy expert projects that Yemen's economy will collapse within four or five years. Unfortunately, there has been little effort made to develop a post-hydrocarbon economy in Yemen.

Depletion of Surface Water and Groundwater. Even more critical over the long term is Yemen's rapid depletion of groundwater and surface water. It is especially severe in Yemen's highlands, where aquifers are being exhausted far faster than they can be replenished. With no public water supply in much of the country, the price of water has quadrupled over the past four-to-five years, and unlicensed private wells have proliferated.

Whereas water tables in Yemen used to be found at three-to-ten meters, the table in some places today is several hundred meters below the surface and dropping more than six feet every year. Some analysts predict Yemen will be out of fresh water in thirty years. Others suggest water on the Sanaa plain could be depleted in five years or less, making Sanaa the first capital city in the world to run out of fresh water.

Meeting agricultural demands seems to be the major reason for overpumping. Qat production, a leading force in the crisis, consumes about 40 percent annually of Yemen's water supplies through irrigation. Additionally, the high population growth, urban migration, and an improved standard of living have vastly increased water use without corresponding conservation measures.

It was only five years ago that Yemen established the Ministry of Water and the Environment to manage the problem, but so far the ministry has little enforcement authority. Creating a legal system to manage equitably the use of groundwater, as has been done with surface water, is one of the first imperatives. Reverting to traditional yet sustainable methods of agriculture and irrigation in lieu of qat production is another of Yemen's best options. Projects to create a sustainable water supply, even if practical, such as collecting surface runoff, desalination, recharging the alluvial aquifer, and reclaiming wastewater have been slow to develop.

According to journalist Robert Worth, as much as 30 percent of Yemen's water is wasted each year through evaporation and runoff, compared to Europe's 7-to-9 percent. Reducing this waste and returning to rainwater collection are other practical steps. Although there are several water projects underway, changes are currently occurring too slowly to avoid eventual catastrophe.

Qat Production, Trade, and Consumption. The qat industry represents about 10 percent of GDP in Yemen, according to a 2006 survey by the World Bank. Unofficial estimates put the figure as high as 30 percent. The World Bank survey sampled more than 4,000 Yemenis and found that 72 percent of men and 33 percent of women chew the stimulant for an average of six hours per day.

An appetite suppressant, qat compromises health and reduces labor productivity by millions of hours each year. With low-income people spending almost a third of their yearly income on the stimulant, there is little left for a balanced, nutritious diet.

Farmers converted some of Yemen's most fertile farmland to qat production after cheap foreign grains began flooding the market in the 1960s. Organic fertilizers and flood irrigation can yield three big crops of high-quality qat per year, and farmers find an immediate cash market for a plant whose shelf life is only 24–48 hours, selling it locally and to neighbors across the Red Sea. One redeeming factor of the qat production is that it creates sorely needed jobs and immediate income for much-neglected rural areas.

With qat use and cultivation increasing by an estimated 10–15 percent each year, the World Bank in 2008 added to Yemen's country assistance program a three-year grant specifically geared to helping the Government of Yemen mitigate the impact of qat and limit its spread. According to Worth and others, the GOY could also help solve the qat problem by eliminating diesel subsidies, loans, and customs exemptions; refusing to buy large quantities for ritual celebrations; and allowing the importation of qat from Africa in spite of threats from the Yemeni "qat mafia."

Lack of Food Security. UN FAO statistics reveal that from 1995 to 2000, 46 percent of Yemen's children were underweight compared to only 15 percent in the entire region of North Africa and the Middle East. The number of undernourished people rose from 4.2 million in 1990–92 to 7.1 million in 2001–2003.

As of 2008 GOY officials estimated that 40 percent of Yemenis live below the poverty line of $2 per day. A doubling of grain prices and drought over the past two years forced another 6 percent of Yemenis (or 1.2 million) into poverty. In June 2008 the World Bank put Yemen on a priority list for food grant support to address immediate food needs.

FAO data indicate a 45 percent decline in the production of cereals (barley, maize, millet, wheat, sorghum) from 1979 to 2003. Today, domestic production of grains is only 8 percent of total local demand. The country continues to import 75–80 percent of its food, with wheat imports doubling since 2004. Factors contributing to this reduced agricultural output are the water scarcity, a limited arable landmass (just over 3 percent), desertification in some areas, soil erosion, periodic droughts and flooding, qat cultivation in lieu of food production, pollution, overgrazing, a lack of investment in the agricultural sector, and the high cost of credit.

Lower Remittances from Yemenis Working Abroad. Historically, Yemen's economy has depended heavily on money sent home by Yemenis working in other countries. When I lived there in the 1970s, one million out of a population of six million were working abroad and sending funds back to their families. The Central Bank of Yemen estimates that remittances in the 1970s and 1980s were $1 billion to $2 billion per year, but they declined to approximately $1 billion in the 1990s, when remittances from the Gulf States and Saudi Arabia ended completely. Those countries expelled over a million Yemenis because of GOY efforts, while sitting on the UN Security Council, to remain neutral over Iraq's invasion of Kuwait in the first Gulf War.

A World Bank report claims that Yemen received more than $10 billion in remittances between 2000 and 2007, a yearly average of over $1.2 billion, or approximately 7 percent of GDP per year. These remittances, which declined considerably with the global economic crisis in late 2008, came from an estimated 600,000–1,000,000 Yemenis working abroad in over forty countries.

After a nearly twenty-year hiatus, neighboring countries are now actively seeking unemployed Yemenis. Yemen and GCC (Gulf Cooperation Council) countries recently signed an agreement to give certain Yemeni laborers priority in hiring. As of January 2010 thousands of Yemenis had been trained in skills needed in the Gulf States. Sixty institutes in Sanaa, Taiz, and Aden were preparing to train up to 40,000 Yemenis in the first quarter of this year, as spelled out in the agreement. Likewise, Saudi Arabia recently decided to favor Yemeni workers in the construction industry. They are also providing funds to create sixty-nine trade schools in Yemen to help develop a semiskilled workforce.

The GCC held a regional meeting February 22–23, 2010, on Yemeni labor and GCC labor market requirements. Participants recommended establishing a higher council for Yemeni manpower to train, qualify, and market Yemeni labor within the GCC; setting an employment quota for skilled Yemenis working in the GCC; and restructuring the education system at all levels to better train Yemenis for jobs in the Gulf economies.

Decline in Tourism. Tourism to visit Yemen's pristine archeological sites and view its unique architecture was a prime source of income from about 1986 to 2000, according to Marco Livadiotti of Universal Tours. This promising economic resource plummeted after the USS *Cole* incident and post-9/11 terrorist activities in the Middle East. Still, over two million Yemeni citizens work in the industry and have lost work because of the decline.

Tourism took a further hit with many tour cancellations due to the June 2009 murders of three of nine kidnapped foreigners near Saada. As a result, GOY officials estimate Yemen's 2009 tourist industry income was down almost half from the $460 million it earned in 2008. As a precaution against increased attacks on tourists, the Ministry of Interior is providing state security escorts for tourist groups (3,654 of them in 2008) and is equipping all tourist vehicles with GPS tracking devices.

Demographic Factors

Key vital and social statistics about Yemen's population add fuel to a smoldering fire. These demographic factors include a high birthrate, increased life expectancy, a steady rate of urbanization, and high unemployment. High illiteracy and an inadequate education infrastructure for the burgeoning population also provide tinder for the fire.

High Population Growth Rate. The average literacy rate of 50 percent, early marriage age of most women, and the traditional preferences for big families and male heirs are major contributors to Yemen's high birthrate (seven-to-eight children per woman). Since 1970, Yemen's population has more than quadrupled, growing from 5.5 million to more than 23 million today. It continues to grow at more than 3 percent annually and some estimates project it will easily surpass 30 million by 2016 and grow to 40 million over the next two decades.

Increased Life Expectancy. In 1970, average life expectancy was 37 years. Today, despite a high infant mortality rate, life expectancy is said to average 62.5 years for both males and females, an increase that puts further pressure on the social system.

High Unemployment. The current rate of unemployment is estimated at 35-40 percent, with as high as 50 percent among youth aged 15–24. Although the typical Yemeni must support a family of seven on average, 25,000 Yemenis enter the job market each year only to find few if any opportunities in the cities, much less in rural areas, according to the CEIP report. Nor does it help that Yemen has become home to as many as 800,000 refugees (74,000 in 2009 alone) trying to escape the violence in the Horn of Africa and competing for nonexistent jobs. In the meantime, half the population is under sixteen and two-thirds are under age 24, all vulnerable. Jihadism, after all, offers work to unemployed youth, and many have taken up the cause of radical Islam.

Inadequate Education Infrastructure. Over 70 percent of women and 35 percent of men are considered illiterate. The population explosion has contributed to severe overcrowding and too few schools, especially in rural areas (only 16,000 schools for 135,000 communities, according to the CEIP report). Whereas ten years ago government school classrooms might have had an average of 85 students, today they get over 140 pupils. Additional problems that need to be addressed include far too few adequately trained teachers, a tradition of rote memorization, the lack of a standardized, useful curriculum, a proliferation in the past two decades of unregulated conservative religious schools with narrow curricula, and poor access to education for women.

Steady Urbanization. Although Yemen's population is still almost 70 percent rural, there has been a steady growth of urban migration to Sanaa, Taiz, Hodeida, and other cities over the last forty-plus years. Sanaa's population has increased in size from the sleepy town of 80,000 I knew in 1970 to more than two million today and is increasing at the rate of 7 percent a year. Migrants moving to cities to seek opportunity and escape rural poverty have propelled the rise in both underemployment and unemployment. The resultant crowding, poverty, restlessness, and minimal basic services put additional strain on an already overtaxed urban infrastructure.

Domestic Security and Related Issues

Political unrest and insurgency abound on several fronts. These frequently violent tensions are exacerbated by a weak central government, growing opposition to President Ali Abdullah al-Saleh and his rule-by-nepotism, corruption at all levels, decline in political participation and women's rights, and the relatively uncontrolled presence of guns. The security issues include:

– A growing secessionist movement in the South stemming from unresolved unification issues left over from the 1994 civil war;
– A six-year insurrection by Zaydi (Shi'a) tribesmen in the North near Saada;
– Kidnappings and attacks on tourists, foreign workers and facilities, and on locals by both insurgent tribesmen and Islamist extremists;
– The infiltration of outside terrorist groups; and
– Insecure land borders and increased sea piracy off the coast of Yemen.

Weak Central Government. A long-standing tradition of fierce tribalism, the mountainous terrain, and an inadequate road system into the hinterland have always made it difficult for the central government to exercise control outside the major cities. Over the years the GOY has tried to play one tribe off against another, buying influence with key individuals through jobs, payments, or pensions, or exercising control by promises of some sort of economic or other development in the region. This patronage system has been the glue that has held the country together for many years. In the past, lawless behavior by tribes occurred as a means to pressure the central government for something they wanted. Today's lawlessness is more violent due to major sectarian differences, the infiltration of foreign agents, and the radicalization of impoverished young people.

As national resources and hence patronage have diminished, the GOY has consciously been ceding its power to regional and local authorities to handle basic services such as medical care, education, road construction, water, and sanitation. In Yemen, residents of remote, rural areas have traditionally had to fend for themselves, thus making them more vulnerable to outside influences, including terrorist recruitment.

Decline in Participatory Democracy. For a time during the 1980s and after the 1990 unification, President Saleh moved Yemen toward greater democracy. The new unity constitution had provided for leadership sharing on a 50-50 basis between North and South. However, the 1994 civil war put an end to this balance of power and jeopardized democratic trends, with the North solidifying its control over the financial and leadership sectors of the new republic. Saleh changed the constitution, claiming increased military and security powers for himself and his family members.

Parliamentary elections were held in 1993, 1997, and 2003. Candidates of Saleh's ruling party, the General People's Congress (GPC), received 58 percent of the vote in 2003, up from 43 percent in 1997. The GPC's increased margin, way up from the early nineties when many political parties threw their hats into the ring, indicates a decline in political participation or possibly fraud at the ballot box.

To counter this trend and the inequities in the 2006 presidential election, the European Union pledged over five million euros in support of electoral reform in the run-up to the spring 2009 elections for the 301-seat parliament. However, the elections were postponed until April 2011, due to pressure from the opposition alliance, because the electoral reforms had not been enacted by early 2009.

Opposition to President Saleh. President Saleh faces greater opposition today than ever in his thirty years of leadership. One of the longest-ruling Arab leaders, Ali Abdullah al-Saleh came from the military and rose to power in Northern Yemen (YAR) in 1978, only six years after we left the country. His two immediate predecessors had been assassinated in quick succession. He assumed the presidency of unified Yemen (ROY) in 1990. The new constitution makes him ineligible to seek another term in 2013, and many believe he is grooming his son Ahmad, who heads both the elite Special Forces and the Republican Guard, to assume the reins of the GPC.

In the 1999 presidential election, Saleh received 96.3 percent of the vote amid claims of fraud. Seven years later, when he received only 77 percent of the vote, he encountered his first serious challenge, from Faisal bin Shamlan, candidate from the Joint Meetings Party (JMP).

Although EU election observers initially viewed that 2006 presidential election as fair and open, they subsequently pointed out flaws in the system. These included unfair use of state resources and obvious bias in the state media, the pervasive exclusion of female participants, detention of opposition supporters, and lack of credibility in the counting process.

In the wake of the many challenges facing the country, Saleh is walking a tightrope. Faced with growing opposition, he must make needed reforms with few resources. He must appease his internal critics, many of whom are vehemently anti-American and have major grievances of their own, and his foreign donors, upon whose financial aid he depends.

Corruption. High unemployment and low wages, among other factors, contribute to the corruption that seems to exist at all levels. Several Yemenis and former American residents of Yemen told me that paying bribes to government officials to get things done is an accepted way of life, something that was not obvious to me in the 1970s.

Khadija al-Salami, an American-educated Yemeni woman in her early forties, is a writer, a diplomat (at the Embassy of Yemen in Paris), and Yemen's first female filmmaker, with twenty television documentaries and a book to her credit. She disclosed to me in a 2007 phone interview that a highly paid cabinet minister makes only about $550 per month, not enough to sufficiently support the typical large, extended family. Lower-wage Yemenis must also find creative means to make ends meet.

Since 2005, Yemen has signed the UN Convention Against Corruption (UNCAC), along with over 137 other nations. The convention uses an index that measures "corruption and lack of transparency in the civil society." Positive perceptions of Yemen's efforts are declining: When compared to approximately 180 other countries, Yemen was ranked 111th on the corruption perception index (CPI) in 2006, 131st in 2007, and 141st in 2008. Although President Saleh has reportedly made noticeable efforts in setting up some monitoring structures to regulate in this area, the GOY must become more transparent in such indicators as public expenditures, the judiciary, education, and access to information.

Limited Rights for Women. Yemeni women were guaranteed the right to vote in the unification constitution written in the early nineties. Even this must have felt like a setback for southern Yemeni women, who had been liberated under the PDRY communist regime in the 1970s. According to Dr. Jon Mandaville, professor of Middle East history and politics at Portland State University, women in the PDRY had more access to schools and public jobs than women in any other Arab country in the Middle East.

Marta Paluch writes that in the first parliamentary elections in 1993, of the more than four thousand candidates forty-two were women, and two were elected. In 1997 seventeen women sought office, and again two were elected. By 2003, only seven ran for parliament, and one was elected. Despite the declining numbers running for office, women hold on average 11 percent of all the high-level leadership positions in the political parties, including 60 percent of the Islah party and 32 percent of the General People's Congress (GPC), according to a September 2008 Women's National Committee report.

Other sources report that in recent years eight women were appointed deputy ministers, and several were elected at the local council level (38 women compared to 7,594 men). A small 6-to-9 percent of women are judges in various courts of the judicial system, inasmuch as women were only allowed to study at the high judicial institute beginning in 2006.

Social attitudes toward women have become more circumscribed over the past two decades, thus limiting their political participation. Khadija al-Salami blames this on social pressure from the still largely tribal society. Social pressure, not legal prescription, now forces the large majority of women to veil in all sectors of society.

Family law, as well, continues to be discriminatory against women. For example, a male relative must accompany a woman out in public or she is subject to arrest. Although a bill to ban marriage of women below age 17 is currently being debated in parliament, it is meeting strong resistance from the religious community. Thus, with no minimum age requirements for marriage, women are often married off prior to puberty, putting their health and lives at risk with teenage pregnancies.

Despite this social pressure, women have increased their visibility considerably in recent years. So far, however, none have achieved leadership positions of real power, according to Dr. Raufa al-Hassan al-Sharki. With a Ph.D. from the Sorbonne, Dr. al-Sharki is a professor of mass media and director of the Women's Studies Center at Sanaa University. In a summer 2007 phone interview, she reported there were two women—out of thirty appointments—serving as cabinet ministers—in human rights and social affairs. One woman sat on the president's consultative council, and several held ambassadorial rank, though at that time only one was serving abroad, as ambassador to Turkey.

Journalists Nicholas Kristof and Sheryl WuDunn state that women represent just 6 percent of the nonagricultural workforce in Yemen today. However, the numbers of women attending school and working outside the home, at least in the cities, have increased since my time there in the early 1970s. Whatever the numbers, current pressures on women, many of whom must support their families, only add to the mounting dissidence throughout the country.

Fawzia, an engineer, works on black box at Yemen Airlines, 1997 (photo by Peggy Crawford)

Limited Control over the Presence of Guns. Estimates from several sources regarding the number of guns in Yemen vary from a high of sixty to eighty million (three or four per person) to a lower figure of sixty-one gun owners per 100 people. Derek Miller did as close to a scientific study as possible in 2003 and concluded that, contrary to public perception, there are only 7-to-10 million guns total in Yemen, or 40-to-50 guns per 100 people. This figure is about half the rate in the United States. However, with weak government control in much of the country, continued smuggling by arms merchants, and the infiltration of foreign agents since the 2003 study, these figures may have greatly increased.

The male population of Yemen has long carried guns as an emblem of manhood, and used them ceremonially and for jubilant greetings, not for violence. Recent attempts by the government to curb the use of illegal weapons, including the outlawing of small arms, have met with modest success. However, the two groups Saleh is most concerned with—the al-Houthi rebels in the north and the discontented southerners—have managed to accumulate sizeable stores of arms, probably through smuggling or by theft from the Yemeni military.

Secessionist Movement in the South. The 1990 unification between North and South more than doubled the geography of Yemen and added two million South Yemenis to the North's then 11–12 million. Their divergent recent histories might make some think it a miracle this unification occurred at all, given North Yemen's millennium of isolation under theocratic rule prior to 1962 and South Yemen's experience with the British protectorate of Aden for 130 years before turning toward communism.

Southern grievances surrounding the violent three-month civil war in 1994 included political graft and corruption by northern officials, lack of jobs and leadership roles for southerners, the confiscation of their land and property, and the imposition by Islamic fundamentalists of restrictions on women. Southerners also resented the north's police, army, and security officers as, in Ambassador Newton's term, "carpetbaggers." Hundreds of southern officers, soldiers, and civil servants were forcibly retired and pensions cut off following the south's defeat in the civil war.

Opposition groups in the south, formed around these unresolved issues, united against President Saleh in the aftermath of
September 11, 2001, when the United States was pressuring Yemen
for help in the war on terror. This opposition coalition grew to include the disaffected soldiers, striking teachers, hospital workers,
and labor unionists, among others, and began in summer 2007 to
stage regular, large, mostly peaceful, protests about their long-
standing grievances.

Largely unreported in the Western press, President Saleh's security forces have used intimidation and harassment, including
numerous arrests and even rocket attacks, against opponents such
as local newspaper editors and foreign journalists trying to cover
the protests. Independent newspapers have been shut down and
several opposition leaders killed. According to Robert Worth, as
of February 2010, more than a hundred people had been killed in
armed clashes with security police, and as many as fifteen hundred
members of the opposition remained in prison. The GOY has been
accused of torture and murder for something as seemingly innocu-
ous as playing a song on a car stereo in support of the "Southern (or
Southern Mobility) Movement," as many now call it.

The movement has no clear manifesto but is organizing its dis-
parate groups behind the leadership of Ali Salem al-Bidh, the ex-
Marxist who led the South between 1990 and 1994 and has since
been in exile in Europe. Tareq al-Fadhli, an Islamic tribal sheikh
whose wealthy family left the South after the communist take-over
in 1970, is an "Arab-Afghan" jihadist, the appellation given to Arabs who fought with bin Laden against the Russians in the 1980s.
He is also related by marriage to President Saleh and was an ally
of the GOY during the 1994 civil war. But now, frustrated by GOY
failure to redress southern grievances, al-Fadhli is aiding al-Bidh,
his former rival during the civil war.

Tensions in the south are near the breaking point. Clashes
between the splintered Southern Movement's separatist arm and
GOY security forces have become frequent and deadly. To celebrate
the twentieth anniversary of unified Yemen on May 22, 2010,
President Saleh announced a general amnesty of both al-Houthi
rebels in the north and southern secessionists and has released
some of both groups. But many remain in jail. Despite offering

various concessions in an effort to pacify the situation, Saleh's heavy-handedness with protesters appears only to have increased discontent throughout the southern provinces.

The Insurrection in Saada. The GOY has been embroiled since 2004 with a major insurgency of fundamentalist tribesmen around Saada, in the north near the Saudi border. Since their Zaydi (Shi'a) cleric was killed that year, hundreds of Yemenis on both sides have lost their lives in the subsequent fighting, for which the government blames rebel leader (and brother of the slain cleric) Abdul Malek al-Houthi. Amidst tribal feuds, open hostilities, and sporadic cease-fires, Saada province appears to many to have become a battlefield for outside forces seeking to gain a foothold in Yemen.

A fragile truce reached in mid-2008 with the promise of a major Saada reconstruction program made slow progress and broke into outright war again in August 2009. Heavy bombing by the GOY military killed many civilians and left refugees unable to access humanitarian aid. Somewhere between 180,000 and 300,000 have been forced to flee their homes since 2004.

Unable to end this rebellion by far-outnumbered tribesmen, Saleh in November 2009 welcomed Saudi entry into the war to put a stop to rebel incursions across their border. For three months the Saudis conducted air strikes and engaged in ground hostilities in which over a hundred Saudi soldiers were killed. Under pressure from donors at the January 2010 London conference, the GOY gave the rebels a timetable to implement a six-point truce to end the war. As part of the truce, by early April 2010, 170 Yemeni and several Saudi government captives and over 50 al-Houthi rebels had been released to their respective sides. In late June 2010, the rebels claimed Saleh had reneged on his promise of amnesty for all imprisoned al-Houthi fighters. Not long afterward, several clashes resulted in the killing of a number of GOY soldiers and rebels. Displaced civilians feared returning to their homes because of the prevalence of landmines and the fragility of the truce.

Porous Borders and Increased Piracy. The land borders are difficult to patrol in the mountains to the north and in the vast desert of the Empty Quarter to the east. As Saudi Arabia and the Gulf States have stepped up internal antiterrorism campaigns, militants have sought refuge in Yemen. Saudis have captured militants entering their country from Yemen. Border clashes between the Saudi military and insurgents operating in Yemen, separate from conflicts with the al-Houthi rebels, are likely to continue.

A return of sea piracy in the Gulf of Aden is plaguing international shipping after a period of relative calm. Al-Qaeda's central leadership announced in April 2008 its goal of establishing naval terror cells and gaining control of the seas around Yemen, where three million barrels of oil pass every day and 25,000 merchant ships each year. Somali pirates who operate in these waters claim they are just trying to protect their seas from illegal fishing.

Yemeni fishermen in their small dhows have been caught between the Somali pirates, who use them as human shields in their attacks on shipping vessels, and the international patrols who mistake them for pirates. Although fish have been Yemen's second largest export next to oil, the piracy has caused a large decline in revenue, as Yemeni fishermen are fearful. Pirates abducted 815 Yemeni fishermen, most of whom were later released, in 72 incidents against fishermen in 2008 and during the first four months of 2009, according to the World Bank office in Sanaa. A small number have been killed.

To help limit piracy and smuggling of humans, drugs, and arms, the GOY recently established a regional antipiracy center. The government also put on trial twenty Somalis accused of piracy who had been turned over to them by international naval forces patrolling the Gulf of Aden. In 2009 Yemen received a four-phase loan from the Italian government to launch radar stations on all of its coasts, with the first in the Gulf of Aden. Also, last year the United States provided $30 million in aid for coast guard patrol and maritime security to combat piracy, and another $25 million for land border security.

Islamist Militants and International Terrorism. Militant jihadists (*mujahidin*) who had left South Yemen after the communists came to power in 1970 trained in Afghanistan to fight the Soviets. Encouraged to return to Yemen beginning in the late 1980s, many of these Islamists (also referred to as "Arab-Afghan fighters") were recruited into the Yemeni security forces and have fought alongside the GOY military against domestic insurgencies in both the south and the north. Other returning Yemeni militants, two thousand of whom fought in Iraq against the United States, along with an influx of foreign jihadists who tend to follow rigid Salafist ideologies have helped to radicalize new and younger Yemeni recruits. According to journalist Victoria Clark, the militants who fought in Iraq represent a third generation of jihadists who are unwilling to make deals with President Saleh as the earlier returnees did.

"Friendly" kidnappings of tourists by tribesmen in the past twenty or so years— as a way to pressure the central government— have taken a back seat to recent deadly attacks by terrorists. Beginning with the 1998 murder of four tourists during a kidnapping near Aden, other fatal attacks on tourists have occurred, especially in the last three years.

Before the June 2009 kidnapping and murder of three foreign healthcare workers near Saada, attacks in Yemen since July 2007 have included several suicide bombings at Marib and in the Hadramawt, in which more than fifteen foreign tourists were killed. At the U.S. Embassy in Sanaa, sixteen people were killed in September 2008, including six suicide bombers. There have also been car bombings, rocket and mortar attacks on both Yemeni and Western targets, and the blowing up of oil and gas pipelines. The Yemen Soldiers Brigades [sic] of al-Qaeda in the Arabian Peninsula (AQAP) has claimed responsibility for most of these. Estimates of the number of al-Qaeda operatives currently in the country range from a few hundred to as many as 1,000–1,500.

Said Ali al-Shihri, a Saudi and the probable instigator of the U.S. Embassy suicide bombing in Sanaa as well as the Saada kidnappings and murders, remains on the loose in Yemen along with other al-Qaeda leaders. Released by the United States to the Saudis from detention at Guantánamo in 2007, al-Shihri made his way to Yemen after participating in a Saudi rehabilitation program for jihadists. He was identified as the new deputy leader of al-Qaeda in Yemen when he and three other al-Qaeda members (including bin Laden's private secretary for six years, Nasser al-Wuhayshi, AQAPs leader, and Qasim al-Raymi, its military commander) announced in January 2009 that Yemen is now its base of operations for the entire Arabian Peninsula.

The Saudis have also released other suspected al-Qaeda operatives and allegedly encouraged them to migrate to Yemen to avert trouble in their own country. Should the approximately ninety-five Yemenis currently housed in Guantánamo be released to Saudi Arabia for "rehabilitation," there is grave concern these individuals could eventually end up back in Yemen working for AQAP.

Since 9/11, the Yemen government has generally cooperated with the United States and other Western countries to fight terrorism—capturing, bringing to trial, and even executing some of the convicted. Despite these positive signs of support, in recent years the GOY has been lax in its treatment of suspected terrorists in several instances. These include suspicious jail breaks of convicted al-Qaeda fighters (e.g., twenty-three from Saana's main jail in 2006 that included al-Wuhayshi and al-Raymi), the release of an al-Qaeda member convicted in the USS *Cole* attack, and the release of more than 170 men suspected of al-Qaeda ties in 2009. Several sources believe there was a tacit nonaggression agreement between the GOY and AQAP and suggest that those released were supposed to help the GOY put down the Saada and southern insurgencies.

In a July 2010 cover story for the *New York Times Magazine*, Robert Worth assessed al-Qaeda strength in Yemen and questioned whether Yemen will be the next Afghanistan. He discusses President Saleh's failed attempts to rein in or make compromises with the younger generation of al-Qaeda, whose goals are to overthrow both the Yemeni and Saudi regimes and create a single theocratic state. AQAP has set itself up in several remote provinces, often protected by tribes that distrust the government, and has used the insurgencies in the south and north to promote its own agenda. These young *mujahidin* have developed an increasingly sophisticated propaganda arm that includes slick Internet magazines in both Arabic and English. Worth states that American policy seeks to use "air strikes and raids to help the Yemeni military knock out al-Qaeda cells, while increasing development and humanitarian aid to address the root causes of radicalism." However, many American officials have told him there is no clear strategy in Yemen, partly because so few have any real expertise about the country.

Solutions to Yemen's Problems

Increased Development Aid. To meet the overwhelming challenges facing this impoverished country strategically located between the Arabian Peninsula and the Horn of Africa, the Government of Yemen needs a major injection of carefully coordinated international and regional assistance. Acknowledging Yemen's critical importance to regional security, foreign governments have been upping their development aid. Saudi Arabia and the Gulf States have provided the largest amount of assistance, including frequent direct budgetary support to the GOY by the Saudis.

In the midst of an aggressive reform effort to stamp out corruption and increase the independence of the judiciary, in November 2006 President Saleh managed to secure approximately $5.5 billion in pledges of development aid at the World Bank–sponsored international donor conference. Coming primarily from the United Kingdom and the Gulf States (GCC), the aid is scheduled to run through 2010.

However, only 58 percent of the aid pledged in 2006 had been released to Yemeni authorities by early 2010, and Yemen had used only 10–20 percent of it on aid projects. The problem of how to spend billions in Yemen was a primary topic at the February 27–28, 2010, donor meeting in Riyadh. The GCC and other donors recognize Yemen's limited capacity for handling large amounts of foreign aid and are seeking solutions to the aid disbursement problem, such as bringing in outside experts to implement particular projects. This donor meeting discussed Yemen's 2011–2015 economic development plan and prospects for donor aid. In addition, Saudi officials met separately with Yemeni representatives on providing $115 million in loans to finance projects in hospital construction, electricity, education, and sanitary drainage.

Compared to others offering aid to Yemen, the United States has been a small donor in recent years, having averaged only $20 million–$25 million annually through 2008, a year in which no U.S. aid was given. Although the United States provided funds for counterterrorism and security training after 9/11, its USAID Millennium Challenge Grants were contingent upon Yemen's meeting certain governance benchmarks. In 2009, Yemen failed thirteen of seventeen governance benchmarks as compared to other eligible recipients in three policy areas (ruling justly, investing in people, and economic freedom).

Despite this failure, the United States in 2009 gave Yemen nearly $70 million in counterterrorism and development aid. This was more than double the three previous years combined. The Congressional Research Service reports that for fiscal 2010 the United States has pledged through the State Department $52.5 million in development and economic assistance to Yemen. Moreover, the Pentagon approved $150 million for 2010 to help train and equip Yemen's security forces, an amount separate from the increased covert U.S. military and intelligence aid being given to help Yemen fight AQAP.

Strengthening Governance and Capacity Building. Most observers agree not only that bolstering Yemen is critical for regional as well as world security, but also that a long-term commitment to development, good governance, and state building is necessary. Given Yemen's importance to U.S. national security, Boucek recommends, in his September 2009 report for the Carnegie Endowment for International Peace (CEIP), that the United States increase its assistance for development, education, and technical cooperation. He also urges capacity building (especially in law enforcement and in the legal and judicial system), institution strengthening, and direct financial assistance.

Other analysts recommend that donors need to help the GOY with English language instruction, teacher training, microfinance programs, and exchange programs for judges, parliament members, journalists, government workers, and academics. Funding ongoing as well as new projects that support water management, diversification of agriculture, reducing Yemen's subsidies on diesel fuel, and securing Yemen's borders are other stabilizing actions needed.

Regional Assistance and the GCC. In addition to major development aid the Gulf States have already offered, bringing Yemen into the GCC fold would help to integrate this poor country into the life of its oil-rich neighbors and facilitate work for unemployed Yemenis. Although Yemen has long sought membership in the GCC, GOY instability, increased terrorist activity instigated from inside Yemen, and the fact that Yemen's population exceeds that of all the Arabian peninsula countries combined poses risks to wary GCC members. Boucek maintains that the GCC should make Yemen's membership contingent on curbing GOY subsidies, reducing corruption, and tightening security.

Minimizing al-Qaeda's Influence and Improving Regional Security. In the aftermath of the aborted December 2009 AQAP-supported airliner attack, Dr. Emile Nakhleh, a Middle East intelligence specialist, testified before the Senate Foreign Relations Committee on January 20, 2010, about the terrorist threat in Yemen. He is adamant that the United States refrain from engaging al-Qaeda in this new arena, because any military escalation of the war on terror there would play right into al-Qaeda's hands. He urges continued counterterrorism efforts to target and neutralize al-Qaeda leaders, operations, and training camps in Yemen and elsewhere. Also needed is a long-term commitment to engaging broader, non-radical Muslim communities, such as in Turkey and Indonesia and the Islah party in Yemen, to de-legitimize the messages of Islamic extremists.

British prime minister Gordon Brown also heeded the alarm and called a summit meeting on Yemen, which convened in London on January 27, 2010. Representatives from the UK, the United States, the Gulf States, the EU, the UN, the World Bank, and the IMF (twenty entities in all) met to garner support for Yemen amid fears the country was becoming a haven for terrorists. The summit called for increased support from the GCC and Yemen's neighbors and for Yemen to pursue needed reforms, including working with the IMF. Several follow-up meetings to this summit geared toward implementing some of the summit's recommendations have been held in the Gulf States.

Resolving the two insurrections, which are an enormous drain on Yemen's limited resources, should improve GOY stability. Stephen Day in the CEIP series of March 2010 urges a political solution in the South that "addresses the unresolved problems from the country's poorly executed unification in the early 1990s." Military reprisal against the secessionist Southern Movement will further anger the southerners and increase support for AQAP. He recommends involvement by Arab leaders to negotiate a settlement. Likewise, the six-point truce between the GOY and the al-Houthi rebels in the north will presumably, with foreign pressure, lead to a redress of northern grievances and defuse tribal animosity toward the government.

Writing in 2010, two authors believe complex cultural, historical, and tribal considerations might preclude AQAP from having an easy time bringing Yemen under its influence. Sarah Phillips in the March 2010 CEIP series maintains there are tribal mechanisms that govern locally in the absence of "formal state control" and that AQAP's push for an Islamic state with a strict religious ideology as well as its penchant for violence against civilians conflicts with local norms and could weaken AQAP's appeal to the Yemeni people and tribes. If Yemen's political system can become less centralized and more inclusive and find political rather than military solutions to its internal conflicts, Phillips sees hope for avoiding undue AQAP influence or control and improving the country's stability.

Victoria Clark (*Yemen*, 2010) cites regional counters to jihadist and AQAP influence. The Zaydi al-Houthi rebels in Saada are vehemently opposed to the Salafism and Wahhabism of militant jihadists. The Hadramis in the south have a strong Sufi tradition as well as "close and profitable" ties with Hadramis who have emigrated to Saudi Arabia, the Gulf States, and Asia or have returned to Yemen. And tribes in Yemen value land and money over ideology or religion. Growing opposition to President Saleh and long-standing northern domination over the south (where Yemen's remaining oil and new LNG plant reside) are the primary uniting forces that might prevent Yemen's fragmentation in the face of economic hardship. Western governments should be careful not to prop up the GOY regime with weapons that could be used against Yemenis opposed to Saleh rather than against AQAP jihadists. Unlike Pakistan and Afghanistan, Yemen is fortunate to be surrounded by wealthy Gulf neighbors who have no desire to see Yemen disintegrate into an al-Qaeda-dominated Islamic state.

With the economic, demographic, domestic security, and leadership crises all coming to a head in the next few years, Yemen is extremely fragile. Increasingly, observers believe the country is deteriorating, some say "collapsing," and could fail. Two years ago, in early 2008, Stephen Day stated: "Yemen has declined from its status among the world's poor developing countries in the 1970s to a level today where it ranks among the deeply impoverished, teetering on the verge of collapse." He states that Yemen could "become a 'failed state,' more like Somalia than its wealthy neighbors on the Arabian Peninsula."

Subsequent observers agree. *Foreign Policy* magazine and the Fund for Peace put Yemen in eighteenth place, just behind North Korea, on their 2009 index of failed states, stating that Yemen is "in danger" but not yet "critical." The year 2010 could well find Yemen in a much higher place on the index.

To counter this downward spiral, analysts believe foreign donors must remain vigilant and committed to addressing Yemen's strategic importance to world stability. They must address the need to prevent the chaos associated with a fragile, failing state from spreading throughout the Arabian Peninsula, the Middle East, and beyond. In return, it is essential that Yemen follow recommendations growing out of the January 2010 London summit and subsequent GCC/donor meetings to meet the challenges outlined here and prevent the country's further descent. Strong leadership by Saleh or his successor and the development of a solid, noncorrupt government infrastructure will also be required to head off the volatile future that could lie ahead for Yemen.

CHRONOLOGY OF YEMEN'S HISTORY

Pre-Islamic Period/Before the Common Era (BCE)

5000 BCE	First village settlements in Yemeni highlands. Descendants of Noah's first son, Shem, and another son, Ya'rub, grandfather of Saba, reputedly settle in Yemen. When Egyptian pharaohs wanted to embalm the dead, Yemen's spice trade began. Initially, goods were carried out by donkeys, then by domesticated camels beginning about 1500 BCE.
1200 BCE	First urban settlements on the edge of the eastern deserts, including Marib.
12ᵗʰ Century BCE to 6ᵗʰ Century CE	Yemen dominated by six successive civilizations—Saba, Ma'in, Awsan, Qataban, Hadramawt, and Himyar—that rival or ally with each other and control the large caravans (as many as 2,000–3,000 camels each) in the lucrative spice trade.
900s BCE	Reign of Sabaen Queen Bilqis, the legendary Queen of Sheba (Saba), who, according to the Bible and the Qur'an, traveled north to meet Solomon, King of Israel (who ruled 970–932 BCE). Sabaens also colonized Abyssinia (Ethiopia).
c. 700 BCE	Sabaens build Awwam Temple (to moon god Ilmuqah) in Marib.

715 BCE	Diplomatic relations with the Assyrians are first documented.
c. 715–600 BCE	Dam at Marib is built by Sabaens over many years. Marib becomes their capital city.
c. 500 BCE	Era of great prosperity in Saba and construction of fine monuments.
c. 400s BCE	Ma'in and southern kingdoms of Qataban, Hadramawt, and Awsan ally against the Sabaens and eventually gain their independence.
450 BCE	Marib dam breaks for second time, but later is repaired.
25–24 BCE	Aelius Gallus, Roman general, leads 10,000 men down the Red Sea and attempts first foreign invasion. They fail to reach Marib due to shortage of water, malaria, and local sabotage.

Pre-Islamic Period/Common Era 50 CE–575 CE

50	Dhamar 'Ali Sharih rules Yemen.
c.100–200	Sanaa becomes center of inland trade route, a royal city, and a joint capital (with Marib) of the Sabaean federation.
200	Aksumites of Ethiopia (Abyssinia) invade Yemen, the second foreigners to do so. They control Tihama through 3rd century but do not reach Marib.
210-250	Great Ghumdan palace for Sabaen kings is constructed in Sanaa. The prototype for Sanaa's tower houses, the site is now a mound of ruins.
c. 275	The Himyars eclipse and annex Saba. The Himyar kings convert first to Christianity, then to Judaism, supplanting polytheism with monotheism. Zafar becomes alternative royal residence after 300 CE.

342	Byzantine Emperor Constantine sends an ambassadorial mission to Yemen, creating an alliance against the Persians. Seeks to convert Yemenis to Christianity and to erect churches.
520	Dhu Nuwas (Jewish Himyar king) leads 120,000 soldiers to massacre Christians at Najran Oasis (between Saada and Mecca).
525	Aksumite Kingdom from Abyssinia (Ethiopia) invades Yemen, at request of Emperor Justinian, due to the persecution of Christians.
537	Abraha, Aksumite general, seizes the Himyarite throne and, with help of Justinian, constructs al-Qalis cathedral, largest Christian building south of the Mediterranean, rivaling the sanctuary of the Kaaba in Mecca
570	Muhammad the Prophet is born in Mecca. Abraha and his army set out for Mecca, taking an elephant with them. Marib dam breaks for the third and final time, triggering a large emigration of Yemeni tribes.
575	Sassanian Persian forces, at request of Himyarite princes, finally expel the Aksumites, but fail in their efforts to rule all of Yemen.

Islamic Period 610–1517 CE

610	The Qur'an is first revealed to Muhammad by God, and Islam is born.
622–630	*Hijrah* (pilgrimage/escape) from Mecca to Medina establishes Islamic community and expands into Yemen during Prophet's lifetime.
632	Death of the Prophet Muhammad; first caliph Abu Bakr becomes the successor and resides in Medina.

634	Army of 18,000 Muslims crosses the Euphrates and forcibly converts Christian tribes to Islam. Many Yemenis are in this army.
638	Although Sassanian governor of Yemen accepted Islam in 628, the Persians were forced to leave Yemen when defeated by Muslim troops.
640	Yemenis rebel against Mecca and Islam but are defeated by 645 and after are ruled for many years by governors appointed by caliphs (successors) in Damascus or Baghdad.
644	The 2nd caliph Umar is assassinated by an angry Persian prisoner of war.
656	Disgruntled Muslim soldiers, followers of 'Ali (Alids), assassinate the 3rd caliph Uthman, installing 'Ali as the 4th caliph, which leads to a 5-year civil war.
661	An extremist of the Kharajite splinter group assassinates 'Ali. The 5th caliph Muawiyyah founds the Umayyad dynasty, rules till 680, moves the seat of Islam from Medina to Damascus, and restores unity. He is succeeded by his son Yazid, who dies in 683 CE.
680	Ali's son Hussein leads his family and a small band of followers from Medina to Iraq and is massacred at Karbala by Yazid's army of Umayyad supporters. This establishes the Shi'a-Sunni split in Islam. Shi'as are followers of Hussein, the grandson of the Prophet.
711	Muslim troops, including 20,000 Yemenis, arrive in Spain, North Africa, and China in the expansion out of Arabia. Advance stopped in 732.
740	Zayid ibn 'Ali, great grandson of 'Ali, the 4th caliph, rebels against the Umayyad caliphs of Damascus but is killed at Kufa. His successors establish their own line called Zaydis within the larger Shi'a group.

750	Abbasids (also Sunnis) stage coup and kill all Umayyad family members and prominent Shi'as to take control and move seat of caliphate by 762 from Damascus to Baghdad, where they create a flourishing intellectual and cultural center.
847	Bani Yu'fir establishes the first independent Yemeni Muslim dynasty, which rules from Sanaa until 1004 CE.
c. 892–897	Yemen separates from the Abbasid caliphate when the Zaydi sect reaches Saada, Yemen, led by Imam Yahya ibn al-Hussein al-Hadi ila 'l Haqq, who becomes first Zaydi imam in 901 and head of the first of four Zaydi dynasties.
c. 922–952	An Iraqi Ahmad ibn 'Isa establishes Shafi'i (Sunni-style) Islam in the southern Hadramawt part of Yemen.
c.1038–1047	Conquest of Sanaa by Sulayhids of Zabid, who follow the Ismaili sect, an exotic offshoot of Sh'ia Islam.
1086–1138	Reign of the famous Sulayhid Queen Arwa, known as the younger Bilqis, from Jibla. She builds a mosque and improves lives of her subjects.
1138–1585	2nd Zaydi dynasty established under Ahmad ibn Sulayman, ruling from Saada, Sanaa, and northern provinces.
1173–1229	Yemen falls under the influence of the Egyptian Ayyubids when Saladin's brothers annex Yemen.
1189	Ayyubids establish themselves in Sanaa, but are later forced to Taiz.
1228	The Rasulid dynasty rules Yemen with Taiz as its capital and considers Sanaa a fiefdom, although Sanaa is periodically visited or occupied by the Zaydi imam.

1323	Zaydis assume control of Sanaa once and for all, pushing out the Rasulids, and eventually establishing control over Yemen's mountainous interior.

Ottoman Period: 1517 CE–1918 CE

1517	Ottomans absorb part of Yemen into their empire, mainly Aden and Lahij. Sanaa and the rest of Yemen continue to be ruled by Zaydi dynasty.
1527	Sanaa suffers a severe plague that takes over 11,000 lives.
1547	Ottoman Turks sack Sanaa, conquering it and killing 1,200 people after a gatekeeper betrays his fellow Sanaanis.
1597–1635	Zaydi imam, Qasim the Great, and his son Hassan challenge Ottomans and finally expel them from Yemen for the first time.
1600s	Coffee becomes the most important export of the busy trading seaport at Mocha. The British, Dutch, French, Venetians, and Egyptians set up operations and consulates on the Red Sea Coast after 1618. Coffee plants are exported to Indonesia, Brazil, and later Jamaica by early 1700s, ending Yemen's monopoly of the coffee trade.
1635–1872	Third Zaydi dynasty under Hassan ibn al-Qasim rules Yemen after Ottoman troops leave in 1635.
1839	British capture Aden seaport to serve as a major refueling station and begin making alliances and treaties in Aden hinterland and Hadramawt. Area becomes known as the Aden Protectorate, continuing until 1967.

1849	Ottomans move back into Yemen along the Red Sea coast. They send a garrison to Sanaa of 1,000 soldiers, who are slaughtered and forced to retreat. Anarchy reigns in Sanaa due to Turkish reprisals against the imam and havoc created by competing tribal groups.
1869	Suez Canal opens, increasing the importance of Aden.
1872	Ottomans occupy the north of Yemen, taking Sanaa as their capital, but face revolt from Hamid al-Din imam and his son Yahya and their followers based in mountains.
1904	Treaty between Ottomans and British establishes a de facto border between North and South Yemen. Zaydi tribes go into full rebellion against both enemies under leadership of Imam Yahya of the Hamid al-Din family, who begins the 4th Zaydi dynasty.
1911	Accord between Yahya and the Ottomans brings peace.

Modern History 1918 CE–Present

1918	Ottoman empire dissolves and leaves Yemen for the second time. North Yemen gains independence and is ruled by Imam Yahya.
1924	Turkey abolishes the caliphate. Subsequently, Muslims struggle to identify religious leaders who follow the traditions of the Prophet, as seen with the Muslim Brotherhood, founded in Egypt in 1928.
1931	Campaign to bring eastern Yemeni tribes under the imam.

1934	Yemen engages in war with Saudi Arabia, but is quickly defeated. Ibn Saud makes treaty with Imam Yahya that demarcates the common frontier, less favorably than Yahya would have liked.
1945	Yemen joins the Arab league and the UN in 1947.
1948	Imam Yahya is assassinated, and son Ahmad succeeds his father.
1950s	Imam Ahmad puts down army mutiny in 1955 and escapes several assassination attempts. He ruthlessly pursues his enemies.
1958	Prince Badr joins with Syria and Egypt in the short-lived United Arab States while his father, the imam, is away in Italy for medical treatment.
1962	Imam Ahmad dies, and son Badr is overthrown five days later by army officers. This republican revolution sets up the Yemen Arab Republic and triggers civil war between royalists backed by Saudi Arabia and republicans backed by Egypt.
1967	British withdraw from Aden, granting independence. Jockeying for power ensues, with the communist People's Democratic Republic of Yemen gaining control in 1970.
1970	The Jidda Agreement settles the civil war in North Yemen, allowing the country to be governed by both Sunni and Shi'a republicans.
1990	Unification of North (YAR) and South (PDRY) Yemen into the Republic of Yemen (ROY), with the YAR's al-Saleh becoming president.
1994	Civil war between North Yemen and rebel parts in the South, with North winning and assuming greater leadership and security control.

2000	The USS *Cole* is bombed in Aden's harbor by al-Qaeda, killing seventeen Americans.
2002	Al-Qaeda attacks French tanker *Limburg* off the Yemeni coast.
2004–10	Shi'a militants (followers of al-Houthi) rebel in the northwest of Yemen around Saada, with sporadic uprisings and killings, ending in a fragile truce in 2008.
2006–08	Mass protests occur in the south against long-standing grievances left over from the 1994 civil war; al-Qaeda-affiliated suicide bombers kill foreign tourists at Marib and in the Hadramawt and attack other Western properties.
2008	Global food crisis puts Yemeni poor at risk of starvation, and the World Bank pledges to put Yemen on a priority list for food aid.
2008	Suicide bombing at U.S. Embassy in Sanaa kills 16 people. Al-Qaeda claims responsibility.
2009	Al-Qaeda in the Arabian Peninsula (AQAP) sets up headquarters in Yemen; nine foreign aid workers are kidnapped and three killed near Saada in June; al-Houthi rebels in Saada and the Yemeni military break their fragile truce, with air attacks and ground battles forcing over 200,000 to flee their homes; the Southern Movement chooses two leaders and gains momentum as demonstrations become more violent; a Nigerian trained by AQAP in Yemen fails in his attempt to blow up a Northwest Airliner over U.S. soil on Christmas day.
2010	The UK hosts a summit in January to gather support for Yemen from its Gulf neighbors and world donors because of fears the country is becoming a haven for terrorists. Participants map out reforms Yemen needs to make and urge

commitments of aid to Yemen for development and counterterrorism. The United States provides training and support but reportedly does not actively engage in Yemen's attacks against terrorists. Under pressure from foreign donors, Yemen government and al-Houthi rebels begin implementing a six-part truce.

GLOSSARY

Arabic Terms and Phrases Used in Yemen

abayah – tube-like black garment that slips over the head and body, held at the top with one hand. It is usually worn with the *lithma* and face veil. Used by younger women in Sanaa and the Middle East today.

Adaysh – How much (does it cost)?

Ahlan wa sahlan – Welcome (literally, "folks and ease").

Allahu akbar – God is great.

asib – a straight, upright dagger, smaller than the curved *janbiyya*, worn in the belt by sayyids, merchants, and other nontribal groups

askaris – Government-trained guards or soldiers

As-salaam 'alaykum – Peace be unto you. Response: *'Alaykum as-salaam* – And peace be unto you.

Aysh ismak? – What is your name? *Ismi* – My name is....

balto – a black raincoat, like a trench coat, worn by some Yemeni women as an outer garment over dresses or pants. Often purchased abroad, they are worn by those women who probably find the old two-piece *sharshaf* cumbersome.

bass – Stop (literally, "enough" or "no more").

bayt – home, house

bint – daughter or girl

bukra – tomorrow. Everything would always happen "tomorrow."

burqa – the face panel of the old style *sharshaf* worn by Sanaani women. The face panel was attached to the *sharshaf* or cape that covered the head, arms, and shoulders.

bustan – garden

diwan – reception or greeting hall on an upper floor of an Arab house but below the *mafraj*; used for large family celebrations.

diya – blood money, paid by one party/family/tribe in retribution for the killing by one of its members of someone in another group/tribe/clan.

futa – man's sarong; an ankle-length skirt made by wrapping material around his waist and securing it with a belt or other material.

guss – the white plaster Yemenis use to outline the ornate stained-glass windows and decorate the exterior as well as the internal walls of a Yemeni building

haflah – party; *tafritah* – special women's party after birth of a child.

hajj – A religious pilgrimage to Mecca, Saudi Arabia, the holiest place in Islam

hajji – one who makes the pilgrimage.

hammam – bathroom, also a public bath for either women or men

iftar – meal served at sunset during Ramadan

Iftah al bab – Open the gate.

Inshallah – God willing.

janbiyya – Sounds like "*jambiyya*" to Westerners; a curved dagger in a holster on a leather belt that Yemeni tribesmen wear around their waists; can also be contained in a silver sheath/holster on a belt.

jebel – mountain

kafiyya – man's head scarf/shawl, often black-or-red-and-white checks in many parts of the Arab world.

kayf – a state of mind, such as the state of Nirvana or bliss achieved by chewing qat.

Kayf Halik – How are you?

khalas – Finished. Time is up. There is no more.

kufi – beanie or skullcap, worn by Yemeni men in the southern part of the country

la – no; *lam* – never

lihfah – striped cotton cloth or shawl worn by a man and thrown over one shoulder to indicate that he is a sayyid, or descendant of the Prophet.

lithma – chiffon scarf, about 4-ft. x 1-ft., that encircles the head to accompany the *maghmuq* and *sitara*. A woman places it on her head, extending it down over the forehead, with the short end in the left hand near the left temple and the right hand drawing the long end of the scarf around the back of the head and bringing it up over the mouth and nose and around the head again, tucking it in on the left temple with the short end.

Mabruk – Congratulations.

Ma'alesh – It's nothing, never mind. The word is Egyptian in origin.

mafraj– the reception or living room in an Arab house, usually on an upper or top floor of the multistoried Yemeni residence.

mansif - A feast of meat and rice where guests sit on the ground under a tent or trees and eat, usually with their hands, from a common dish. It is a typical way for Bedouins in the desert to entertain.

Marhaba – Hello.

maydan – square, public square; Persian word for a parade ground, an open space for men and horses, often with a reviewing stand. It can also mean a battleground.

moghmuq – tie-dyed light cloths in red and black and white with bulls' eyes in the design. Worn with a *lithma* and a *sitara*.

nabi – prophet

qabili – tribesman

rais – cap or hat that looks like a pillbox, worn by married women over the *lithma*.

riyal – a unit of Yemeni money (in 1973 about 7 riyals to one dollar).

Sabaah al-khair, or *Sabaah an-nour* – Good morning. *Masaah al-khair* – Good evening.

sayyid – descendant of the Prophet Muhammad

Sharia – the body of Islamic religious law

shadrawan – a Persian word for water fountain, usually located in a courtyard.

sharshaf – the traditional black cape that covers head, shoulders, and arms of a Sanaani woman. A *burqa* or double veil is attached to the front half of the cape that covers the forehead and face and is secured at the back of the head with a tie. A long black skirt covers the lower half of the woman's body. This type of *sharshaf* is a remnant of Turkish colonialism.

Shukran – Thank you.

sitara – the Indian print bedspread-type cloth that has a paisley print in reds, blues, blacks, and whites, often dull in color or faded; frequently worn by Sanaani women, rather than the black *sharshaf*, when they go out in public.

swiyah – little, small

tammam – good, okay; *mush tammam* – no good.

tannur – an oven. Coming in several sizes, this clay oven, cylindrical or shaped like a pottery jar, has an opening at the bottom for inserting small firewood and an opening at the top through which bread dough can be slapped on the insides for cooking. The opening may be topped with a clay cover or grate.

'urf – customary law

wassakh- filthy, dirty

zinna – an ankle-length dress worn by men, usually belted at the waist with a janbiyya

Foods of Yemen (and Ethiopia)

bamiya – okra

bint al sahn – "daughter of the pan or dish" or "daughter's cake;" a pastry served with butter and honey; a round strudel-like layered egg bread, sprinkled with blackened cumin seeds and drenched in a mixture of honey and clarified butter or ghee.

café *bunn* – strong coffee made from the coffee bean itself

doro wot – Ethiopian chicken in a hot pepper (*zigani*) sauce

ful – broad beans, eaten at breakfast with bread; not eaten at Ramadan

hilba – national dish, a meat sauce made from fenugreek seeds soaked in water, ground into a powder, and whipped by hand to a frothy consistency to remove the bitterness.

injera – Ethiopian moist spongy-like bread made of *teff*; a damp flatbread, similar to a crèpe, that is served with a mixture of hot ghee and fermented cow's milk

khubz – bread, usually round, like thick pancakes; a staple of the Yemeni diet.

lahuh – thin, flat, sourdough millet or buckwheat pancake with holes in it, like a soft Indian naan bread; used for dipping into *shafut*, a green yoghurt sauce

qishr – a brew made from the ground husks of the coffee bean and spiced with cardamom and ginger; a drink for poor people.

salatah – Salad, made from tomato, red onion, and lettuce greens, often served with *shafut*

salta – Rice paste made of crushed leeks, mint, and spices (garlic, chilies, thyme), into which bread is dipped; it is like *hilba* with broth and vegetable stew.

shafut – a tasty green sauce of yoghurt (*laban*/buttermilk), milk, garlic, chilies, and chopped coriander leaves into which one dips lacy buckwheat, whole wheat, or sourdough pancakes (*lahuh*). It is served especially at Ramadan.

shai – tea; *shai ahmar* – tea without milk; *shai halib* – tea with milk.

teff – small grain from lovegrass, similar to millet, grown in Ethiopia

zigani – Ethiopian hot pepper

People, Places, and Other Relevant Concepts/Ideas

ABU DAOUD – name used by Muhammad Oudah as the team leader of the PLO splinter group (Black September) that orchestrated the assassination of Israeli athletes at the 1972 Olympics and conducted other terrorist activities, including the assassination of three diplomats in Khartoum in 1973.

AGRÉMENT – a French term used in diplomatic circles for agreement, consent, approval, usually in writing.

'ALI IBN ABI TALIB – cousin and son-in-law of the Prophet Muhammad. He and his wife Fatima produced two sons, Hassan and Hussein. 'Ali's followers assassinated the 3rd caliph (rightful successor to the Prophet) in 656 CE, and 'Ali assumed rule as the 4th caliph. Followers of the third caliph in turn assassinated 'Ali in 661 CE and regained the caliphate for the Umayyad family, who ruled until 750 CE and who established the Sunni line of Muslims. 'Ali's son Hussein and his descendants continued the Shi'a line, while the older son Hassan was the progenitor of the Sunni Hashemite Kingdom of Jordan.

ADEN – capital city of the PDRY until its 1990 unification with northern Yemen; a major seaport on the Indian Ocean on the southern end of Arabia, at one time second only to New York in terms of yearly ship visits; seat of the British government rule under the Aden Protectorate from 1839–1967.

BAKSHEESH – tip, present, gratuity, often money for a bribe in Arab world.

BEDOUINS – tent-dwelling Arab peoples who live in the deserts of southwest Asia/Arabia and North Africa and are dependent on animals for their subsistence; nomads, wanderers.

BILHARZIA (or schistosomiasis) – An endemic disease in Yemen and elsewhere caused by a liver fluke or flatworm that lives in the liver of a snail residing in still water. It works its way into the body tissues through a crack in the heel, often making the person lethargic and itchy. The person eventually dies from liver failure if the disease is left untreated.

BLACK SEPTEMBER – A splinter group of the PLO that carried out terrorist activities, especially in the 1970s; named to commemorate September 1970, when Jordan's King Hussein confronted Palestinian terrorists operating in his country and, with the help of his military, drove out the PLO, sending them to Lebanon in 1971.

CALIPH – title given the political successors of the Prophet Muhammad. Except for the 4th caliph, 'Ali, the successor caliphs in the Sunni branch of Islam were not directly related to or descended from the Prophet. Caliphs Abu Bakr and Uthman were fathers-in-law of Muhammad.

CASBAH – the older, traditional Arab core of a North African city, with a suq, narrow streets, and cul de sacs, as in Algiers.

DHOW – any of various sailing vessels used by Arabs, usually with triangular lateen rigging on two or three masts.

AL-FATAH, or FATAH – the secular political party founded by Palestinian leader Yasir Arafat in 1959. Under Arafat, Fatah took control of the PLO in 1969. In the early 1970s, several groups affiliated with the PLO, including Black September, carried out international terrorist attacks until being forced in the mid-1970s by international pressure to restrict their attacks to Israel.

FRONT FOR THE LIBERATION OF OCCUPIED SOUTH YEMEN (FLOSY) – A collection of groups and organizations that united to obtain the independence of the Aden Protectorate from Britain in 1967.

GENERAL ABDULLAH AL-SALLAL – trusted officer of Imam Ahmad, who became the first leader of Yemen following the Egyptian-supported coup that ousted Imam Badr in 1962. Sallal, viewed as a puppet of the Egyptians, was ousted in the mid-1960s, with Qadi al-Iryani taking over as president in 1967.

HADRAMAWT – a large area of land that overlapped the southern border of the YAR and the northern border of the PDRY prior to unification in 1990; mountainous and inhabited by the Hadrami people.

HASHID TRIBE – the largest of three major tribes (along with Bakil and Madhaj) in Yemen. Sheikh Abdullah al-Ahmar, paramount sheikh of the Hashid tribal federation, who was head of the Islah Party and speaker of the democratically elected Parliament, died in December 2007, to be succeeded as the new tribal leader by his son Sadeq, a Shoura council member. Abdullah's death, as well as that of Mujahid Abu Shawarib, also a Hashid sheikh, gave President al-Saleh another challenge in maintaining his tribal allegiances and GOY stability.

HASHEMITE KINGDOM – The lineage of Jordan's late King Hussein and his son King Abdullah directly from the Prophet Muhammad through the Prophet's grandson al-Hassan, eldest son of the Prophet's daughter Fatima and her husband 'Ali ibn Abi Talib, the 4th Caliph. The Hashemites are Sunni.

HENNA – a red vegetable dye used to color hair and paint hands

HODEIDA – primary Yemeni seaport on the Red Sea in coastal zone known as the Tihama

IMAM – prayer leader who officiates at a mosque; title for a Muslim leader or chief; one of a succession of divinely inspired leaders of the Shi'ites. In Yemen, it also refers to the Zaydi religious ruler prior to the 1962 revolution.

IMAMS YAHYA, AHMAD, and BADR – The successive religious leaders of the Zaydi Shi'a Muslims in Yemen, descended from the Hamid al-Din family. YAHYA and his father fought the Turks for many years in the mountains of Yemen. Born in 1869, he came to power in 1904 upon his father's death and was Yemen's titular leader through the final downfall of the Ottomans in 1918 up until he was assassinated in 1948. His son AHMAD, to avenge his father's death, sacked Sanaa brutally with thousands of loyal tribesmen and set up his capital in Taiz, where he served until his death in 1962. Ahmad's son BADR was in power for only five days when the Egyptian-supported General Sallal, head of the Yemeni army, surrounded the palace and launched the Republican Revolution of September 1962. Badr fled north toward Saudi Arabia, where he led the Royalist opposition for several years, supported with Saudi gold. With the 1970 peace settlement, some Royalists were allowed back into Yemen and into positions of authority, but all members of the Hamid al-Din royal family (who had not been killed) were barred from return. Badr lived in exile in London, where he died in 1996.

ISLAH – The political party led by the paramount sheikh of the Hashid tribe was formed in 1990 as a conservative counter to the south's Marxist YSP; by 2005, it had joined a coalition with the YSP and other smaller parties to form the JMP as a counter to Saleh's GPC. Today Islah is Yemen's fastest growing party, according to Victoria Clark.

ISLAM – A monotheistic religion founded by the Prophet Muhammad in 610 CE when he received a vision and teachings from God. His teachings were codified into the Qur'an after his death in 632 CE.

ISMAELIS – A sect of Shi'a Islam that follows the son of the sixth Imam Jafer as Sadiq Ismael (died 760 AD) rather than his brother Musa al-Qasim. Ismaelis first appeared in Yemen around Hajja, but due to conflicts between two men vying for control did not succeed in spreading Ismaeli belief until Ali ibn Muhammad ibn Ali al-Suleyhi established the line in the early 11ᵗʰ century CE around Jibla and followed the Fatimi caliph in Egypt. The line ended with his daughter-in-law Queen Arwa's death in 1138. There are only a small number of Ismaelis, who reside around Manakha and in the Harraz mountains today.

JIHAD – meaning "struggle" or "strife" in Arabic; a holy war on behalf of Islam, prescribed as a religious duty by the Qur'an; a vigorous, emotional crusade for an idea or principle.

JIHADIST, or MUJAHID (plural mujahidin) – in Arabic both from the same j-h-d root, meaning one who wages jihad against the enemy, primarily in a religious sense.

JINN (plural of JINNI, also djinni or genie) – in Islamic myth, any of a class of spirits, lower than the angels, capable of appearing in human and animal forms and influencing humankind.

KALASHNIKOV – a renowned assault rifle, one of the first ever manufactured; made in Russia and known as the AK-47 (for "Kalashnikov model automatic rifle of 1947"); named for the weapon's Russian designer; the most widely used weapon in Yemen and many parts of the developing world.

KOHL – a dark, finely grained antimony sulfide powder, used by Yemeni women as eyeliner and eye shadow.

LEGATION – a foreign diplomatic mission led by a minister and staff, following an age-old tradition adopted early in our country's history. Legations mostly did commercial and consular work. Taiz was one of the last legations the United States established.

MARIA THERESA THALERS – Named for the archduchess and later empress of Austria (1740–1780 CE), these large silver coins, especially the widely minted 1780 thaler, were the only currency Middle Eastern countries accepted and trusted in matters of trade. The thalers were brought to Yemen by the Ottomans and continued to be used as Yemen's main currency until the 1962 revolution, after which Yemen finally issued paper money.

MARIB (pronounced Ma'rib) – the ancient seat of the Queen of Sheba, ruler of the Sabeans; located to the east of Sanaa about 100 miles toward the Empty Quarter of Saudi Arabia.

MASLOW'S HIERARCHY – a theory of human motivation developed by Abraham Maslow.

MUEZZIN – The person/crier who broadcasts the call to prayer for Muslims five times a day from the mosque. Nowadays this is done mostly with recordings. The puritanical Zaydis in the north do not think the call to prayer should be musical. People on the coast and in the southern parts of Yemen are more likely to "sing" the call to prayer.

NARGILEH – literally "coconut"; refers to the round part of a water pipe, also called a hookah, which used to be made of a coconut. Expatriates (probably British) called it a hubbly bubbly. Water passes over the hot charcoal and tobacco that burn in the perforated clay holder at the top of the stem. Smoke passes down the stem into the bulbous round bottom of the pipe, which holds the water. The steamy smoke is sucked up through the narrow tube that extends out the side of the pipe into a long hose with a mouthpiece. People sit around the pipe with its snaking hoses and pass the mouthpiece from person to person to smoke tobacco.

NOTE VERBALE – French term for a type of official diplomatic correspondence between one government and another.

OFFICIAL PASSPORT – a maroon-colored U.S. passport that falls between a black U.S. diplomatic passport and a blue U.S. civilian passport. Under the terms of the Vienna Convention, a host government grants diplomatic immunity to the bearer of a diplomatic passport but not to the bearer of an official or a civilian passport. USG military and other officials not assigned as diplomats to a particular country generally carry an official passport.

OLIGARCHY – a form of government in which power is vested in a few persons or in a dominant class or clique. In the case of Yemen, power was vested in the imam and his sayyid advisers.

ONE-TIME PAD – Sent to post by classified pouch, this 8"x10" writing pad/tablet had a unique cipher inside the cover of the package. An officer would very tediously encrypt his messages into groups of five English letters each and take them to the local telegraph office for transmission to the State Department at a cost in 1960 in Yemen of $1 per group of five letters. The cipher was burned after use. The department also sent messages this way when there was no communications code room at post to receive them. For obvious reasons messages tended to be short!

PALESTINE LIBERATION ORGANIZATION (PLO) – The PLO is the political and military organization founded in Jerusalem in 1964 by several hundred Palestinian national figures. The organization's original goal was the liberation of Palestine through armed struggle but was modified in 1988 to support a two-state solution. As of October 1974 the Arab League regarded the PLO as the "sole legitimate representative of the Palestinian People." Arafat was chairman of the PLO and of Fatah until his death in 2004. Hamas, a rival Palestinian political organization that does not recognize Israel, has emerged as a major competitor to Fatah and the Palestinian Authority, under President Mahmoud Abbas, since winning the 2006 legislative elections. In February 2009, conflict between Hamas and Israel in the Gaza strip came under a cease-fire. Israel has recently begun to allow some supplies into Gaza following the international outcry over its May 31 blockade of a flotilla carrying supplies to Gaza in which one of the ships was boarded and, in the ensuing melee, several Turkish participants were killed. Tensions remain high.

PDRY – People's Democratic Republic of Yemen, also known as South Yemen, was formerly the Aden Protectorate ruled by the British from 1839 until 1967, when the FLOSY gained its independence from the British. Within three years a Communist regime came to power and established the People's Democratic Republic of Yemen (PDRY), which ruled until unification with the YAR in 1990.

PERSONA NON GRATA – an official term designating a person, usually a diplomat, unacceptable to the host country's government. Diplomats so designated normally must leave the country.

PHALANGISTS – a Lebanese Christian political party with a military arm; one of many such parties in Lebanon.

PIED NOIR – Meaning "black foot" in French, this label was given to French settlers in Algeria, especially to military families, both men and women, who wore black shoes, in contrast to yellow *babouches* (i.e., slippers with no backing at the heel worn daily throughout the Muslim world, thus allowing the wearer to remove them easily for prayers without touching them).

QADI – religious judge; the judge's decisions in a Muslim community are based on *Sharia*, Islamic religious law. In Yemen *qadi* also refers to a learned class of *Sharia* scholars descended from Qahtan of the ancient South Arabian tribes. Apparently, the *qadis* (President al-Iryani, 1967–74, was one) do not care for the sayyids of the al-Hadi and Zaydi line. Although the sayyids are direct descendants of the Prophet, they are of Northern Arabian Adnan stock rather than of South Arabian heritage.

QAT – mildly stimulant leaf, tasting of tannic acid, which Yemenis chew generally every day, usually in the afternoon. It allegedly makes one think more clearly.

QUR'AN (KORAN) – the Muslim holy book. This sacred text of Islam is divided into 114 chapters, or suras. It is revered as the word of God, dictated to the Prophet Muhammad by the archangel Gabriel from 610 CE over a period of twenty-plus years until Muhammad's death in 632 CE. The Qur'an is accepted as the foundation of Islamic law, religion, culture, and politics.

RAMADAN – the ninth month of the Islamic calendar. During this holy month, Muslims adhere to a daily fast from dawn until sunset. At sunset they partake of a special *iftar* meal. This period of fasting ends with a big feast called the 'Id al-Fitr.

ROY – Republic of Yemen, the new name of the country after the 1990 unification between the YAR and the PDRY. The Government of Yemen (GOY) refers to unified Yemen, whereas YARG refers to the government of the YAR prior to unification.

SANAA (pronounced San'a) – capital city of Yemen, in the highlands at an estimated altitude of 7,225–7,500 feet (almost 2300 meters); seat of Yemeni government and Zaydi (Shi'a) influence in the north.

SAADA (pronounced Sa'da) – the original seat of the Zaydi imamate in northern Yemen. Al-Hadi mosque, named for the first Zaydi imam, still stands in Saada.

SALAFIS – an Arabic term that means "predecessors" or "ancestors" and refers to the first three Muslim generations, beginning with the Prophet Muhammad. The term is applied to Sunni Muslim fundamentalists who believe that Shi'a are "heretics." Literalist/ strict constructionist readers of the Qur'an, Salafis mistrust the *Hadith* (stories about how the Prophet lived and what he said and traditions of the early followers of Muhammad) and the four schools of traditional Sunnism. Generally, they are opposed to modern life, which they consider full of evil innovations, and want to go back to the fundamentals of Islam. Although mainstream Muslims consider Salafis extremist, only some Salafists incline to violence. Dissatisfied Salafis are likely targets for terrorist recruitment. Indeed, most of today's terrorist recruiters and leaders are Salafis.

SERVICE (pronounced "serveese") – a taxicab common in Lebanon and Jordan that carries a number of people along a specified route, usually more cheaply than a private taxi.

SHAFI'I – The Sunni Muslim sect of Yemenis who reside primarily around Taiz and in the south of Yemen. While other Sunni groups settled in the Zabid area at an early date, the Shafi'i sect was brought to the Hadramawt in southern Yemen in the early tenth century by an Iraqi named Ahmad ibn 'Isa. He was a follower of Imam Muhammad ibn Idris al-Shafi'i (768–820 CE), who founded one of the more conservative of the four schools of Sunni Islamic law (the others are Maleki, Hanafi, and Hanbali).

SHARIA – the body of Islamic religious law, which means the "way" or "path to the water source." This canon law is based on the Qur'an and the *Hadith*. as well as centuries of debate, interpretation, and precedent. Especially among Shi'a fundamentalists (mostly in Libya, Iran, and Afghanistan today), it forms the legal framework regulating public and many private aspects of life.

SHEIKH – In Arab countries, the patriarch or chief of a tribe or family.

SHI'A MUSLIMS – Those who believe that 'Ali, the son-in-law and cousin of the Prophet as well as the 4th caliph, was the rightful heir and leader of the Muslims. The only true heirs descend from 'Ali and his son Hussein. However, the 12th imam, the young son of the deceased 11th imam, "disappeared" in 873 CE, and, according to some believers, reappeared when Ayatollah Khomeini came to power in Iran in the 1970s. However, other Shi'a, known as the "twelvers" are preparing for the 12th imam to return, believing that the Mahdi, the rightly guided one, has already been here and will return from hiding.

SUNNI MUSLIMS – Those who believe that the heirs of the first three caliphs were Muhammad's rightful successors. The 3rd caliph Uthman, who began the Umayyad line, was assassinated in 656 CE by followers of 'Ali, who became 4th caliph. 'Ali was assassinated in 661 CE, and the caliphate reverted to the Umayyads, who ruled until the Abbasids defeated them in 750 CE and moved the seat of the caliphate to Baghdad. The Sunni caliphate continued in several locations and under competing lineages until it was finally abolished in Turkey in 1924. Now Sunnis follow various lineages. They believe that the Mahdi, the rightly guided one, has yet to appear.

SUQ (SOUK) – marketplace, generally in the older part of the city, where merchants sell their wares from covered stalls or open booths.

TAIZ (PRONOUNCED TA'IZ) – The commercial center and second largest city in the YAR; seat of Shafi'i (Sunni) influence in the south.

THEOCRACY – a form of government in which God or a deity is recognized as the supreme ruler; a system of government by priests claiming a divine commission. The Zaydi imams of Yemen claimed to be directly descended from the Prophet Muhammad through his son-in-law 'Ali, husband of Muhammad's daughter Fatima, and their son Hussein.

TIHAMA – the coastal area of Yemen along the Red Sea, approximately thirty miles wide.

VEIL – for Yemeni women, the veil is not a symbol of oppression to them, but one of keeping themselves special, pure.

WADI – dry valley; the channel of a river or watercourse that is dry except during periods of rainfall; the watercourse itself; in Spanish, an *arroyo*.

WAHHABIS – Followers of Muhammad ibn Abd al-Wahhab, a Sunni reformist judge-preacher of the mid-17th century Hanbali school of law, considered the most conservative of the four established schools. The Saudi clan, which followed his ideology, had firmly established their rule over most of present day Saudi Arabia by 1800. Today 80 percent of Saudis are followers of al-Wahhab's teachings, which have been modified into a comfortable, distinctive adaptation to modern life. The mostly Sunni Saudis are uncomfortable with Shi'ism, although approximately 10 percent of the Saudi population are Shi'a, living mostly in the Eastern Province. Many Muslims in Kuwait, Qatar, and the UAE are also Wahhabis, some having converted as far back as the 17th century. Wahhabism appeared more recently in Yemen. Wahhabis are conservative for the most part and generally not "extremists" or militants. Since the 1970s, however, many observers lump Wahabbis and Salafis together as followers of a conservative Muslim extremism, despite the two groups' different origins and practices.

YAR – Yemen Arab Republic, the name for North Yemen before its 1990 unification with South Yemen (PDRY), the former Aden Protectorate. The Ottoman Empire ruled North Yemen until its breakup after World War I, while the British controlled the port of Aden in South Yemen until 1967.

ZAYDIS – The branch of Shi'a Muslims named for Zayid ibn 'Ali Zain al Abidin, great grandson of 'Ali, the 4th caliph, brought to Yemen in 897 CE by al-Hadi ila 'l-Haqq, who is considered the first Zaydi imam of Yemen. He established the first Zaydi dynasty. Three subsequent dynasties over the next thousand years generally controlled the government in Sanaa prior to the 1962 revolution. Zaydis continue today to be a major force in the government. They have traditionally lived in the mountainous, northern part of Yemen.

BIBLIOGRAPHY

Books

Al-Aini, Muhsin. *50 Years in Shifting Sands: Personal Experience in the Building of a Modern State in Yemen.* Translated by Hassan al-Haifi. Edited by Ghassan E. Ghosn. Beirut: Editions Dar An-Nahar, 2004.

al-Salami, Khadija, with Charles Hoots. *The Tears of Sheba: Tales of Survival and Intrigue in Arabia.* New York: Wiley & Sons, 2004.

Armstrong, Karen. *Islam: A Short History.* New York: Modern Library, 2002.

Bamford, James. *The Shadow Factory: The Ultra-Secret NSA from 9/11 to the Eavesdropping on America.* New York: Doubleday, 2008. See also the NOVA PBS-TV production of *The Spy Factory,* released February 3, 2009, based on this book.

Bethmann, Erich W. *Yemen on the Threshold.* Washington, D.C.: American Friends of the Middle East, 1960.

Cleveland, William L. *A History of the Modern Middle East.* Boulder, Colo.: Westview Press, 2004.

Clark, Victoria. *Yemen: Dancing on the Heads of Snakes.* New Haven and London: Yale University Press, 2010.

Colburn, Marta. *From the Queen of Sheba to the Republic of Yemen: K-12 Resource Guide and Classroom Ideas.* Ardmore, Pa.: American Institute for Yemeni Studies, 2007.

Costa, Paolo, and Ennio Vicario. *Arabia Felix: A Land of Builders.* New York: Rizzoli International Publications, 1977.

Crawford, Peggy. *An American in Yemen: Travel Notes of a Photographer.* Paris: Éditions Nicolas Chaudun, 2005.

Daum, Werner, ed. *Yemen: 3000 Years of Art and Civilization in Arabia Felix.* Innsbruck: Penguin-Verdag, 1988.

Dresch, Paul. *A History of Modern Yemen.* Cambridge: Cambridge University Press, 2000.

Fayein, Claudie. *A French Doctor in the Yemen.* London: Robert Hale, 1957.

Gunter, Ann C., ed. *Caravan Kingdoms: Yemen and the Ancient Incense Trade.* Washington, D.C.: Smithsonian Institution, 2005.

Hansen, Eric. *Motoring with Mohammed: Journeys to Yemen and the Red Sea.* New York: Random House/Vintage Books, 1991.

Ingrams, Harold. *Arabia and the Isles*. London: John Murray, 1966.

International Women's Association, ed. *International Recipes from the Land of the Queen of Sheba*. Sana'a, Yemen: International Women's Association, 1985.

Lewcock, Ronald B. *The Old Walled City of Sana'a*. Paris: UNESCO, 1986.

Little, Tom. *South Arabia: Arena of Conflict*. London: Praeger, 1968.

Mackintosh-Smith, Tim. *Yemen: The Unknown Arabia*. Woodstock, N.Y.: Overlook Press, Peter Mayer Publishers, 2000.

Maréchaux, Pascal, and Maria Maréchaux. *Arabia Felix: Images of Yemen and Its People*. Woodbury, N.Y.: Barron's, 1980.

McClintock, David W. "The Yemen Arab Republic" and "The People's Democratic Republic of Yemen." In *Governments and Politics of the Middle East*, edited by Abid al-Marayati, 317–48. Belmont, Calif.: Wadsworth/ Duxbury Press, 1972.

McMullen, Christopher J. *Resolution of the Yemen Crisis, 1963: A Case Study in Mediation*. Washington, D.C.: Institute for the Study of Diplomacy, Georgetown University, 1980.

Newsom, David D., ed. *Diplomacy Under a Foreign Flag: When Nations Break Relations*. Washington, D.C.: Georgetown University, Institute for the Study of Diplomacy, and New York: St. Martin's Press, 1990.

Oppersdorff, Mathias. *Under the Spell of Arabia*. Syracuse, N.Y.: Syracuse University Press, 2001.

Paluch, Marta, ed. *Yemeni Voices: Women Tell Their Stories*. Sana'a, Yemen: British Council, 2001.

Peipenburg, Fritz. *Traveller's Guide to Yemen*. Sana'a: Yemen Tourist Company, 1983.

Quin, Mary. *Kidnapped in Yemen*. Guilford, Conn.: Lyons Press, 2005.

Robinson, J. Brian D. *Coffee in Yemen: A Practical Guide*. Sana'a: Ministry of Agriculture & Water Resources, 1993.

Schaffer, Howard B. "Brokering a Yemen Settlement." In *Ellsworth Bunker: Global Troubleshooter, Vietnam Hawk*. ADST-DACOR Diplomats and Diplomacy Series. Chapel Hill: University of North Carolina Press, 2003.

Searjeant, R. B., and Ronald Lewcock. *Sana'a: An Arabian Islamic City*. London: The World of Islam Festival Trust, 1983.

Singer, Caroline, ed. *Yemen: In the Land of the Queen of Sheba. Guide to Events*. London: Pallas Athene Publishers, 2002.

Stark, Freya. *The Coast of Incense: Autobiography 1933–1939*. London: John Murray Publishers, 1953.

———. *The Southern Gates of Arabia: A Journey in the Hadramaut*. New York: Modern Library, 1936, 2001.

Swanson, Lealan. "Historical Considerations in Yemeni Vernacular

Architecture: Houses from the Sulayhid Dynasty (439/1047) in the Modern Period." Ph.D. diss., Ohio State University, 1997.

———. *Project Yemen*. Seattle, Wash.: Society Expeditions (723 Broadway East, Seattle, WA 98102), 1985.

Walters, Delores M. "Women, Healthcare, and Social Reform in Yemen." In *Feminism and Antiracism: International Struggles for Justice*. Edited by France Winddance Twine and Kathleen M. Blee, 71–93. New York: New York University Press, 2001.

Weir, Shelagh. *Qat in Yemen: Consumption and Social Change*. London: British Museum Publications, 1985.

Professional Journal and Magazine Articles/Institutional Reports

al-Sharki, Raufah Hassan. "Public Sphere Headgear Swinging between Culture and Religion." In *Cultural Development Programs Foundation*. Sana'a, Yemen (April 2006):1–28.

Burnham, Anne Mullan. "Silver Speaks." In *Saudi Aramco World* 55, no. 6 (November/December 2004):8–16.

Burrowes, Robert D. Review of Rashid A. Abdu, MD, *Journey of a Yemeni Boy*. In *Yemen Update: Bulletin of the American Institute of Yemeni Studies*, no. 48 (2006): 40–45.

Cockburn, Andrew. "Yemen United." In *National Geographic*, April 2000, 36–53.

Hansen, Eric. "Crossing Yemen." In *Travel and Leisure*, July 1997:76–87.

———. "Sana'a Rising." In *Saudi Aramco World* 57, no. 1 (January-February 2006): 24–33.

Nist, Ted. "Back to the Future—The US Mission in Kabul Reopens." In *State*, no. 454 (February 2002): 14–17.

Ransom, Marjorie. "My Research in Yemen: The Disappearing Tradition of Silver Jewelry." In *Yemen Update: Bulletin of the American Institute for Yemeni Studies*, no. 47 (2005): 14–22.

Newspapers/News Bureau Articles

Cooley, John. "Arabian Tensions Ease: Peace Platform." *Christian Science Monitor*, August 1, 1970.

Downey, Tom. "Yemen's Exotic Secrets." *New York Times*. Travel, December 30, 2007.

"Dr. Mario Livadiotti, Imam Badr Private Physician." Culture, *Yemen Times*, vol. 10, no. 42, October 16–22, 2000.

Hopkins, John. "Yemen's Islamic Heritage, Architecture Rediscovered." *Arab News*, March 15, 1984.

Kubic, Milan J. "Yemen: Our Socialist Friends." *Newsweek*, May 25, 1970.

"Rains Came but Too Late: Hundreds Starve in Yemen." *Los Angeles Herald Examiner,* August 19, 1970.

Sherman, George. "U.S. Boosting Famine Aid to Yemen." *Washington Star,* August 2, 1970.

"U.S. Diplomat in Yemen First Time in Two Years." *New York Times,* April 10, 1970.

"Yemen Premier Quits; Killed Man in Dispute over Phone Call." United Press International, September 7, 1971.

Unpublished Resources

Foreign Affairs Oral History Program. Association for Diplomatic Studies and Training, Arlington, Va. Oral history transcripts, 1988–present. Also available as *Frontline Diplomacy* on the Library of Congress Web site.

Numerous emails and interviews with individuals referenced in the text.

SELECTED REFERENCES FOR "YEMEN'S CHALLENGES TODAY"

Books, Magazines, Journals, and Professional Publications

Alkaff, Huda F. "Water Scarcity Problem in Yemen." In *Yemen Update: Bulletin of the American Institute for Yemeni Studies*, no. 42 (2000): 51–54.

Boucek, Christopher. "Yemen: Avoiding a Downward Spiral." Carnegie Endowment for International Peace, September 2009.

Carnegie Endowment for International Peace. *Yemen: On the Brink.* Four-part Carnegie Paper Series. Authored by Christopher Boucek, Stephen Day, Alistair Harris, and Sarah Phillips. March 2010 ff.

Day, Stephen. "Updating Yemeni National Unity: Could Lingering Divisions Bring Down the Regime?" In *The Middle East Journal* 62, no. 3 (Summer 2008): 417-436.

Dunbar, Charles. "Yemen's Parliamentary Elections: A Step, but in Which Direction?" In *Yemen Update: Bulletin of the American Institute for Yemeni Studies*, no. 45 (2003): 7–8.

Johnson, Gregory. "Yemen: Empty Economic Reforms Slow Bid to Join the GCC." In *Arab Reform Bulletin*, Carnegie Endowment for International Peace, February 2007.

Kristof, Nicholas D., and Sheryl WuDunn. *Half the Sky: Turning Oppression into Opportunity for Women Worldwide.* New York: Alfred A. Knopf, 2009.

Miller, Derek B. "Demand, Stockpiles, and Social Controls: Small Arms in Yemen." Occasional Paper No. 9, a publication of the Small Arms Survey, May 2003.

Nakhleh, Emile. "Yemen: How Understanding the Challenges Can Help Us Undermine al-Qaeda and The Radical Paradigm." Testimony on Yemen and al-Qaeda before the Senate Foreign Relations Committee, January 20, 2010.

Sharp, Jeremy M. "Yemen: Background and U.S. Relations." Congressional Research Service, July 7, 2009, and January 13, 2010.

Newspapers and News Services

Associated Press, February 9, August 28, 2009.

Burns, John F. "After Failed Attack, Britain Turns Focus to Yemen." *New York Times*, January 2, 2010.

Erlanger, Steven. *New York Times*, January 3, 4, and 5, 2010.

Finkel, David. *Washington Post*. Three-part series on Yemen. December 18–20, 2005.

Fleishman, Jeffrey. "Yemen Becomes Increasingly Unstable." *Los Angeles Times*, August 24, 2009.

Friedman, Thomas L. "Postcard from Yemen." *New York Times*, February 7, 2010.

Heenan, Bill. "Saving Yemen." *Albuquerque Journal*, January 17, 2010.

Hill, Ginny. *BBC News*. August 15, 2005; March 4, 2006; February 5, April 2, 2007; September 17, 2008.

Holmes, Oliver. "In Yemen, Women Protest Delay on Child Marriage Ban." *Christian Science Monitor*, March 23, 2010.

Hull, Edmund. "Al-Qaeda's Shadowland." *New York Times*, Op-Ed, January 12, 2010.

Kamber, Michael. "On Assignment: Minders, Fixers, Troubles." *New York Times*, Lens, February 9, 2010.

Kasinof, Laura. *Christian Science Monitor*, June 14, 23, 2009.

Lancaster, John. "Women Take to the Polls in Male-Dominated Yemen." *Washington Post Foreign Service*, April 26, 1997, A01 (www.clark.net/pub/alkebsi/news.html).

Priest, Dana. "U.S. Military Teams, Intelligence Deeply Involved in Aiding Yemen on Strikes." *Washington Post*, January 27, 2010.

Whitelaw, Kevin. "On a Dagger's Edge." *US News and World Report,* March 13, 2006.

Worth, Robert F. *New York Times*, January 28, February 27, June 29, September 18, 2008; January 23, May 5, November 1, 2009; February 28, 2010.

———. "In Yemen's South, Protests Could Cause More Instability." *New York Times*, February 27, 2010.

———. "The Next Afghanistan? A Journey into Volatile, Fragile, Militant Yemen." *New York Times Magazine,* July 11, 2010.

Yemen Times, September 2008–February 2010.

Online Publications/ Websites

http://earthtrends.wrl.org/
http://UNstats.un.org/
Johnsen, Gregory. "Waning Vigilance: Al-Qaeda's Resurgence in Yemen." Policy Watch #1551, July 14, 2009. www.washingtoninstitute.org

Knights, Michael. "US Embassy Bombing in Yemen: Counterterrorism Challenges in Weak States." Policy Watch #1404, September 24, 2008. www.washingtoninstitute.org

Kohlmann, Evan. "In Too Deep: Terrorism in Yemen." National Review Online, January 17, 2003. http://article.nationalreview.com

Murphy, Caryle. "Aid to Yemen: Money Well Spent?" www.globalpost. com/print/

Novak, Jane. www.globalpolitician.com/, June 26, 2006; www. longwarjournal.org/, April 7, July 11, 2008; http://janenovak. wordpress.com/, February 13, 2009; www.armiesofliberation.com, February 10, 2010.

www.allAfrica.com

www.arabnews.com

www.cnn.com

www.economist.com/agenda/

www.FAOSTAT.org

www.globalpolitician.com

www.google.com

www.infoplease.com

www.islamandinsurgencyinYemen.blogspot.com (Waq al-Waq)

www.mcc.gov

www.meepas.com (The Middle East Economic and Political Analysis Company)

www.nationsencyclopedia.com

www.news.bbc.com/

www.news.yahoo.com

http://www.npr.org/

www.oxan.com (Oxford Analytica)

www.realclearworld.com/

www.republicofyemen.com

www.state.gov

www.tajaden.org

www.thestar.com/

www.waqalwaq.com

www.washingtonpost.com/

www.zawya.com/

www.wikipedia.com

www.yemenpost.net

www.yemen-today.com

www.yobserver.com (Yemen Observer)

www.al-bab.com (Yemen Gateway)

INDEX OF PERSONAL NAMES

A

Abdul (cook), 36, 182
Abdul Kadir. *See* Farhan, Abdul Kadir
Abdullah (cook), 52, 142
Abdullah (guide), 195, 200–201; photo, 196, 199
Abu Daoud, 62
Abu Luhum, Sheikh Sinan, 72, 159, 181
Ahmad, Imam, 77, 124–125, 131–133, 155, 207, 209
al-Aini, Azziza, 143, 180–183; photo, 182
al-Aini, Muhsin, 72, 117, 126, 143, 159, 181; photo, 129
al-Amri, Hassan, 73, 132
al-Aulaqi, Anwar, 215
al-Bidh, Ali Salem, 228
al-Fadhli, Tareq, 228
al-Hadi ila 'l Haqq, Yahya ibn al-Hussein, 124
al-Houthi, Abdul Malek, 229
Ali, Hashim, 90
'Ali ibn Abi Talib, 123, 199
al-Iryani, Abdul Rahman, 117, 128, 137; photo, 136
al-Raymi, Qasim, 231, 232
al-Salami, Khadija, xx, 224, 225
al-Saleh, Ali Abdullah, 222–224, 228, 229, 232, 236
al-Sallal, Abdullah, 132
al-Sa'r, Sheikh, 128, 173, 175; photo, 175

al-Sharki, Raufa al-Hassan, 226
al-Shihri, Said Ali, 231
al-Wuhayshi, Nasser, 231, 232
Anderson, Kathleen, 203
Arafat, Yassir, 61
Armstrong, Neil, 137
Arwa, Queen, 65

B

Badr, Imam (formerly Crown Prince), 125, 131, 133, 154
Baracchi-Tua, Ambassador, 155
Bergus, Donald, 9, 135–136
Bertaud, Alain, xxi, 88–89, 108, 145, 148–150, 156, 195, 198, 200; photos, 88, 199
Bertaud, Marie Agnes, 89, 108, 148–150; photo, 88
Bertaud, Veronique, 148; photo, 147
Bertaud, Yann, 148; photo, 147
bin Laden, Osama, xviii, 231
bin Shamlan, Faisal, 224
Blanche, Lesley, 8
Boucek, Christopher, 216, 234
Brown, Gordon, 235
Bunker, Ellsworth, 125
Busby, Horace, 5

C

Case, Sam, 112
Charlie (Khalil), 7
Clark, Victoria, xx, 231, 236
Colburn, Marta, 76

Cole, Diane, 31, 54, 89, 183
Cole, John, 31, 54, 89, 92; photo, 188
Cortada, Jim, xx
Costa, Paola, 156
Crawford, Peggy, xxi, 76
Crawford, William, xx, 137, 176, 179
Curran, Marcia, 182
Curran, Robert (Ted), xx, 131–133, 182

D
D'Amico, 21, 22
Day, Stephen, 235, 236
Dhamar Ali, 156
Doar, Ruby, 80

E
Eagleton, William, 134
Eilts, Hermann, xx
Erbach, Jerry, 63; photo, 64

F
Faisal, King, 125
Farhan, Abdul Kadir, 17, 55, 56–58, 80, 112, 129, 164; photos, 57, 165
Fayein, Claudie, 56, 90, 155–156; photo, 155
Foster, Dr., 133
Fuller, Graham, 63; photo, 64

G
Griggs, Lee, 157

H
Hagen, Tony, 20
Hamami, Chief of Protocol, 107, 130
Hamshari, Ali, 58–59, 84
Harnett, Monsignor, 79, 143, 159; photo, 143
Hassan, Muhammad, 80
Himyar, 122

Hizam, Ahmad Ali. See Quedens, Billy
Hud, Prophet, 119
Hussein, King, 61
Hussein (grandson of the Prophet and son of 'Ali ibn Abi Talib), 42, 123

J
Jaghman, Yahya, 143
Jazaery, Ali, 73
Jocton, 119
Johnson, Lyndon B., 5, 21, 181

K
Kennedy, John F., 125, 126
Khalil (Charlie), 7
Kissinger, Henry, 60
Koehnen, Larry, 83
Koehnen, Sue, 83, 102
Korn, David, 61
Kristof, Nicholas, 226
Kubik, Milan, 157

L
Leach, Hugh, 157
Lewcock, Ronald B., 40, 187, 190
Livadiotti, Jana, 154; photo, 142
Livadiotti, Marco, xxi, 154, 220
Livadiotti, Mario, xxi, 35, 68, 83–88, 153–154; photo, 86

M
MacArthur II, Douglas, 12
MacArthur, Laura "Wahwee" Barkley, 12
Mackintosh-Smith, Tim, 120
Mandaville, Jon, 225
Maresca, Dick, 71
Massa-Bernucci, Romualdo, 10, 22, 141, 155
Mawry, Vic, 81

McClintock, Anna, 97–102, 111, 153; photos, 53, 110, 153
McClintock, David, xvii, xix, xx; photos, 12, 98, 107, 136, 199
  arrest in Syria, 73–75
  Chinese school diplomatic fiasco, 130
  early career, 6
  famine relief trips, 159–169
  illness, 84–87
  leisure initiatives, 105–112, 116
  presentation of moon rocks, 98
  Susan's Christmas accident, 91–94
  thesis writing, 104–105
  Yemen assignment, 3–4
  Yemen fact-finding trip, 9–11
McClintock, Lesley, 73-75, 95, 97, 99, 102–103, 111–112; photos, 88, 104, 176
McClintock, Susan, photos, 98, 113, 142, 151, 188
  abduction in Syria, 73–75
  birth tea party, 103
  Chinese school diplomatic fiasco,130
  Christmas accident, 91–94
  duties as Foreign Service wife,138–147
  Mrs. al-Aini's women's group, 180–184
  pregnant with Lesley, 95–97
  as principal officer's wife, 146–147
McConnell, Fran, photo, 113
Miller, Derek B., 227
Moore, George C. (Curt), 61
Morris, Willie, 95, 161
Muhammad Abdul Ghani. *See* Nagi, Muhammad Abdul Ghani
Muhammad, the Prophet, 122, 123
Murphy, Richard (Dick), 144–147

N
Nagi, Muhammad Abdul Ghani, 10, 17, 20, 22, 30, 35, 55–56, 58, 67, 80, 102, 110; photos, 57, 68
Nagi, Rashida, 20, 56, 58
Nakhleh, Emile, 235
Nasser, Gamal Abdel, 125–127
Newsom, David D., 134
Newton, Christa, 95
Newton, David, 33, 80, 95, 98, 129, 134, 179, 210–211, 227
Nixon, Richard M., 137
Noel, Cleo, 61
Nu'man, Abdul, 23, 47, 50, 52; photo, 53
Nu'man, Ahmad, 177; photo, 136
Nu'man, Assia, 177, 179; photo, 178
Nu'man, Azziza, 177; photo, 176
Nu'man, Maha, 177
Nu'man, Muhammad, 176–177, 179

O
O'Donnell, Jack, 31, 54, 55
O'Grady, Peg, 55, 98, 102
O'Grady, Walt, 55, 98
Oppersdorff, Mathias T., 156–157

P
Paganelli, Bob, 3, 7
Pahlavi, Shah Reza, 12
Paluch, Marta, xx, 225
Peipenburg, Fritz, xx, 121
Pennacchio, Fausto, 10, 15–17, 155
Percque, Aimé, 150–151, 159–160, 162
Petree, Richard (Dick), 114
Phillips, Sarah, 236
Phillips, Wendell, 156
Polansky, Edward, 151–152; photo, 151
Porter, Dwight, 139
Priest, Dana, 215

Q

Qahtan, 119
Qassim, Muhammad, 58, 186;
    photo, 190
Quedens, Billy, 77–79, 83;
    photo, 79
Queen of Sheba (Saba), 119, 120
Quin, Mary, xx, 76

R

Radub, Muhammad Abdullah,
    35–36, 38, 52
Ransom, David, 45, 47, 213
Ransom, Marjorie, 210, 213–214
"Rashid", 62
Rauh, Rick, 54, 55, 72, 172, 185;
    photo, 79
Reade, Lew, 207–209, 210
Reed, Richard, 76
Richardson, Anne, 13
Richardson, Elliot, 12
Rogers, Mrs. William, 181
Rogers, William, 129, 130, 137
Rusk, Dean, 21
"Ruth," 157–158

S

Saad, Abdullah Muhammad, 33–
    35, 39, 52, 142
Saba, 119
Sabbagh, Isa, 133
Salah, 67, 69; photo, 68
Samura, 67
Sayf (cook), 36
Schreyer, Helmut, 153
Schreyer, Jutta, 153
Schreyer, Kai, 153
Searjeant, R. B., 187, 190
Seibert, Tom, 89, 108, 164; photo, 165
Selassie, Haile, 113
Sharih, Dhamar Ali, 156

Sheba (Saba), Queen of, 4, 119, 120
Sheehan, Michael, 156–157, 161
Shem, 119
Shu'ayb, Prophet, 199
Singer, Carolyn, xx, 120
Sobke, Allison, 96
Sobke, Marilyn, 96
Solomon, 120
Stanissis, Mr., 159
Steffan, Manfred, xxi
Sterner, Michael, xx
Stoltzfus, William (Bill), xx, xxi,
    100, 101, 125, 132; photo, 208
Swanson, Lealan, 63, 69, 194, 210,
    211–213; photos, 43, 212

T

Talib, 'Ali ibn Abi, 123
Terry (TDY technician), 23, 25
Thatcher, Nicholas G., 97

V

Varisco, Dan, xx
Vestring, Alfred, 53, 110, 152, 162;
    photo, 153
Vestring, Ulrike, 52, 152; photo, 153

W

Wiley, Marshall, xx, 133, 209
Wolle, William (Bill), xx, 132
Worth, Robert, 217, 228, 232
WuDunn, Sheryl, 226

Y

Yahya, Imam, 124, 156
Yost, Robert, 114
Young, Jim, 83

Z

Zabara, Muhammad, 103

www.ingramcontent.com/pod-product-compliance
Lightning Source LLC
Chambersburg PA
CBHW020657270326
41928CB00005B/156